JAZZ
ON THE
BARBARY
COAST

This book is published jointly by the San Francisco Traditional Jazz Foundation, the California Historical Society, and Heyday Books.

The San Francisco Traditional Jazz Foundation seeks to foster and preserve high-quality traditional jazz, regionally and worldwide. The Foundation supports live jazz and educational events, and sponsors recordings, publications, and other media applications. Organized in 1981 as a non-profit, the Foundation maintains a growing private archive of items relating to the traditional jazz revival beginning in San Francisco about 1939. For more information, please contact:

San Francisco Traditional Jazz Foundation
650 California Street, 12th Floor
San Francisco, CA 94108
Telephone: 415/522-7417
Fax: 415/922-6934
www.sftradjazz.org

Since 1871, the California Historical Society has dedicated itself to collecting, preserving, and presenting the account of California's remarkable, multi-cultural heritage. Through its historical library full of original manuscripts, first editions, and rare books; archives of over one-half million historic photographs; art collection; lectures, tours, and symposia; and quarterly publications, the Society makes the legacy of California's past available to all Californians. For more information, please contact:

California Historical Society
678 Mission Street
San Francisco, CA 94105
Telephone: 415/357-1848
Fax: 415/357-1850
e-mail: info@calhist.org

Heyday Books publishes high quality books on California history, literature, natural history, and culture. For a free catalog, please contact:

Heyday Books
P.O. Box 9145
Berkeley, CA 94709
Telephone: 510/549-3564
Fax: 510/549-1889
e-mail: heyday@heydaybooks.com

JAZZ ON THE BARBARY COAST

By Tom Stoddard

Introduction by Douglas Henry Daniels

HEYDAY BOOKS • BERKELEY
in conjunction with the SAN FRANCISCO TRADITIONAL JAZZ FOUNDATION
and the CALIFORNIA HISTORICAL SOCIETY

Library of Congress Cataloging-in-Publication Data:

Stoddard, Tom.
    Jazz on the Barbary Coast / Tom Stoddard ; introduction by Douglas
H. Daniels.
      p. cm.
    Originally published: Chigwell, Essex : Storyville, c1982.
    Includes bibliographical references and index.
    ISBN 1-890771-04-X (pbk.)
    1. Jazz—California—San Francisco—History and criticism.
  2. Jazz musicians—California—San Francisco—Biography. I. Title.
  ML3508.8.S26S76 1998
  781.65'09794'61—dc21   98-10989
                                          CIP
                                          MN

Cover Design: Jack Myers, DesignSite, Berkeley
Interior Design and Production: Rebecca LeGates
Editing: Julianna Fleming
Editorial Assistant: Simone Scott
Photo Research and Permissions: Peter Johnstone
Printing and Binding: Publishers Press, Salt Lake City

Orders, inquiries, and correspondence should be addressed to:
Heyday Books
Box 9145, Berkeley, CA 94709
510/549-3564; Fax 510/549-1889
heyday@heydaybooks.com

Printed in the United States of America

10 9 8 7 6 5 4 3 2 1

B1700746

CONTENTS

INTRODUCTION

by Douglas Henry Daniels

Tom Stoddard's *Jazz on the Barbary Coast* is a modest work, but herein lies its significance and similarity to jazz, which is often presented modestly, without fanfare or the support of leading institutions. By permitting the participants to speak for themselves and express their opinions, this book distinguishes itself through its firsthand accounts of the music, personnel, and nightlife of the Barbary Coast, presenting differences among musical generations and changes in the character of the music.

There are a number of important ideas embedded in this work. One of them is the leading role that African-Americans played in the emergence of California jazz—not only the music, but in the evolution and popularization of jazz dance as well. Another is the early appearance of jazz on the West Coast—before World War I, in fact. Then there is the dominant role played by the leading West Coast vice district, the Barbary Coast, drawing African-Americans along with other migrants from places like New York, Chicago, Des Moines, New Orleans, and even the Caribbean and the distant Cape Verde islands off the coast of West Africa. *Jazz on the Barbary Coast* is also noteworthy because it places the music within the appropriate historical and social setting, characterizing jazz as a national phenomenon.

Jazz was a significant component of the American urban culture that emerged early in the twentieth century, with important contributions made by cities like San Francisco, as well as Los Angeles, New Orleans, New York, and Kansas City. *Jazz on the Barbary Coast* helps correct the New Orleans bias concerning the music's origins in so much of the historiography.

According to popular notions of jazz history, the dispersal of this music from New Orleans came after the closing of Storyville, the Crescent City's entertainment district, during World War I. The facts of the case are more complex, because singer-pianists Tony Jackson and Jelly Roll Morton were on the road long before 1917. *Jazz on the Barbary Coast* recognizes the presence of leading New Orleans musicians out west before Storyville's demise, and their singular influence on musicians in San Francisco.

Stoddard notes that Will Johnson's Creole Band came out in 1907 with Ernest Coycault on trumpet; Will's brother, Dink, migrated west a few years later, as did Jelly Roll Morton around World War I and King Oliver shortly thereafter. Indeed, cornetist Bunk Johnson, who helped to spark the New Orleans revival in California from the early 1940s, arrived on the West Coast as early as 1905. The ragtime pianist Tom Turpin, from St. Louis, came about the same time. Freddy Keppard appeared in 1914. Because other New Orleans musicians—not only Kid Ory and Papa Mutt Carey, but Wade Whaley and Clem Raymond—migrated to San Francisco before 1920, we can not only appreciate the Crescent City's significance for providing important musicians ("All of them played that Creole jazz like Wade"), but consider San Francisco as an attractive entertainment spot because it drew them west early in the music's history.

While the San Francisco musicians profiled in this book note New Orleans' influence, their stories together with Stoddard's research indicate the creativity found among the early San Francisco musicians and dancers. Some of these artists used San Francisco as a springboard to other West Coast cities and abroad, just as New Orleans and New York musicians migrated to different regions of the United States and occasionally sojourned or became expatriates in Europe.

As Stoddard points out, there were similarities between San Francisco and New Orleans. Each was a large city, dominating its region, and a major port with international connections. Each metropolis had its own vice district, the Barbary Coast and Storyville respectively, vying for the attention of patrons and tourists alike.

Differences existed, however. New Orleans' black population was quite large—77,714 in 1900—overshadowing San Francisco's much smaller contingent of barely 1,654 in a city of one-third million. Also, many black New Orleans residents were descendants of slaves and newcomers to the city; others were French-speaking with a heritage of freedom—the Creoles who gave jazz so many artists. One city was in the Deep South, near several million African-Americans, the other was on the rim of the Pacific with no significant black population closer than Texas.

Still, San Francisco's unique setting drew a variety of black residents— seamen, Pullman car workers, miners, merchants, laborers, and cooks, some from the gold rush era. They adapted versatile, shifting roles as the economy and their fortunes fluctuated. They were institution builders as well. As the largest black contingent on the Pacific Slope, they played a major role in founding the California Colored Convention, a newspaper (*Mirror of the Times),* three churches, and three fraternal orders during the 1850s. They formed other newspapers, societies, and civil rights organizations in subsequent decades. The fact that they were a small population of one to two thousand did not prevent them from pursuing their dreams for fortune and, failing that, the security of a good job, comfortable home, and loving family.

The true city-dwellers, often single individuals, preferred a San Francisco residency, but those who wanted to buy homes and raise families gravitated across the bay toward the suburban milieus of Oakland and Berkeley, where homes and rentals were more affordable. This process began even before the 1906 earthquake. Many black suburbanites continued to work in San Francisco. Wherever they lived, many of these urbanites were devotees of black music culture—ragtime, blues, and jazz music and dance.

Although distant, they were not isolated from mainstream Afro-America thousands of miles across the continent. Many were migrants from Eastern and Southern cities; also, their churches and societies linked them to African-

American organizations in the East. Moreover, like many mobile Californians, they visited their original homes from time to time. Most importantly, the city attracted not only migrants but traveling musicians and dancers, some of whom played major roles in the history of jazz.

Jazz on the Barbary Coast portrays the experiences of native-born Californians, such as pianist Sid LeProtti, and those who were migrants, such as nightclub owner Lester Mapp and saxophonist Reb Spikes. Together, the native-born and newcomers sustained a profoundly rich black cultural tradition within their churches, nightclubs, and dance halls, attracting highly mobile entertainers and providing a launching pad for forays into the interior and along the West Coast. Stoddard's work reveals the degree to which African-American culture in general, and jazz music and dance specifically, were national, at least by the beginning of this century.

Stoddard's work also helps us appreciate jazz's international character from the very beginning. Some readers may know that James Reese Europe, of New York City's Clef Club and then band leader in the black infantry regiment that fought in France during World War I, popularized the music overseas, paving the way for touring black road shows and jazz bands in the 1920s and 1930s. At the same time and in the same year (1917) as Europe's journey overseas, San Franciscans like Sid LeProtti and Reb Spikes played in Hawaii, which at that time was not one of the states. Moreover, musicians like Bo Diddly (not to be confused with the modern bluesman), "the first scat singer" that Reb Spikes "ever heard...[who] was scat singin' before Armstrong," went to Japan, "and on out through there." Others, such as saxophonist Earl Whaley and pianist Bill Powers, went to Asia as well. In fact, "we had a lot of guys who would come here from the East on their way to the Orient," indicating how the music became international from both coasts early in the music's history.

Besides the globalization of this music, the different cultural influences and the international character of the American society also nourished jazz. Significantly, European training, like that of LeProtti's German music teacher, which emphasized classical traditions, enabled his So Different Band to diversify its repertoire so as to meet the tastes of different audiences with classics, quadrilles, waltzes, ragtime, and blues. This European music culture accompanied the European languages that were already part of the black

American culture, an aspect of African-American history that is not usually appreciated. For example, Morton and Ory spoke French or French Creole, LeProtti's grandmother spoke German, Spikes had a French grandfather and French-speaking mother, and Adam "Slocum" Mitchell came from French and Creole-speaking Martinique.

Other musicians on the West Coast had West Indian connections which draw our attention to the international character of San Francisco and the people who sustained jazz. From the nineteenth century, the city possessed a significant black foreign-born population of about 10 percent, most of them from the West Indies. Louie Gomez's, a West Indian night club, was where San Francisco's Antilleans met regularly in the early twentieth century. Banjoist Alfred Levy's grandfather came from the West Indies; LeProtti's euphonium-player and flautist, Gerald Wells, was from Port of Spain, Trinidad; Charlie Uter, who ran The Squeeze Inn, was also a West Indian; and Lester Mapp, proprietor of the So Different on Pacific Street, hailed from Barbados.

African and Southern folk aspects and instrumentation also enriched the development of the music. *Jazz on the Barbary Coast* deftly delineates those rhythmic elements that distinguish the jazz tradition, tracing its roots to minstrel performers on bones and banjo, an African instrument, and in such overlooked institutions as the medicine show. This highly rhythmic aspect, sometimes called syncopation, involves an approach to music in which the band swings the dancers, who in turn influence the musicians. Stoddard's analysis of jazz dance, including the Cakewalk, Grizzly Bear, and Shimmy (or Shimmeshawobble), highlights the dynamic dimension of the music, in which dance movements are essential expressions of the beat's swinging character.

Through the lens of the Barbary Coast, Stoddard allows us to view important artists in the music's history, as well as lesser-known musicians, including his informants, Sid LeProtti, Reb Spikes, Alfred Levy, and Charlie "Duke" Turner. Their firsthand accounts draw attention to individuals who do not usually appear in jazz histories. Spikes tells us about Wesley Fields, from Des Moines, Iowa, who was "a devil of a piano player"; trombonist Frank Withers, described as "the best jazz trombone player I ever heard in my life"; and Slocum Mitchell, a regular in the LeProtti band, who "was kind'a the king of clarinet jazz."

Families played important roles in the early music education of these jazz musicians. Some of them played together, the Spikes brothers and the Levy brothers, for example, and the husband and wife team of Justin "Sax" and Grace Sexius. But as Sid LeProtti's testimony reveals, a musician's growth, as well as the development of jazz, was influenced by a variety of factors. LeProtti knew how to read music, but other musicians taught him things about improvisation and "freak fingerin'" that permitted him to present ragtime and jazz more effectively. These ear musicians like Wesley Fields and Frank Shievers ("He could read what the man said and then blow his own soul and tell you what he wanted to say") assumed an important role in West Coast music just as they did in other spots in the nation. In other words, jazz could be taught, but not by the academies and the professors of classical music.

LeProtti also explains the music's development from two-beat to four-beat, the New Orleans style introduced by Will Johnson and others. The pianist and others were amazed to see Johnson pick the bass rather than bow it. "That's where I got the idea of the four beats," LeProtti recalled, and as early as 1912, this San Francisco band leader also "switched to the New Orleans type of instrumentation." These changes permitted the San Francisco black musicians to compete with New Orleans musicians like Wade Whaley and the others who "kept stickin' to the Louisiana beat" after World War I.

Stoddard makes it clear that there were differences between the various generations of musicians, and this played an important role in distinguishing jazz styles. Fields, Spikes, and LeProtti were among the early pioneers in the new music, attuned to New Orleans innovations, while Al Levy and Charlie Turner were beneficiaries of the jazz and swing decades of the 1920s and 1930s and influenced by Fletcher Henderson's and Louis Armstrong's bands. Also, some Bay Area musicians made it to the big time, becoming full-time musicians who traveled up and down the coast, while others, like Sid LeProtti and Duke Turner, worked day jobs and stayed close to home for that reason.

This fascinating glimpse of the Barbary Coast also allows us to appreciate other individuals who were part of the San Francisco scene. Willie "Strut" Mitchell led So Different entertainers when they danced to the song "Shimmeshawobble"; another dancer, "Old Folks," an ex-jockey, "was the greatest soft shoe dancer" that LeProtti ever saw; and a San Francisco dancer named "Rastus" so impressed a judge with his dancing that he was freed from all charges when arrested for fighting. Stoddard also chronicles the singularly important role that criminals played in San Francisco's early history, not to mention the respective roles of crime, municipal corruption, and reform in the story of the Barbary Coast.

The district's society, music, and dance was a magnet for the city's elite and fascinated natives as well as tourists from throughout the world. The informants make it clear that well-known white personalities from the business, political, and entertainment world delighted in slumming on the Barbary Coast, and at least one Russian ballerina, Anna Pavlova, learned a new dance, the Turkey Trot, at a black night spot, Purcell's, and vowed to "take it to Russia and...introduce it throughout Europe."

This was in 1910, years before other jazz dances, the Charleston and the Lindy Hop, became popular during the jazz decade of the 1920s. The fact that the Turkey Trot was one of several dances that started in or was popularized in a black San Francisco resort should not be lost on readers who have heard more about New York and Chicago dance spots. Nor should the fact that film stars and celebrities such as William Randolph Hearst and Sarah Bernhardt sought out the music and dance at Nigger Mike's to revitalize their staid lives be lost on contemporary readers who are aware that the vast majority of today's rap records are bought by white Americans.

But not all jazz musicians were entrenched in this raucous scene. Members of the So Different Band were not themselves participants in the excesses of Pacific Street. They neither drank ("We just didn't have any drinkers in the band") nor smoked. Spikes went straight home after the job. Because they did not conform to the stereotypes of the high-living jazz musician, they lived a long time—Spikes into his nineties— permitting Stoddard to record their reminiscences, as well as LeProtti's wife's.

The historical analysis in *Jazz on the Barbary Coast* adds context and even greater value to these stories from jazz musicians. "Blacks in the West" includes material known by California historians but not so much by the public, such as the role of the first black man to enter the west in 1538, the black presence among other early Spanish adventurers and sailing crews, and the migration of blacks as slaves and freedmen during and after the gold rush. Delilah Beasley's *The Negro Trail Blazers of California* (1917), not included as part of this book, expands on the historical information about black pioneers in the state. More recently, the works of Rudolph Lapp, Douglas Daniels, and Al Broussard have deepened our knowledge of blacks in Northern California in the nineteenth and twentieth centuries, and those of Tom Reed and Bette Yarbrough Cox enhance our knowledge of Los Angeles jazz and Central Avenue's unique history, in particular.

Stoddard's work also draws our attention to Peter Tamony's research, namely the fact the word "jazz" first appeared in print in a San Francisco newspaper in 1913. This has extraordinary significance for the history of the term and its use, as does the fact that white musicians who claimed to play jazz—Ferde Grofe, Art Hickman, and Paul Whiteman—performed in the city around World War I and were influenced by the Pacific Street music scene. Also, this is one of the rare works that notes the presence of the famous black vaudeville team, Bert Williams and George Walker, and their early careers in San Francisco before they gained national renown.

The inclusion of historical photographs of musicians and the interiors and exteriors of nightclubs and dance halls allows readers to visualize the dress and decorum of the artists themselves and the physical settings in which they performed. Yet because of the musicians' testimony and Stoddard's inclusion of historical material, *Jazz on the Barbary Coast* goes beyond the usual photo histories of jazz with their few captions and brief summations. In this and other respects, Stoddard's work is pioneering.

Jazz on the Barbary Coast deserves our close attention. Stoddard permits the musicians to present their views in their own words, continuing in the tradition of some of the best chroniclers of the music's history, Bill Russell, Alan Lomax, and Larry Gara. At the same time, Stoddard admits that the music itself is the best source and refrains from analyzing the few existing records — such as Curtis Mosby's from the late 1920s — or the reprinted composition, "The Big Three Rag," of Sid LeProtti.

One of the ways to gauge a work's value is whether it encourages deeper research. For example, Stoddard suggests the topic of jazz in the Far East might be worthy of a book. Closer to home, with its catalogue of musicians' names and nightclubs, not only in San Francisco, but in Oakland, Sacramento, Martinez, Monterey, and Los Angeles, this work gives a patient researcher the raw material to recreate the California jazz scene with the aid of newspaper articles, city directories, and fire insurance maps. Such a work, inspired by Stoddard's research, would permit greater appreciation of the music and dance which was simultaneously not only regional, but American and international around the time of World War I.

Douglas Henry Daniels is Professor of Black Studies at the University of California, Santa Barbara. He is the author of Pioneer Urbanities: A Social and Cultural History of Black San Francisco *(U.C. Press, 1990) and the co-editor of* Peoples of Color in the American West *(D.C. Heath, 1993).*

PREFACE

During the mid-sixties, I began traveling around the San Francisco Bay Area recording conversations with early jazzmen. Initially I worked with the white musicians of the New Orleans revival. At the outset, I was idly collecting information, asking some questions about the essence of jazz, and unearthing rare jazz records of the twenties. As I proceeded, I discovered there were many blacks who played jazz in San Francisco during the twenties, and I began to concentrate on recording their stories. In this period. I began to publish a few articles about the lives of these early jazzmen.

My interviewing and research were interrupted between 1967 and 1971 while I worked on the life story of George Murphy "Pops" Foster, eventually published as *Pops Foster—The Autobiography of a New Orleans Jazzman*. I then returned to work on black jazz in the Bay Area. Eventually, I concluded that black jazz in the twenties had spread to Canada and the Pacific Northwest; throughout the Southwestern states, including Arizona and New Mexico; and to the Far East, in particular to China, Japan, and the Philippines. I also discovered that there were a few black jazzmen around during the late teens, most of them well-known New Orleans musicians such as "Kid" Ory, Wade Whaley, Neny Coycault, "Papa Mutt" Carey, Dink Johnson, Freddie Keppard, Frankie Dusen, Will Johnson, and so on. Every time I turned up a solid useful lead on a black jazzman who played before the twenties—or on those who were referred to as the "oldtimers"—it would soon end up in a blind alley. After a hundred blind alleys, I finally located Mrs. Louis Sidney (Mamie) LeProtti and discovered the material Sid LeProtti left behind. This exciting breakthrough eventually led to Reb Spikes and focused my interest on the earlier period from 1900 to 1920. The results of this interest are what you have before you in this book. I believe that it may change some of our perceptions about the beginning and early dissemination of jazz in America.

This kind of research has its high and low points. On the high side is the satisfaction of discovering material virtually untouched by other researchers. The photographs included in this volume, for example, have never previously been published. My early expectations for the research have been exceeded several times. On the low side, much of the source material has disappeared, and leads to new material were scarce and often useless. Even the promising avenues often had to be abandoned for lack of sufficient information. As a researcher, I had been constantly whip-sawed between the exhilarations of discovery and the depression of defeat. The exhilarations won.

Many a good historical book never gets published because the author is continuously dredging up new facts and working them in. He never reaches the point where the research is complete and probably never will. There is always one more person to see, another library to go through, a book to read, and so on. It is the same with this book. Although it is incomplete, it is a beginning, and my hope is that the material can be added to and, eventually, the whole story reconstructed.

This volume attempts to survey the black music of the San Francisco Bay Area and Northern California from 1850 to 1940. For the period before 1900,

I relied entirely on information I culled from various historical sources. For 1900 to 1920, I provide firsthand reports; this is the area of greatest concentration.

The book opens with an autobiographical sketch of Louis Sidney "Sid" LeProtti, who was born in 1886 and played on the Barbary Coast from 1906 until 1921. I call this an autobiographical sketch because it is written in the first person, but it derives from a number of sources. I try to use the phrases, expressions, and syntax that Sid used in the autobiographical material he left. His story comes first because it is the most complete—he played the Barbary Coast and Northern California all his life—and it gives us the most basic information. There is a brief remembrance of Sid by his widow that sheds some light on him as an individual but not as a musician.

Sid's life story is followed by a piece on Benjamin M. "Reb" Spikes. Born in 1888, Reb visited the Barbary Coast in 1907 and 1908, but was not a musician at the time, and then returned in 1914 as a musician in Sid LeProtti's So Different Jazz Band. Reb lived in Los Angeles and traveled the Southwest and Midwest during his absence from the Barbary Coast from 1908 to 1914. After his Barbary Coast period, he returned to Los Angeles in 1921 to carve out another historically important career. Thus, Reb gives us an important view of the Barbary Coast, provides a good summary of jazz in the Southwest and Los Angeles during several periods, and, finally, is blessed with an unusually accurate memory.

Next, we have a brief biographical sketch of Wesley Fields, done by Harry Mereness in 1940. Word for word, it is the most important material in the book. It is maddeningly short.

The autobiographies of Alfred Levy and Charlie "Duke" Turner, covering the post-Barbary Coast era, offer a marked contrast to those of LeProtti and Spikes. Levy and Turner were asked about every known Barbary Coast musician; a few were remembered and commented on. The absence of any mention of a musician indicates they did not know him. For the black jazzmen who came along in the twenties, Kid North, Oklahoma Red, Juicy Payne, Slocum Mitchell, Wesley Fields, Clarence Williams, and many others simply did not exist. There are distinct generations of musicians in the Bay Area. Levy and Turner represent the generation after the closing of the Barbary Coast. Levy offers a view of a full-time musician, a profession he entered while with the Peacock Melody Strutters. Most of the musicians

Levy played with were full-time professionals and they give similar accounts of their lives. Turner was a part-time musician who played weekend gigs and rarely ventured far from home because of time limitations. Turner's part-time gigging was the more usual pattern for Bay Area black musicians during the twenties and thirties.

The book continues with two background chapters—"Blacks In The West" and "The Barbary Coast." Most prospective readers of this volume will be jazz buffs and will want a brief cultural and historical setting for the music. "Blacks In The West" offers a brief summary of the black man's place in the West and how it compared with his place in the rest of America. "The Barbary Coast" focuses on the flavor and setting of the Barbary Coast. The two chapters combined, plus the biographical material, give a good idea of what black life was like in general, and on the Barbary Coast in particular. Neither chapter pretends to be significant historical research, and far better materials are suggested in the bibliography. The best of these are *The Black West* by William Katz and *The Barbary Coast* by Herbert Asbury.

The next chapter is a historical summary of black music in Northern California. It is titled "Jazzin' 'n Dancin'." The primary emphasis is on the period 1850 to 1900, which precedes the biographical material. Material from this period is scarce. There is some information covering our primary period of interest (1900 to 1920), and much of this confirms the biographical material.

Concluding the book, I have presented some facts, fiction, commentary, prejudices, speculation, and/or insight, in "Comments Out of My Mind." This is the material I had the most fun and the easiest time with. I have to admit at this point that I am not a musician and, therefore, may have missed or misunderstood many of the technical musical points. I would add that I love jazz and would prefer being a jazz musician, but never could get the hang of it, and, instead, write about jazz as my contribution.

The Barbary Coast is used as the hub of this narrative. All of our major sources played there, and it was the location of more music than any other place in the Bay Area or the western United States. This concentration does not exclude other places in Northern California or the West, and what we know about other places is included.

The material for the Sid LeProtti monograph was graciously provided by Mamie LeProtti. It derives from a variety of sources left by Sid, including newspaper articles, acetate recordings, lists, tapes, photographs, programs, letters, and notes. This is the most valuable material in the book and made this book possible. The LeProtti material led directly to Benjamin "Reb" Spikes and the subsequent inclusion of considerable material from Spikes. Let me publicly thank the gracious Mrs. Louis Sidney (Mamie) LeProtti for making this book possible.

Long before I contacted Mr. Benjamin M. "Reb" Spikes, I knew of him and of his connection with the Los Angeles jazz scene. He had been interviewed a number of times for jazz publications in connection with his Los Angeles activities. I was unaware of Mr. Spike's connection with the Barbary Coast and was very excited when I realized that he had played on the Barbary Coast with one of the earliest black bands in the area. I contacted Reb Spikes in early 1972 and had three fairly long interview sessions with him. The three sessions resulted in about twelve hours of tape. Mr. Spikes is a thoughtful and gracious man with an outstanding memory. His eyesight is failing and identification of photographs is difficult, but he still reads considerably with the help of a magnifying glass. Mr. Spikes lives in a large comfortable apartment house furnished in the upper middle-class manner and is blessed with a lovely wife. He tells us how he was in the business end of music, and this resulted in investments that have made his future secure. His time is spent managing his investments and in writing and composing. At eighty-four years of age, Mr. Spikes is more active than most twenty-five year olds. My thanks to this musical pioneer for his help.

Some will question this book's focus on blacks. Most jazz experts agree that blacks are responsible for the creation of jazz. This book is going to work on that assumption and proceed with the business of adding to our knowledge of its origins. There is no conscious effort to avoid whites in the book, and they are included where they are brought up by black sources. On the other hand, no effort has been expended in researching white musicians and white jazzmen. If I came across unrelated historical material on whites, I skipped over it.

A great number of people are mentioned by Sid LeProtti and Reb Spikes. Some are identified as black and some as white. There are a number of well-known whites that I do not identify further and some people whom I feel the context explains whether they are white or black. It is reasonably safe to assume, in the absence of information one way or the other, that the subject is black.

There are a number of errors and inconsistencies in the text. These are by design. I have long held the notion that historians took a bad turn in the road twenty-five hundred years ago when they followed Thucydides instead of Herodotus. I believe that a certain amount of inconsistency adds to the charm of a work. Of course, some of the inconsistencies could be cleared up if the sources were alive today. Others are the conflicting views of different people. For example, Sid LeProtti states that he played on the Barbary Coast for twenty years from 1906 to 1921, and gives us conflicting information on which joint he started in and on the makeup of early Barbary Coast bands. Most of these I have preferred to leave in. Reb Spikes I found to be the most internally consistent of anyone I have ever interviewed; his story checks out completely with external sources. Jelly Roll Morton I found the most subject to the shifting winds of his mind. It is curious that we have three versions of Jelly's leaving the Bay Area. The reader may want to read them in sequence to get the full impact. I did not have the advantage of asking Sid LeProtti questions as I did Reb Spikes, and a certain number of the errors and inconsistencies in the LeProtti material could be due to my misunderstanding of it. It has been my overall purpose to present a historical work that is more exciting than a laundry list.

I would like to thank a number of people for their efforts in helping me to complete this book. I have already thanked Mamie LeProtti and Reb Spikes. I also thank: Alan Lomax for letting me use the Jelly Roll Morton material; Harry Mereness for use of his Wesley Fields article; Douglas Daniels for his hundreds of hours reading black newspapers and sharing his research with me; Al Levy and Charlie Turner for their interviews; Bob Gicker for photographing the Barbary Coast today; the California Historical Society Library and Archive staff; the Wells Fargo History Room staff; the Bancroft Library staff; the University of California Library-Newspaper Room staff; the many Bay Area black musicians like Ike Bell, Ethel Terrel, Freddie McWilliams, Neva and Tibb Pierre, and Norris Hester, who indirectly helped with leads and material; Joline DuBois and Glory Bayne, who typed the manuscript; Roberta, Ann, Hill, Marc, and Jana Stoddard for a pinch of patience; the indefatigable Laurie Wright for his patience, understanding, and superior printing; and finally, all the great black musicians who made the book possible in the first place.

Tom Stoddard
San Anselmo, California, 1982

Preface to the republishing of *Jazz on the Barbary Coast*

This book was, thanks to Laurie and Peggy Wright and Storyville Publications, London, England, first published in 1982. At that time, my turbulent and difficult marriage was coming to an end. My principal concern was to get the book in print so that Barbary Coast and West Coast jazz would be preserved for future generations. Laurie and Peggy, who published many of my articles in their magazine, were willing to print it without a lot of effort and time on my part. To them, thanks again for preserving an important part of jazz history.

I hoped the book would someday be published with more photos and better photo reproduction. I call this a republishing instead of a reprint because some material has been changed and some photos that I can no longer retrieve have been dropped. These photos are principally of the physical Barbary Coast as it stood in 1974 when my dear, deceased friend, Bob Glicker, took them; they are now lost. They are of only marginal importance to the musical history of the time and place, and, fortunately, because the area is preserved as a historical district, the same buildings appear today much as they have looked since the time of the 1906 fire. For those who would like to walk through the distict, walk east on Pacific Street, from Kearny to Battery.

Today I am in far happier circumstances, married to my loving and helpful wife, Loretta, with whom life has become a cakewalk. Loretta has taken time to review the text and assist with the republication. She has done all the hard work on two books written since *Jazz on the Barbary Coast,* and because of her, they are excellent productions. Both publications are still available from us with details available on my biographical page.

My thanks to Bill Carter and the San Francisco Traditional Jazz Foundation, who had discovered this volume and have been the driving force in this republication. Thanks also to the California Historical Society for joining with this republication effort and, thereby, indicating its importance to California history.

Petaluma, California, 1998

*Sid LeProtti, 1953,
as photographed
by Harry Bowden*

Sid LeProtti

THAT
BLAZE
OF ELECTRIC
LIGHTS

The Barbary Coast is gone, but one good thing, it didn't take me with it. I played there from 1906 until they closed it down in 1921. Let me give you a few stories about the people and the characters and the gamblers and the music back then, and everything that went with it. I'd like to tell you about a gambler named Catfish and how he cut off Baby Face's head. Then there was musicians like Russ Morgan, my trombone player, who could hit sixteen notes clean as a lick; Will Johnson's New Orleans Jazz Band that come visitin'; that character Mr. Jelly Lord; King Oliver and his tobacco-chewin', wall-spittin' bunch; and my famous Sid LeProtti's So Different Jazz Band that played at Purcell's. We had hop fiends, or opium fiends as you might call them today, and a bunch of beautiful girls who danced and was prostitutes.

9

The electric lights of the Pacific Street clubs, c. 1910

The Barbary Coast was famous for Purcell's, which was founded by Lew Purcell and Sam King, two Negro ex-pullman porters. Purcell's was one of the most famous Negro dance halls in the country and was located at 520 Pacific Street in one of the first buildings put up after the fire of 1906. They had started up on Broadway and then had moved down to Pacific Street. Pacific Street was the main stem of the Barbary Coast. We used to call it Terrific Street. I can remember the time you could come across San Francisco Bay on the ferryboat, and you could pick out that blaze of electric lights on Pacific Street. There wasn't any neon in them days, just millions of electric lights. There was The Midway, The Hippodrome, The Thalia, Louie Gomez's, Parenti's Saloon, Griffin's, Spider Kelly's, The Bella Union, and a slug of other places like that. You could see all the lights from them for miles in any direction. I've seen good times on Terrific Street when the street was so crowded with people nobody could go through there in an automobile, and I remember the night the officers of the law come in and closed

Exterior of Spider Kelly's, c. 1913

everything down. The last number I played was "Four O'Clock," one of my own numbers I'll tell you about.

This is my version of the old, famous Barbary Coast. As I said, the main street was Pacific, but originally it was Broadway one block north. The Barbary Coast was bounded on the north by Broadway, on the south by Clay Street, on the east by Sansome Street, and on the west by DuPont Street, which is now Grant Avenue and the main street of Chinatown.

I broke into the Barbary Coast in 1906, right after the earthquake and fire. I started playing at Sam King's at the afternoon session from two 'til six. We just had piano and drums. They had a very fine piano player by the name of Fred Vaughn who was playin' the afternoon session for them. He took a trip to Chicago, and I took his place while he went, and he's still goin' as far as that job goes. The music readin' era was comin' in about that time, which before that was mostly all fakers or improvisers. Fred couldn't read any music, and when he come back he couldn't make it afterwards. By then, all the bands was playin' from music.

They liked my playin', and they put me playin' the piano in the evenings with the orchestra under a fella by the name of Jack Ross. He'd been an old soldier and put several enlistments in the army, playin' in an army band. He played the violin, and there was a very peculiar thing about the way he played it. He strung the violin up right-handed like you usually do, and he played it left-handed, and he could play it. When I first started playin', the tunes we played were marches, mazurkas, two-steps, and waltzes of the day, and once in a while some character would come in and ask you to play a polka or schottische. The customers there would ask Jack to play a slow drag, or the blues as they called them. He was very stubborn and hard-headed about playin' tunes, and he'd just ignore them. So when he'd step out to the restroom, the gang would say to me, "Play the blues" or "Slow drag!" I'd play the blues and the floor would be full'a people dancin'. Well, Sam King, it was very characteristic that he always stood at the head of the bar all night and greeted the customers as they come in and shook hands with everybody; he noticed it. He put old Jack on the spot. He told him he'd have to play more blues and ragtime tunes. Old Jack said, "I'm runnin' the orchestra, and if you don't like the way I'm runnin' it, that's just too bad." They give him the customary two weeks' notice and let him go. There wasn't no union in them days, and that was it. They made me leader of the band, and that's how I got to be leader, and I went on from there.

I got rid of the violin as I seen that we didn't have no bass fiddle. From what I know about instrumentation, your violin goes fine when you have some of your other string to go with it. You got to have your bass fiddle to bring your fiddle out, because it's all in the same family. If you've got a fiddle against cornets, clarinets, trombones, and all that stuff and another, it don't jive. We had clarinet, cornet, trombone, piano, and drums.

Sam King and Lew Purcell split up early—before I started on the Coast. Sam was down at 468 Pacific Street and had a joint that went on for years. I played down there for him first. The music in the places usually started off with piano and drums; then it worked up to four pieces and then six pieces. The Thalia, which was one of the biggest places, had eighteen pieces at one time.

A fella named Willard Jones come to San Francisco right after the earthquake of 1906. He was a mighty fine piano player and brought some good tunes and had a very fine style. After Leroy Watkins, he's the first one I heard playin' boogie woogie. I'll tell you about Watkins when I get into my growin' up. There wasn't very many piano players that played that stuff. Mostly they played rags and blues. A very popular number in those days was "The Preacher and the Bear." Willard played "Frankie and Johnnie," "Shreveport Blues," "Texas Blues," and "Shimmeshawobble." Willard played a fancier style than I'd heard before and did a lot for me.

The front of the saloons and dance halls was all open, and they was open twenty-four hours a day, 365 days a year. The only time they closed up was election day. They'd either nail some boards across the door, or they'd take some wire and wire the swingin' doors together. Then some of the employees would stand around durin' the day. Those swingin' doors were up there in front goin' all the time, 'cause they never closed up. They had a lot of fights, and it was nothin' to see the carpenter, every once in a while, replacin' some swingin' doors because some beer bottles or bodies had gone through them. I want to tell you about a couple of them fights, like when the Ninth Cavalry come to Purcell's.

I'll tell you a little bit about the personnel of the place. As you come in, on the left was the bar, and on the other side there was a partition. The partition was open, and the girls all stood up there in front behind it. As you went in, you selected your girl to dance with. You bought little copper checks for twenty cents apiece, and then you gave one to the girl every dance. The girls turned the checks in at the end of the night. Ten cents went to the girls, and ten cents went to the house. You took the girl out and started dancin'. The floor manager come and took your order while they're dancin'. "What do you want to drink?" he'd say. You'd say, "Whiskey," "Wine," "Beer," or "Cigar," and he'd call this out to the bartender. Then the floor manager would blow the whistle, and the minute he blew the whistle, you had to stop the music right now, wherever it was. Then he'd say, "Play a waltz," then fine, you'd play it. They didn't waste any time when business was good. Course, when it was slow, we'd slow up.

When business was good, we used to play between twenty-six and thirty dances an hour. It was nothin' for the piano player to have tape on the end of his fingers and wear out a good piano in a year. It was the same with all the piano players around. They called them good pianos, but they'd generally go get a second-hand piano that was maybe half-worn out when you got it.

The Hippodrome, c. 1936, was one of the biggest and most popular dance clubs on the Barbary Coast. Pictured here is the revived nightclub, not the original.

Most of the bands started off with piano and drums, and then work on up. My famous band there started with piano, drums, clarinet, and baritone euphonium. Then we added bass fiddle, flute, and piccolo.

The gamblin' in those days was mostly dice; that was the big thing. They gambled all over, and we had a gamblin' room like everybody else. They played poker in some of the pool halls, but they didn't go so much for poker right around the Barbary Coast. Up at the Dixie Hotel, they mostly went for craps, and Catfish ran that game; and down at the Squeeze Inn craps was the main thing on a billiard table. I don't believe they ever played a half-a-dozen games of billiard on that table, because them characters stayed up all night shootin' craps. Naturally, they didn't get up until late in the day, but there wasn't much billiard playin' goin' on during the day; there was generally a canvas cover over it. Blackjack was another game that went on in all those places. Of course, there was Old Fong the Chinaman; he used to come around and write the Chinese lottery tickets.

There was other famous places on the Barbary Coast outside of Purcell's. The Chinatown guides used to bring the tourists into the main places, and they'd give the guides a little fee for bringin' them in the place. They'd bring them to The Hippodrome, The Thalia, Purcell's, and sometimes they'd go in The Midway, but, as a general rule, they just made about the three most prominent places. The Hippodrome, I think, of all the big dance halls, was the biggest. There was a big celebration at The Hippodrome any time the soldiers or the fleet come in.

You talk about your present day B-girls and what's goin' on with them; we had practically the same thing in those days but not so rough. The bottle of beer was fifty cents, and, when one of the boys got groggy, the waiter brought the beer for the girl. She never touched it, and, when he wasn't lookin', the waiter took it away, and the same bottle came back again. So the same things that went on in them days is goin' on now. I think that people in them days were livin' better than they do today, because we didn't have such vicious people in them days that would kill people for nothin'. Don't get me wrong about the Barbary Coast. We had some of the best people in town to frequent the place. They wanted to come out and see the sights. Of course, there was the characters and hang-arounds, too.

We had Red Kelly's across the street from Purcell's; it was a very famous place for its blondes and Filipino customers. We had a smaller place down the street, Louie Gomez's. He was a Portuguese-Negro boy. Over there, they had a piano, cornet, and drums. The cornet player was the brother of my clarinet player, Adam Mitchell. His name was Buddy Mitchell, and, if it was a quiet night, you could hear him blowin' up at Kearny and Pacific. We used to call it the cornet band. We don't know what the piano player was doin' there, because he blew him out.

One time we had a bad shootin' scrap over at Louie Gomez's. How that drummer didn't get shot, nobody knows! This customer got in a fight and pulled a gun and started shootin'. As you keep your foot on the drum pedal, there's a ball goes up and hits the drum. One of the bullets went right through the bass drum and hit that pedal and busted that ball all to pieces. The only thing I can figure out, the drummer never played the drum with his foot on it straight; he always played it kind of on the side. They killed that fella as he went out the door; the bartender reached over and hit him with a bottle full'a whiskey, and then, after he hit him, the fella staggered, and the bartender jammed the rest of the broken bottle in his neck. That cut his jugular veins and his throat, and he fell over and bled to death.

As I say, there was lots of famous places there. There was Parenti's Saloon on the corner, owned by the Parenti brothers. Griffin's was owned by the famous old-time San Francisco referee. He refereed some of the most prominent fights, and his place was where all the boys got their checks cashed.

We had a fella around the Barbary Coast named Irwin Jones who used to play banjo. I never seen it, but they said he could put a whole pie in his mouth at once. There's another fella I must tell you about. He hung all around the Barbary Coast, down around Third and Howard, and the Townsend District; he was all over San Francisco. They called him Giles County, and he played the banjo. He'd play for those parties that would come in Purcell's and the different places. He was a character; he played the banjo and rode it like a horse. He had the banjo neck reinforced so he could ride it, and he got on it and rode it, and he was plucking the banjo all the time. Everyone knew Giles County; he went to all the places.

The Bella Union was up on Kearny Street. It was kind of a mysterious place in my estimation. The man that run it was an old sea captain, and he catered strictly for seafarin' people. Little Egypt appeared at the Bella Union in 1893 and did her famous dance. As far as I knew of, I never heard of any music in the Bella Union outside of an electric player piano. It's an old type

AT THE BELLA UNION.

Dancers at the Bella Union, the most renowned theater on the Barbary Coast from the gold rush until after the 1906 earthquake, c. 1890

with the metal discs that drop down over the strings, and they make a sound like a banjo. You can play them with a player roll or just play them; there are very few of them left. I had an opportunity to play one up at Brentwood until I played it full'a holes, and they finally got another one.

In those days, they didn't look at servicemen like they do today. It was terrific the way they used to beat them in them days; everybody hated a soldier and hated a sailor. Why, I didn't know. Everybody today, it's a different story, the boys goin' out there bravin' all them bullets to fight for the cause. That's one thing that's gotten better. If anybody beats up servicemen today, you're just likely to get in dutch. Most of the street fights was with soldiers and sailors. Anytime they'd come down to the Barbary Coast, if they got unruly, they'd work out on them. Them guys were out at sea or in one of them camps, then they'd come down there and get all

Little Egypt at the Bella Union, c. 1893–1906

loaded up, get boisterous and rowdy, then a fight'd get started. All they would have to do is a fistfight get started; that'd settle it, everybody would get in it. They got one started in The Thalia one night, and it come on out in the street. It was between the sailors and the civilians. They got out in the street, and I mean, it was a fight, they were layin' all over Pacific Street. It was mostly fists in them days, and there was no danger of gettin' run over because there was only a handful of automobiles. I don't know how many sailors they carried out of there, but I know four civilians that got badly bruised up. Somebody phoned into the Hall of Justice right down on Kearny Street, and here come a whole wagonload of cops. They blocked Pacific Street off; there was fightin' from gutter to gutter. All the police in them days wore shoes with double soles on them, and they done a might fine job of kickin'. They started kickin' everybody into them wagons and took fifteen or twenty wagonloads down to the City Hall and locked them up. After it was all over with, some of them was back the next night, drinkin' and havin' a good time. There's a Negro fella named Bill Green, who used to run the Aloha Club in Martinez, who was shinin' shoes in The Thalia at the time, and he used to tell me about some of the fights in there.

The sweetest music I ever heard this side of heaven was down at a little Negro joint, in the second block down Pacific Street, called Charlie Coster's. It was just a harp and violin, and both the boys that played them was from Portugal. One was what you'd call a light-type Portuguese who played the harp, and the violin player was an Armenian, but his folks had come from Armenia and settled in Portugal. I knew the boys very well and used to go

Six belles of the Bella Union, c. 1890

listen to them any chance I got. One of their tunes that was beautiful was George M. Cohen's "Popularity." What was so wonderful about their music was the harp player was great at improvisations in them days. He didn't pick to play strictly chords; he played a lot of obbligatos in his music. I don't know where the violin player learned to play at, but he sure could play. I've heard a lot of violin players in my life, but I never heard a fella that could get his 'tonation on it; it was tremendous, especially on the heavier strings. He just had great 'tonation and technique. "I'm Ruth" was one of their sweetest tunes.

All of the traffic was around Kearny and Pacific streets, and even after you got down in the second block of Pacific Street, between Sansome and Montgomery, you were gettin' out of the Barbary Coast. Even though the boundaries was like I give you. That included the houses of ill-fame, the saloons, the dance halls, the Chinese gambling joints, the Chinese hop joints, and everything that went with them. I don't know today why they ever called it the Barbary Coast. I've never seen nothin' very barbary about it, with the exception of the fights, and we still have fights today. That was just the name it got because of the seafarin' men. That was their rendezvous and quite a rendezvous for the old-time shanghaiers that shanghaied the men for the boats.

Sid LeProtti

"Ma, Sid's Playin' Ragtime"

I've heard my grandmother tell friends of the family about me, "That's the pop-eyed rascal that burnt up my turkey," because I was born Thanksgiving Day, November 25, 1886, at 3:15 in the afternoon. In all the excitement of my bein' born, they forgot about the turkey. I was born and raised in Oakland in the part that's called Watts Tract. That's just a tract that a man by the name of Watts settled in the early days, and it's in North Oakland. I went to school there at the Clausen School, and my grandparents raised me.

My grandmother was a famous contralto in San Francisco in 1860. She was the first Negro woman to sing on stage in the state of California. She was married to Richard Marsdon but sang under the name of Amelia Francis. She used to tell me about those days. They sang in open-air theaters, and the Spanish caballeros took out their six-shooters and shot in the air for applause. She had several sets of silverware she'd gotten in them days for singin'. When my uncles and aunts grew up, they had a singin' group they called the Marsdon family; they used to sing at the Sage Horn Hall in Oakland.

After I started to grow up, I started piano. Naturally, my grandmother bein' a singer, and my father playin' the harp, I had to start. In them days, everybody that had a grandfather, grandmother, uncle, aunt, or anybody in the family that played music, as the kids come along, it was customary for them to play music. There's been millions and millions of dollars wasted on children who have music lessons because of that, and after they grow up, they don't know a clarinet from a bassoon; they forget all about it. My grandmother was born in Philadelphia at Fourth and Lombard streets, and she spoke German very well and had lots of German friends around. They used to be always telling her, "Oh, Marsdon, you should start that boy out, his father could play the harp and blah, blah, blah."

I finally got a German music teacher about eighteen or twenty years old, named Marva. She was one of the grandest players I ever heard. She played all of Liszt's Hungarian Rhapsodies, all fourteen of them, from memory alone, and there's thirty-two pages in number two. I learnt like all youngsters do, my scales first. Well, I could'a spit in their faces as a kid because, when come time after school to practice, I liked to go out and play.

My grandmother would say, "Well young fella, you better get over there and practice," then she'd lay down on the sofa. I'd be sittin' there foolin' on the piano, and I'd think she's asleep. Then she'd open her eyes and say, "That don't sound like much practicin' there to me." I'd set the clock up and everything else to keep from practicin'.

After while, I begin to do well. Then Miss Marva had one great criticism: that was to learn to play everything from memory. She said you were just like a machine when you had to sit there with the music in front of you all the time. I used to kind of revolt against her on that.

She'd say to me, "Do you know this piece?"

I'd say, "Yeah."

She'd say, "Play it."

I'd play it and make one mistake, and she'd say, "You don't know it."

I'd say, "I know it."

She'd say, "In Germany, where I came from, you either learn something or leave it alone. Now, if you don't want to play the piano, it's all right; I'll tell your grandmother."

She'd turn around to my grandmother and *sprechen Sie Deutsche* [speak in German] so I wouldn't understand what they meant. Then my grandmother would get on me. That's what I come through, and I went along and played music. I revolted against memorizin' everything, but if Miss Marva were alive today, I'd hug and kiss her. Today, I can sit down and play from sunup to sundown and wouldn't play the same thing. I can play three or four hundred pieces, memorized. Sometimes I forget the bridge or somethin' like that, but I can remember them.

The first time I heard ragtime, I was about eight years old; that was in 1894 or 1895. A Negro boy by the name of Leroy Watkins came out west because his mother was here, and she'd since married a man named Crouch. My mother, uncles, aunts, and what few Negro people there was in Oakland in them days—you could name most of the families on two hands—would come to my grandmother's house, as we was considered rich in them days because we had a piano. It was an old four-legged Stedman; it really wasn't old, it was modern in them days. We gathered there to hear this fella Watkins play ragtime, and he was the first ragtime player we'd heard. It was straight ragtime. There wasn't any fancy doin's in his playin'. He also played boogie woogie, and that was the first time I'd heard it.

A couple of years after Leroy Watkins came, Blind Tom come and we heard him play at the Presbyterian Church at Thirteenth and Clay in Oakland. He sure was somethin'. It was a few years after that that Blind Boone played here.

I still believe the best preparation for a jazz piano player is to study classical music. I think anyone, if they play the piano, cornet, clarinet, trombone, bass fiddle, or sax, should have a classical training at first. You've heard of Bach; there's no time, no air, no melody. I don't particularly care for it, but I have to take my hat off to anyone playin' it. It's all technique. There's a great Negro player named Hank Jones, and that's how he got his start. You can't get the piano or any instrument right without knowledge unless you're a genius like Art Tatum or Erroll Garner or Blind Tom. Some of them who played by ear took piano lessons, and it ruined them.

I never will forget the first ragtime piece I ever played. In them days, the *San Francisco Examiner* used to come out with a piece of popular music in the paper every Sunday, like the comic strip today. When I was eleven or

"Ambolena Snow" sheet music cover,
Sunday Examiner Magazine, *1897*

twelve years old, they came out with a piece named "Ambolena Snow." So naturally, I read music and sat down and played it. My grandmother was married four times, and one of them was an Indian; my uncle whose father was the Indian went in the kitchen and says to my grandmother and told her, "Ma, Sid is playin' ragtime."

My grandmother came in and kind of pulled me over the coals about it. She said, "I spend the money for your music lessons, and here you're playin' ragtime." So, after that, she got to talkin' to old man Lorenzo—he was a German and was a great dancer—and they got talkin' about me playin' ragtime. Then my grandmother comes to me and says, "Old man Lorenzo told me he thought it was fine you were playin' ragtime." Well, that was a nice way to tell me I could go on and play ragtime, and I went on and played the ragtime.

Grandma died when I was sixteen, not quite seventeen, and I started livin' with some people on Fortieth Street in Oakland, and I was on my own after that. It boiled on down to where I started workin' in the rollin' mill in the Judson Iron Works. The old Judson Iron Works is still there in Emeryville, but they have open hearth furnaces now. In them days, it was all wrought iron, and there's a lot of difference between wrought iron and steel. On wrought iron, there's a slag as stuff came out of the furnaces, and as it was squeezed together, there was flashes out of it that would just take your shirt off. I worked on the rollin' mill on the hot bed. We had to use all woolen clothes to keep from gettin' burnt up. I've still got marks on my hands and arms from workin' there, and how my hands have kept as supple as they have after all that, I don't know.

I worked there a while, and I met this boy who was a pretty good piano player. He says to me: "There's a fella down at the corner of Fortieth and San Pablo who wants me to play piano. He's got this piano in his joint and wants me to play, but my mother won't let me play. Why don't you go down and see him?" I had the gall to go up there and ask for a job playin'. They hired me. I played with two fellas by the name of Martin and McDonald.

I played the "Maple Leaf Rag" and "Peaceful Henry"—that's the only ragtime pieces I could play—and then "Ambolena Snow," which was just a song but was characteristic of the instrumental numbers in them days. Then I'd sit and play waltzes, "The Blue Danube," classics, and all that stuff. Then I'd go back and play the "Maple Leaf Rag" and "Peaceful

Sheet music cover for an early edition of Scott Joplin's "Maple Leaf Rag," 1899

Henry," and then some more classics, then the "Maple Leaf Rag" and "Peaceful Henry." I played there from seven o'clock to ten o'clock at night. I had to quit then because the racetrack was in Emeryville then, and the jockeys and exercise boys all lived upstairs and had to get up at three or four o'clock in the morning to exercise the horses. That's the way I started.

Then I went down in the country with them to a little town called Purisima on the San Mateo Coast. They went down there and took me along. They brought the farmers from all around to Purisima. They'd never heard a ragtime piano player down there, and I made me a hatful of money down there playin' ragtime. We came back in 1904, and I went on up to Angels Camp playin' in a whorehouse. I went to bed one night, and it got so cold that I got up and took the rugs off the floor and threw them on the bed to keep warm. Next morning, I looked out the window, and there was seven inches of snow coverin' the ground. I finally came back home and then got a job playin' in Salinas. Durin' the earthquake of 1906, I was right out in the main street of Salinas with my nightclothes on. Right after the earthquake and fire, I came up to Oakland and got a little job playin' in a sportin' house.

Then came this man into my life, old Henry Stewart, an old singer with the minstrel shows. He just came right out in plain English and said, "You know kid, you can play all the notes in the world they put up there in front of you, but you ain't playin' nothin'. That music is just mechanical; the only thing that keeps all the mechanicalism out of it is you play from memory. Did your teacher learn you that?"

I said, "Yeah, there's where it come in, she made me memorize everything."

He said, "If you really want'a play somethin', you know what you want'a do?"

I said, "What?"

He said, "You want'a get around some of them ear piano players; you want'a learn to listen and pick up some of their stuff. What you got to do is learn to fake and fill in."

We called it fakin' in those days, but today we'd possibly call it improvisin'.

Then he tells me about the songs, "You also got to learn to pick up a song from the boys. It's just a matter of ear trainin'. Then, when they walk up to you and ask you to play a song, you can play it by ear."

So I went along and that's what I done. I tell anybody, like my grandmother used to say, two heads is better than one, and I don't care how old you are, and makes no difference how much you know, you can always learn some more. Naturally, I learned a lot with my band. Now there's a lot of the late-style playin' that we have to do; I don't particularly care about it, but that's what the people want, and you have to go along with the times. A person that grows up and gets to be sixty years old and tries to choke everything down somebody's throat, like when he was a boy, why, he's just antique—put him in the garbage pile! As times go along, you've got to be modern. That's the reason I play all the tunes, but I don't try to keep up with the modern-day style; I play my style. I tell all the piano players that come along, the kids and everybody, after you learn to play, play your style. Somebody'll like your style and somebody won't; the president of the United States don't please everybody.

So I went along and learnt how to fill in and fake. Then one boy came along and told me, on some numbers, you have to do a lot of freak fingerin'. He said the way to finger the tune I was playin' is like that, and he showed me the way to do it. It was the effect you get playin' that stuff; it sounds better with freak fingerin'. It also takes the mechanical touch away from it, and I learnt how to do it. So, my teacher Miss Marva taught me to memorize, old Henry Stewart got me to learn fakin' and fillin' in, and this other boy taught me freak fingerin', and that's how my style come along.

Later on, we had a Negro boy named Juicey Payne, who played at this place called the Squeeze Inn on the Barbary Coast. I used to go in there sometimes after work and play for tips and kicks. Juicey was a piano player who couldn't play a thing without music. I tried to learn Juicey. He was a nice piano player, played nice, had a nice touch and everything, and he was a lovely fella with it, but I couldn't seem to get it in Juicey's head that he could pick up fakin' by ear. His playin' sounded nice, but it was dead. It just went boom, jing, boom, jing, all night long. There was nothin' in between it, and I told him you gotta fill it up. Juicey never did learn to fake and fill in.

I have a terrible time now givin' kids lessons or tryin' to show anybody anything. When I play any of the popular numbers, I'm liable to play it this way now and then play it a dozen different ways. Then I can't go back and show them how I wanted them to play it. Sometimes it sounded good the first time, and I really want'a try it again, but I forgot all about it.

Sid LeProtti

Rastus Danced
Out of the Courtroom Doin' the
Buck and Wing

Now you'd like to know a little something about some of the famous acts that came out of Purcell's. We started off with one entertainer, Dick Robertson. He was a kind of bartender and would sing songs [circa 1906–08]. Then the ladies come. The first official entertainer that come out was Nina Jones [circa 1908–09]. She made plenty of money with the customers throwin' silver halves and dollars at her.

There's quite a history to that. We used to send for our entertainers to Chicago and New York. After they'd get out here and I'd get acquainted with them, I'd ask, "How do you like it out here?"

They'd say, "Man, this is it!"

I'd say, "It's all right then?"

I remember one girl tellin' me, "You know, back in New York we'd do a verse and two choruses for the house, and as long as anybody threw a nickel, you had to do another chorus and a dance. I'll never forget one fella who used to come in with a handful of nickels when I'd dance and sing, and he'd just keep throwin' those damn nickels."

So the honey that drawed the flies out here was the half-dollars and dollars, all silver—there practically wasn't any paper money then. Nina Jones, she broadcast it all over.

Then we got such prominent entertainers as Nettie Lewis, Bricktop, and Lillie Rose. I'll tell you about Nettie Lewis and her husband Glover Compton, and what they done to me, later. Glover was the one who learned a tune I composed and taught it to the guy who wrote it up and made it world-famous. Nettie went under her maiden name. I made seventy-five dollars one night playin' for Vincent Rose. Nettie sang this song that he liked, and when I got done, I had seventy-five dollars he give me. That's the most tips I ever made in one night, and that was somethin'. I played "Separation Blues," that was quite a number them days, and a gentleman tipped me thirty-five dollars. We had the famous Bricktop, who runs a cafe in Paris, France, today. One of our top girl entertainers, Lillie Rose, traveled all over Europe with two Negro boys. She spoke French, Italian, German, and Russian. She done the Russian dance, the part where you get down knee-bendin' and whirlin' around. She done that in tap steps, and those entertainers had to dance; there was no foolin' around.

In Purcell's we used to do what we called a team song, and one of the tunes we did it to was "Shimmeshawobble." All the entertainers would gather together on the dance floor. Willie "Strut" Mitchell would be out in front with his little cane, to lead them, and the rest of them in the background. They'd be doin' all kinds of steps. The steps was improvised with Willie leadin' them. The people would love it, and they'd do as high as ten different choruses. Sometimes they danced to what we used to call stop-time. You'd play and stop for six bars, play, stop for four bars, and so on. The point of it was you could hear them steps clean. Now, as a general rule, the band plays straight through, and they use cleats and chunks of iron and everything else on them. These boys I'm talkin' about danced with their shoes on, and you heard the steps. They'd go on and on in the team song until Willie would stick up the cane; then we'd cut. That was the signal for the last chorus.

"Old Folks" was the greatest soft shoe dancer I've ever seen. I never saw anybody, on or off the stage, to equal him, and he should'a been on the stage. He was a little bit'a Negro fella and skinny. He was smaller than me, and he'd been a jockey. My mother knew him very well when I was a baby. Then I come along as a young man, and he was up there in the years. He only had one eye; a horse kicked him in the other eye and put it out. You think imitation skatin' like they do on the Ed Sullivan and Kate Smith Show is new, but I seen Old Folks do it years ago, and he did it soft shoe. The way he danced soft shoe is what I call real dancin'. You ask somebody to do some real soft shoe dancin' and see what they'll do. They'll do it, and I'll admit they have some marvelous dances and some marvelous steps, but I seen all them steps, and done better, by Old Folks on the Barbary Coast. Like our great Negro dancer, Bill "Bojangles" Robinson, the way he danced in New York up the stairs to the stage, that's where he got the name "The World's Greatest Dancer," but I seen Old Folks do the same things.

After the police tightened down on the Barbary Coast and stopped the dancin', they hired Old Folks to stand on the door out in front to watch for the cops. It was always cut and dried that when the cops would come, he'd come in and wave twice and stop the music. The waiters would go tell the patrons to go sit down and take it easy, that everything would be all right in a few minutes. After the cops went by, we'd start up again. When people like Mose Guntz and the Chinatown guides would come in, they'd bring Old Folks in to dance. They tell me Old Folks was close to eighty when he died. That fadin' of the Barbary Coast is some story I'll tell you later on.

We had another little Negro boy here who was a fine dancer. He was as straight up and down as he was wide. I never did know what that boy's name was; we all called him Rastus. He'd come from the Emeryville Race Track in the horse racin' days. He was a marvelous Buck and Wing dancer. He got arrested for fightin' in Oakland and got hauled before the judge. He was a Jewish judge, Judge Samuels—Oakland only had one or two judges in them days—and the judge asked him what he did for a livin'. Rastus said he danced for a livin'. The judge asked him to dance and said if it was pretty good, he'd let him go. He started dancin' there in the courtroom, and the judge liked it, so he waved him right on out the door, and out the door he went, doin' the Buck and Wing. Later on he got to be a victim of dope, and that's pitiful. The last time I heard of Rastus he was up around Spokane,

Washington. I must tell you about a beautiful Irish girl I know who got on dope, and how I helped her get off it.

Speakin' of Spokane, there's someone I want'a bring up, a very fine piano player up there named Porkchops. He used to play everything very slow. Porkchops just never would hurry a tune. He was also a great fella for playin' a long and distinctive bass. When I heard him hittin' back licks on the bass, that was the first time I'd ever heard it. I picked up a few licks from him that I use.

We had some great piano players. Some of the most famous of those days was Ragtime Charlie, Arthur Rickman, Fred Vaughn, Wesley Fields, Harry Couch, and Oklahoma Red.

The musicians got along better than they do today. In those days, everybody would get along. I used to make a lot of money helpin' the other piano players. I'd go down to Sherman Clay's and get sheet music. I was the only piano player for ten years around there that read music; all the other fellas was ear piano players. Fred Vaughn, Wesley Fields, and I would go up the Wesley's house. I finally moved up to Wesley Field's house and lived with him and his wife. We had a piano up there, and I'd sit down and play the tunes. That's the way they'd learn them. After they'd learn the tunes, and we'd practice awhile, we'd go down to the Il Trovatore on Broadway and have one of those Italian dinners. That's the way we got along. Now a guy steals a tune like my "Canadian Capers," and they put him in San Quentin.

Ragtime Charlie played strictly ragtime and could only play one or two numbers. The other fellas I'm tellin' you about could accompany any song at all that you knew. If you could just hum it, they could play it. Ragtime Charlie wore a watch-chain big enough to hold a good-sized dog. He had a watch on it that possibly the present generation doesn't know much about; he wound it with a key. Everytime you saw Charlie he had his pipe in his mouth. I imagine you could'a put a half a can of tobacco in it because the bowl was so big. I asked him one day, I said, "Charlie, what's the idea of that pipe? The bowl on that thing looks like a steam shovel."

"Well little fella," he says, "you know if you got a small pipe you have-ta fill it more often. I got this one made up in Montana by a pipe maker up there. I told him I want a pipe I won't have-ta be fillin' all the time. You know if you're sittin' playin' the piano and smokin', you can't be stoppin' to fill your pipe all the time."

The fine piano players was Fred Vaughn, Wesley Fields, Arthur Rickmeyer, and Oklahoma Red. They was the best players of them all. Oklahoma Red played boogie woogie. He's a guy that could really play. Wesley Fields was left-handed and had a marvelous bass hand. We had a very fine piano player named Jay Roberts. He was a tall fella, as I remember, and he composed the "Entertainers Rag." He was the guy that used to play "Dixie" on one hand and "Marching Through Georgia" on the other. Some of the tunes that was popular in those days was "Some of These Days." You might not think it's that old, but it is. Shelton Brooks wrote it, and he wrote "Darktown Strutters Ball."

I don't see much difference in the good piano players in them days and the good ones today. I think the reason they got away from ragtime was because it was too much work. You listen to the bands playin' ragtime in them days, or today, and they're really playin'. There's no rhythm section, sax section, brass section, to take down and look all around, play a lot of half notes and whole notes to a bar, weak tunes. In those days, every man had to work. I get quite a kick out'a the piano players today; you see the right hand flyin', but the left hand is just once in a while hittin' the chords. The piano players in the Barbary Coast days had the left hand doin' as much work as the right, sometimes more.

We had another piano player, a little Jewish boy known as Mike Bernard; he came to San Francisco, and he was quite a pianist. I owe somethin' to Mike. He watched me play one night and said, "Sidney, I notice your fourth finger is a little weak."

I said, "Yeah."

He said, "I want'a show you an exercise that will help it."

He showed me an exercise that finished on the fourth finger, and I practiced it. Sure enough, it did get my finger in shape.

Mike was another two-handed piano player. He played "Stars and Stripes Forever" on the right hand and "King Chanticleer" on the bass.

Bert Williams came to San Francisco every so often and played uptown in the big theater. I think he played the Columbia. They had a show of Williams and Walker. I knew Bert Williams personally and played for a dance he had here. That dance was in 1911, the same year I had smallpox. What a dance! Everybody was there, and they served nothin' but champagne.

There was an awful lot of fine piano players on the Barbary Coast in those days. We never had any piano playin' contests like they did in the eastern cities. We all got along peaceable and quiet here in the West, fine bunch of fellas, show you anything they knew, and would be glad to do it. We were all good-hearted at swappin' tunes, but there was one time I was sorry I was bein' so good-hearted. That refers to when I had part of "Canadian Capers" stolen from me.

When I used to finish with my regular job at Sam King's or Purcell's, I sometimes used to go down to a little joint on Pacific Street called the Squeeze Inn. I used to pick up a few extra nickels there playin' for late parties.

One mornin' it was rainin' terrific, and I didn't want to go home in it, so I went down to the Squeeze Inn and played. I sat there and played this number of mine over, and everybody was crazy about it and wanted to know what it was. I didn't have no name for it; I'd just made it up and played it once in a while.

Bert Williams & George Walker's "The Voo Doo Man," sheet music cover, Sunday Examiner Magazine, *1900*

One of my entertainers was there, and she says, "Would you mind learnin' it to my husband sometime?"

I said, "Sure, Nettie."

Her name was Nettie Lewis; that was her maiden and stage name. She was married to Glover Compton, the piano player. Glover was playin' out on the beach—him and a very famous entertainer, Evelyn Joyner. So Nettie, she brought Glover down, and I learned it to him and never thought nothin' about it.

Then this gentleman, George Bryant, with Ferdon's Medical Show, we made a score of it and sent it off and got it copyrighted. We also had our twelve-piece orchestra to play it.

Sheet music cover of the 1921 edition of Sid LeProtti's composition, "Canadian Capers"

Next thing I know, I'm in Sherman Clay's at Kearny and Sutter Street. One of my piano player friends was there, and he says, "Say, Sid, you know that number you was playin' here awhile back that you said was yours?"

I said, "Yeah, why?"

He said, "Is that yours?"

I said, "So far as I know, it is."

He said, "Well, looka here. Here's a piece of music called 'Canadian Capers.' Look it over; there's something in here sounds like something you played in your number."

Sure enough, there was a strain of mine in there. I never had a name for my number, but that was my strain, and I was hot.

Later on, when we moved to Los Angeles to play in Byron Long's Tavern, as it was known then, this fella come in. I'd met him previous in San Francisco, and his name was Henry Cohen. He come over, and he said hello to the band.

I said, "Henry, that tune you got, 'Canadian Capers,' where did you get that at?"

He said, "That's quite a tune, ain't it?"

I said, "Yes," and then reached up in the music pile, and I had the piano part of the manuscript right there.

I said, "Did you ever see this?"

I said, "This strain here!"

He looked at me and turned two or three different colors and says, "This could cause a lot of trouble."

I said, "That's right! Where did you get it at?"

He says, "I got it from Glover Compton. You know how all the gang of piano players get together back in Chicago jammin' around together. Well, Glover was there, and he played it. I asked him if he'd play it over for me, and I asked him if I could take it down. Glover said, 'Yeah,' and that it was his tune."

Cohen said, "That's as far as I know about it. But," he said, "I'd like to see you about it. Can you come up and see me?"

I saw he felt kind'a bad 'cause he took it and all that. We talked some more, and he wanted to know if we could get together, and he could pay for his mistake. To make a long story short, I just told him, "That's all right, forget it this time, but be careful next time." And that's my story of "Canadian Capers."

One of the worst fights I ever seen was when the Ninth Cavalry came into Purcell's. They was Negro soldiers that was enroute to Honolulu [circa 1915]. It was one of those nights when the taxicabs and others would just have to worm their way through Pacific Street, back and forth from one side to the other. Lester Mapp, who just passed away in 1951, was the gentleman who took over after Lew Purcell passed away. He was a well-known fella, who was originally from Barbados in the West Indies. Mapp was a heavy-set man with a powerful wallop in each hand, and when he hit them, they went down and stayed down. I've seen him knock dozens of them down. When he hit them, that's all there was to it.

So these Negro soldiers got in an argument, and Mapp picked out a guy about six-foot. He popped him right on the point of the chin and knocked him back. The guy come back, and he hit him again. Well, he knocked him down for keeps the second time. About that time, one little fella jumps up on one of the benches and yells, "Look what they're doin' to our boys!" Then the fight was really on. George Purcell, Lew Purcell's son, come out from behind the bar with a little pearl-handled pistol. I don't know whether it was loaded or not, or whether he shot it, there was so much noise. The last time I saw the pistol it was goin' through the air like a jet plane. Beer bottles were flyin' around there like bullets, and people were gettin' knocked out through the swingin' doors; everybody was fightin'. Finally, patrolmen Bolin and Cavanaugh come in with the military police and got them boys down and hauled them off. When they left, the place looked like a good-sized wood-yard, with all the chairs and tables smashed up.

Sid LeProtti

DOIN' THE
TEXAS TOMMY

Up on Pacific Street above Stockton was the old Dixie Hotel. It was the Negro hotel where a lot of the characters roomed. They had a crap game goin' most of the time in the back room. A fella named Catfish ran the game around there. Catfish was a short, heavy-set man, about five-foot-eight. When Catfish was runnin' the game, this guy Baby Face used to come around pickin' on him [circa 1910]. Baby Face was a powerful-built Negro fella, about six-foot-six. I went up to the Dixie Hotel once in a while, to kill some time before goin' to work or to see someone.

One evenin' I was up there, I didn't gamble. I looked at the game, talked some with Catfish, and walked on out. When I got up the next mornin', I walked down the street to get something to eat. I seen the police and everybody on Pacific Street goin' up the street. I saw this little boy by the name of Whinny; we called him Whinny because he was always whinnying with his voice when he talked.

I said, "What's the matter?"

He said, "Man, didn't you know that Catfish cut Baby Face's head off last night?"

I said, "No."

He said, "Baby Face was pickin' on Catfish, and Catfish just blowed up. He took his knife and cut him from ear to ear, clean across."

Then he said, "Looka here!" and he showed me a trail of blood goin' up the street. It went right up the street, from in the middle of the block on Pacific Street, between Stockton and Dupont, to almost Griffin's Saloon, on the corner of Pacific Street and Montgomery. After Catfish had cut Baby Face, he run that far and left a trail of blood. He dropped there, and there was a pool of blood where he died.

I said, "My God, they'll hang Catfish."

Whinny said, "Yeah, if they ever catch him."

They tell me he just took that knife, wiped it off, and put it in his pocket and says, "I'll see you all later." He walked out the door on down to the Ferry Building, got on a ferry, went over to Oakland, and caught a freight train. That's the last of him. Until today they haven't caught him.

The entertainment like the quadrilles were very interesting because they was a little bit different than the quadrilles what they used to dance in the white dance halls. In Purcell's, Sam King's, Louie Gomez's, and Charlie Coster's place, they were a little different from the ordinary weekend country-dance quadrilles. First, they played a few bars of fast music; then, the floor manager would say, "Okay, okay, you boys let's go! Get your partners!" and they'd all get out on the floor, collected together. Then they'd dance. The first part of the dance was fast, and then the floor manager would signal to stop, and we'd stop for the intermission. The bartender had the glasses all on the bottom bar, and the floorman would go around to the customers and take their orders for drinks. He'd call the drinks to the bartender—"Whiskey," "Wine," "Beer," "Cigar," "Beer"—and the bartender would set the glass up. After the drinks was called, we'd play again, and they'd dance. Then, when the bartender finished pourin' the drinks, he'd yell, "All made!" The floor manager would blow the whistle and that would end the dance, and they'd pass out the drinks. In the white dance halls, they'd dance and then go to the bar and order.

Texas Tommy Swing

VOL. I.   SAN FRANCISCO, CAL., JANUARY 1, 1911.   50 cents.

PAVLOWA ENDORSED TEXAS TOMMY SWING.

CHARMED BY OUR DANCE, RUSSIAN BALLERINA WILL MAKE IT INTO BALLET.

DANCES IT ON THE "COAST."

With Society Folk Goes on a Slumming Tour Following Russian Dinner.

San Francisco has produced, in the famous "turkey trot" dance, a novelty in terpsichorean art, which is to be exported to the imperial palace of the Czar of the Russias for the entertainment of Nicholas II and his court, and then it is to be the basis of a new ballet which, it is expected, will create a furor in the capitals of Europe.

Anna Pavlowa, the delightful Russian artist, who has dazzled at the Valencia Theatre for the last week was delighted with the novelty. She tried it herself on the floor of the dance hall where she saw it, and after learning it declared that it was the best and most original terpsichorean production, delightful to behold and artistically satisfying.

"I will take it to Russia," she said, "and I will introduce it throughout Europe."

Pavlowa was on the "coast" as a member of a big party, in which were some local society people, in addition to the celebrated danseuse who admired the "trot," Mordkin, the latter's wife, Madame Pazitszkaia, Count Centenani, Stanley Sharp, Theodore Stier, the orchestra conductor, and other leading members of the company.

"The turkey trot is a wonderful dance," said Pavlowa, after she had seen it, admired it, learned it and tried it in one of the Pacific-street dance halls. "It is something quite different from anything I have ever known before. I like it. I will use it. I am going to dance it and introduce it in Russia and throughout all Europe. It is full of possibilities. The life and intensity of it appeal to me very strongly.

"I will have a great and beautiful ballet made of it, a ballet that will astonish the world. That is a wonderful dance. It is the only American dance I have seen that is original, in which there is no evidence of borrowing from something else. Such dances are rare, and I feel that I have made a discovery here."—*San Francisco Examiner, November 29, 1910.*

VAL. HARRIS

Composer of "Kid You've Got Some Eyes," "The Sheriff," one of the best rube songs ever written, "Keep on Lovin' Me Kid," "Oh, You Kid, I'll Get

THE DANCE THAT MAKES THE WHOLE WORLD STARE

AS ORIGINALLY FEATURED IN VAUDEVILLE BY NORINE and HARRIS

THE STORY OF THE DANCE

A BREATH FROM THE COTTON FIELDS—THE GRIZZLY BEAR, THE LOVING HUG, THE WALK-BACK AND THE TURKEY-TROT ALL BLEND IN TEXAS TOMMY SWING.

The Texas Tommy Swing invades the north and east like a dainty zephyr from the perfumed cotton fields of the sunny South. The rhythm of the Grizzly Bear, the inspiration of the Loving Hug, the grace of the Walk-Back and the abandon of the Turkey-Trot all blend in the harmony of the Texas Tommy Swing, which was really the parent of all the others.

The dance originated more than forty years ago among the negroes of the old Southern plantations. Every little movement has a meaning all its own to the heart truly in tune with nature. The graceful harmonies of the song and dance reflect the joyous spirit of the negro race, the care-free actions of the Dinahs and the Sams who gathered outside the cabin doors on moonlit nights and to the twang of the banjo or the scrape of the fiddle, vented the rhapsodies of mind and body in a purely natural way.

Here and there a raucous discord like the squawking voice of a chicken in distress breaks in upon the frivolous melody of the theme or a plaintive note brings a reminder of the tear always so close to the laugh in the negro nature.

Southern darkies brought the dance and a suggestion of the melody to San Francisco several years ago, and there upon the Barbary Coast it was rounded into perfect harmony. It took the place by storm. Eastern people interested in dancing took it up. Stage favorites seized upon its absorbing rhapsodies.

Society men and women accepted and adopted it. Pavlowa, the Czar's favorite dancer, went into raptures over it and incorporated it in her repertoire. Leaders of the four hundred all over the country regard it as one of the sights of San Francisco and endorse it to their friends on their return.

In tangible and concrete form this inspiring, historic and dramatic song and dance is now presented to the public for the first time, is Texas Tommy

MRS. OELRICHS LIKED TEXAS TOMMY SWING.

INTEREST AS GREAT AS PAVLOWA'S IN EXHIBITION OF CLASSIC AT BEACH

GOES TRIPPING HERSELF.

With James D. Phelan as Partner Newport Is Forgotten in Swing of Barn Dance.

Hearing how Pavlowa, the great Russian dancer, had discovered new styles of dancing in San Francisco that she intended to take to Russia and show to the Czar, Mrs. Theresa Oelrichs, who is making her annual pilgrimage here from New York and Newport, went out to the beach last night and saw the "turkey-trot" performed.

Mrs. Oelrichs appeared to be as much interested in the eccentric two-step as Pavlowa was, and after it was performed the evening was brought to a close by the members of the party accompanying her taking part in a barn-dance, through which she tripped daintily with James D. Phelan.

Mrs. Oelrichs had seen the Apache dance in Paris and the other talked-about dances in other European capitals, and when she came to San Francisco she decided that she wanted to see the style of dancing that the Russian had promised to incorporate in the imperial Russia ballet for the delectation of the Emperor Nicholas.

The trip to the beach last night was made by Mrs. Oelrichs, following a dinner at the St. Francis. In the party were Mr. and Mrs. Rudolph Spreckels, Mrs. Oelrichs, two other women, James D. Phelan, Joseph S. Tobin and Thomas Magee.

Dancing at Roadhouse.

The party rode in automobiles to the beach. A gay company was assembled at the roadhouse, and the orchestra was reeling off lively music as attendants placed chairs at the disposal of Mrs. Oelrichs and the party. Mrs. Oelrichs inquired about the "turkey-trot" as soon as the orchestra had finished playing.

"I read what Pavlowa had to say about this dance," she explained, "and I would very much like to see it."

Mrs. Oelrichs is herself a very graceful dancer, and she judged the dancers critically as they glided through the measures of the two-step that has created so much talk.—*San Francisco Examiner, December 29, 1910.*

SID BROWN

Composer of "I'll Cheat On You," also the original writer of "My Ever-Lovin' Southern Gal" now featured by Hedges Bros. and Jacobson; also composer of the classic ballad, "The Bee and the Rose" and many other popular

---

The "Texas Tommy Swing" originated at Purcell's and other Pacific Street clubs in 1911, and later became an international dance craze.

Right after the quadrille was over, the floor manager would say, "Drag 'um!" Then you got down to your slow music. They had several boys that hung around the place that was very good dancers, and they would put on this show. In this second part, the money would start rainin' while they danced everything from a Hootchy-Kootchy on up. There was plenty of money, mostly halves and dollars, all in silver. After the dance, they'd pick up the money and divide it up. The musicians always got two dollars out of it.

One of the famous dances which practically originated out of Purcell's was the Texas Tommy dance, and it was danced all over [circa 1906–11]. We had several fellas that did it very good, like Johnny Peters, Dutch Mike, and Pet Bob. Johnny was a waiter in our place and was an Oklahoma boy. His father was a Baptist preacher, and the Baptists didn't believe in dancin'. He liked to dance so, naturally, he sold out and run away from home.

He said to me one time, "Why, that Texas Tommy dance is common down home; it originated in Texas."

I said, "Where did it get its name, Johnny?"

He said, "I don't really know. The first time I ever heard of it, my uncle made a trip to Galveston, Texas, and he come back teachin' everybody the Texas Tommy."

So we know where the Texas come in, but we don't know where the Tommy part come from. One of the best tunes we used to play for it was "King Chanticleer."

Dutch Mike, as we called him, was a Scandinavian boy; he didn't fit the nationality of Dutch at all. He come around the place practically every night. He danced with the Negro girls, Mary Dusen and Little Bit, who were very good Texas Tommy dancers, and he was very good. Another boy that was very good dancin' the Texas Tommy dance was Pet Bob. He got really famous with the old dance "Ballin' The Jack" that come along next. "Ballin' The Jack" was Chris Smith's tune. He come over the Orpheum Circuit once about 1911 and played the piano, and he was more on the comedian order. Actually, myself, I think Pet Bob was a better dancer than Johnny Peters. Johnny was more graceful, but Pet Bob looked like his dancin' was just natural.

Well, naturally, the Texas Tommy dance spread all over, like any famous dance. The mayor of San Francisco, Mayor McCarthey, who was very famous in them days, and the other officials would send parties down with a personal card, and we'd entertain them with the Texas Tommy. They danced it for such famous characters as Mose Guntz, who was a little gray-headed fella, and the other Chinatown guides. They were the licensed guides in San Francisco that used to bring the tourists through Chinatown to see the hop joints and to the famous places on the Barbary Coast.

It was something similar to your Gray Line sightseeing buses today, only they brought them on foot. It used to be as interestin' for us to see them as for them to see us. I never will forget one bunch that come from Indiana. The best part of them happened to be followers of Carrie Nation, the lady that was so famous for bein' against the saloons.

When they walked in and sat down, one lady jumped up and says to the guide, "This is just about enough of this. This is going too far. We didn't expect to come here to a place like this. I wish you would get our party together and come out of here."

After a few seconds, she said, "If you won't take us out, we'll voluntarily leave."

So she went out very indignant. That always stuck out how they didn't like the idea of comin' in a place like that.

All of the prominent show people, when they come to San Francisco, their hangout was the Barbary Coast and the night spots there. Al Jolson came here on one of his shows. I can't just remember the name of the show, but anyway he come down to Purcell's. He seen this Texas Tommy dance and liked it very much. He decided to get a couple of the dancers and make it part of his show. He had several auditions and interviews, and finally picked Johnny Peters and Mary Dusen to go with him. He even paid the band once to come down in the afternoon to play so the dancers could rehearse to get this act ready to take to New York. On the way to New York, Mary quit, or somethin' happened, and Johnny taught a new girl to open with him. So they danced on quite a tour back to New York. When they got to New York, their dancin' went over big at the theater; I think it was the Strand. They were only there for a month or six weeks. This was in 1908 or 1909, and in them days, if you were a singer, you must dance, and if you was a dancer, you must sing. And, what I mean, you had to do both of them and very good. I don't mean get up there and cut a few steps; you had to dance. Well, Johnny and this girl couldn't sing and didn't have any monologue they could do, so they went on and danced. They were out after the show run out.

I've seen all kinds of brawls and fights and what-not around Purcell's, but there's one thing on the old Barbary Coast that always stuck out above a lot of the other things. As old a man as I am, I haven't seen nothin' as mean as this. It was around ten o'clock on Christmas Eve [circa 1910–12], and this gentleman who come in once in a while come in with some bundles under his arm. This smaller, tough-lookin' character was standin' at the bar. These two started drinkin' and talkin' together, and one drink brought another, and one word brought another. The first thing you know, they got in an argument and then a fight.

One of the employees of Purcell's came out and tried to separate them, and as he did, the gentleman's bundles fell on the floor. The tough-lookin' character hit the gentleman and knocked him down, and then he kicked him in the face. The tough character started kickin' the bundles around. They were just wrapped in flimsy paper that came off, and they was toys this gentleman was takin' home to his children. The character stood there and started stompin' them toys to pieces under his feet. When he stomped them all, he kicked the man in the head again.

About that time, the head floorman, Big Boy, come in to work. Some of the employees was workin' on the gentleman, and they'd kind'a partly revived him.

Big Boy grabbed the tough customer and said, "I know this fella; he comes in here and dances with the girls. Look what you've done to them toys for his children. Have you got any children?"

This character says, "No, I'm on the ship. I sail the seven seas. Why should I care about children?"

Big Boy said, "Well, look what you done here—broke up all this gentleman's toys for his children. Don't you wonder how he feels? This is Christmas Eve, and possibly he can't get any more toys. I know you've had some brothers and sisters, and you must feel somethin' bad about it."

The character said, "I don't feel nothin'," and commenced to give Big Boy some lip. In a few seconds he was layin' on the floor like the other gentleman was, and they drug him out.

I happened to be in Sherman Clay's music store one day. They sold all kinds of instruments and music, and they're still goin' today. The gentleman in the sheet music department always laid aside new music for me to try out.

When I went in, he said, "Here's a peculiar thing. I've been all through the East and South and to New Orleans, and I've been to Basin Street, but I never thought we'd have a tune like this named after it."

He handed "Basin Street Blues" to me and said, "Take it on upstairs and try it."

They had a little mezzanine room up there, and I went and played it. I said to the gentleman, "This is pretty good," and I took it over to my boys. We went over it with the band and started playin' it in Purcell's. It got to be pretty popular around for a while, and then all of a sudden, it died out.

Well, "Basin Street Blues" come back again when Will Johnson's New Orleans Jazz Band come here playin' it. They were the first New Orleans jazz band I ever heard of. He went east from New Orleans and then come out here. Will Johnson was quite a character. He was a real light fella, and he always had a cigar in his mouth, chewin' it. I don't ever remember seein' a cigar in his mouth lit. He played the bass fiddle with a glove on it, and we was kind'a amazed out here in the West to see a man pick a bass. We knowed that in theater and symphony orchestras they picked them, and it was generally what they called pizzicato on the bass. To see him in a jazz band pick it like that was somethin'. That's where I got the idea of the four beats.

I listened, and I says to the fellas, "You know that old heavy two beats we play—you know we've got to get that four beats like them boys."

I can hear that rhythm; I can hear the difference in that rhythm that was changin' them days. Nowadays they play the two beats, and they play it a little more solid than we did in them days. So I stuck a bass in there because that was the Louisiana-type.

In the early days, the Louisiana-type bands, like Will Johnson and King Oliver, didn't have no pianos. I didn't know whether they didn't allow them to have any pianos in the South or what. From what I seen, and fellas like Wade Whaley told me, when they first started to play, they went around from place to place with the bass fiddle, guitar, fiddle, cornet, clarinet, and trombone.

So I told my boys we were gonn'a start playin' to four beats. I had a drummer, Old Pete; he'd traveled for twenty years with Richard and Pringel's Minstrels, the Old Georgia Minstrels. He could read all the notes that you could put up there in front of him, but he wasn't much on fakin'. His fakin' was kind of raggety, as we called it.

When I told Old Pete I wanted him to play the four beats, he got kind of imminent and said, "Man, you don't know how much work that is!"

I said, "Well, you know the man's payin' us to work."

The Georgia Minstrels, 1876. Note the double bass and violin with mixed brass.

Well, we had a little boy around there by the name of Georgia Huddleson who was a terrific drummer. Oh! He was terrific. We finally got rid of Old Pete and got this Huddleson boy, and he played four beats and played them good.

I told the rest of them fellas. I said, "You either got to do that, or we'll have to get some more musicians."

Finally, we weeded on out and weeded on out until we got the So Different Orchestra that's in the picture about 1916. Them fellas could play everything. After Huddleson joined the band, and we weeded out, well, gee, everybody thought this is another band, four beats. Jesus, it was great. It was along about 1912 when we switched to the New Orleans type of instrumentation.

That's the bunch that played the overtures. We had a little six-piece band with piano, drums, string bass, clarinet, a fella who played flute and piccolo, and baritone euphonium, at first. My baritone euphonium player caught $2,500 in the Louisiana Lottery, so he got too rich to work, so we had to change over and get Reb Spikes to play baritone saxophone with us. We worked on them early in the evening at Purcell's, when there would be nothin' doin'. We went to work at eight o'clock, and it'd be possibly ten o'clock before we'd get a crowd. What we would do, we would take the first movement of a piece and play it to see how far we could go, and then we'd take the second movement of it, and then we'd take the whole tune and go over it. We'd just memorize them, and my memory for them is just as good in 1952 as it was for them in 1912. The help at Purcell's enjoyed them, and sometimes we'd have quite a standin' crowd. Of course, sometimes a customer would want to dance, and we'd play dances in between if somebody wanted them.

Imagine us fellas playin' such overtures as "Poet and Peasant," "Semaramidi," "Morning, Noon and Night in Vienna," "William Tell," and "Pique-Dame"; and we played every one of them and every part from memory. A gentleman by the name of George Bryant was wintering here one year with Ferdon's Medical Show, and we used to have the fellas from his show and my band get together once a week and have a rehearsal. With my six-piece band and his six pieces, it made a twelve-piece orchestra to play them. We also played my "Canadian Capers." Them overtures come in very handy later when we went to play for C.O. Swanberg at the Porta La Louvre in San Francisco, at the corner of Powell and Market streets, and at the Alexander Young Hotel in Honolulu. Those overtures fit in right well durin' the dinner hour.

Take Adam Mitchell, my clarinet player in them days; he could play anything. He was from Martinique in the West Indie Islands and one of the finest clarinet players I ever heard. The only one that compares to him is Benny Goodman. We called Adam "Slocum." In those days, they used the A and B clarinets; you used the B when playin' the flats and the A when playin' the sharps. He used the B-flat clarinet; make no difference where he was or what he was playin'. In those days, we played a lot of waltzes, such waltzes as "Wedding In The Wines," "Tu Sur Ami" (sic) (which means forever and ever), "Tu Sur Fedile" (sic), Emil Waldteufel's waltzes (which is beautiful waltzes), Strauss's waltzes, and them old boys who composed them didn't care what key they put them in. They didn't stick in B-flat and E-flat. They went all over with three sharps and four sharps and five sharps. Slocum

Sid LeProtti's So Different Jazz Band, San Francisco, c. 1915 (L to R: Clarence Williams, string bass; Reb Spikes, baritone sax; Adam "Slocum" Mitchell, clarinet; Sid LeProtti, piano/leader; Gerald Wells, flute; unidentified on drums)

though, he'd just take that clarinet of his and play any of them. He played the old Albert System; it's all Band System now. He stuck to that Albert System of thirteen keys, and it was late that he finally switched to the Band System. He's the first man I ever heard slur on a clarinet like you do on a trombone. And he played the worst clarinets you ever looked at; I still got one out in the barn as a relic. When a spring broke, he'd use a rubber band, and when something would happen, he'd stick some gum in the holes and go right on. How he got all that music out, I'll never know. He finally got an E-flat clarinet too, and he used it on "Tiger Rag" with all the squealin' goin' on there.

Sid LeProtti

ALONG COME
MR. JELLY LORD

We met Mr. Jelly Lord or Jelly Roll Morton in Los Angeles when I was there with my famous LeProtti So Different Orchestra [circa 1916]. Jelly was quite a character; he was just as ornery as he was good. I can see him now with that overcoat on. He was a kind'a thin-featured fellow and had quite a lot'a gold in his teeth, which was characteristic in them days. When you first looked at him, his mouth was twisted like he'd had some kind of a slight stroke, but I don't think it was that—it was the way he held his mouth. He'd also always kind'a squint one eye.

I'll tell you what a character he was. Reb Spikes was in our band, and Reb traveled with Jelly when they was around carnivals and tent shows in Oklahoma. Reb tells this story when they was playin' this kind'a open-air tent show, and Jelly and his girlfriend had been fightin'. Most of the time,

Jelly walked around with a Colt .45 pistol in his pocket. About the time they walked out on stage this girl cursed him, and he just took out his Colt .45 and hit her across the head with it. Naturally, down she went, and everybody thought it was part of the act and very funny. As the old sayin' goes, the show went on, with girl lyin' there all the time. It really takes Reb Spikes to tell about it because he was right there.

In Los Angeles, Jelly played in the hotel. He played the blues a hundred and one times and never played it the same way twice. He was a wonderful player, and there's no doubt that he has the background to say that he was the originator of a lot of the present-day piano styles. I can hear the piano players as they go down the line, and I can hear Jelly right in there—some of his improvisations, some of his licks, and things like that.

For some reason or other, Jelly took a likin' to me.

One day, he said, "You got a pretty good band."

I said, "Yeah, I think so."

He said, "It'll do."

That's just the way he was—one of them kind that didn't want'a give nobody credit for nothin'. We did have a very fine band.

He said, "I've got some good numbers; I'm gonn'a let you look them over."

So he gave me this number and said, "Here's one I want'a give you."

The manuscript looked like some kid had dropped ink on it and then the chickens had scratched on it. There was a white boy in Los Angeles who was a pretty good piano player, and he'd studied a little bit of harmony and could do some arrangin'. He said he'd help me figure it out, and so we finally figured it out and played it. It was "The Crave." Jelly played it, but he was pretty cagey; he'd play it one way, then he'd change it and play it again. One day I caught him playin' it and heard him say to a fella, "Well, this is the way I play it when I'm playin' ad lib." I copied it after the way he played it then. I took the tune and run over it with the boys. The boys I had in them days were all very professional and pretty fly-ey. We went ahead and played it out at the place, and, my God, the bunch was just crazy about it, especially Jack Pickford, Mary Pickford's brother, who never got very prominent in the movies, Fatty Arbuckle, and Max Schlerman, and they broadcasted it all over Los Angeles. Everybody was sayin' that you ought'a go out and hear those boys play "The Crave."

The original manuscript for Sid LeProtti's unpublished composition,"The Big Three Rag," n.d.

People would walk in there every night and say, "They tell me you play a number called 'The Crave,'" and we'd play it for them.

After we got done playin' our regular job, we'd come down to Murray's Cafe—which was the leading Negro cafe, in fact the only one in Los Angeles in 1916—and play. We was down there playin', and the joint was just rockin', just steamin'. We were playin' "The Crave" and Jelly walked in. You could've cooked an egg on his head, he was so hot. The next day he jumped me.

He said, "Hey, what do you mean to do? God, man lend you a number and you try to steal his stuff. You're a heck of a guy; that's all I hear, 'The Crave,' 'The Crave,' my stuff!"

That was a great word for your own numbers, if you had them, in those days, my stuff.

I said, "What do you mean, stealin' your stuff?"

He said, "When I lent you that tune, I didn't want you broadcastin' it all over. The next thing I know, you'll be tryin' to publish it."

I said, "Jelly, I got the brains enough not to publish your tune. When you gave it to us, you gave it to a mighty fine band. Not me, but the rest of the band, the horns; them's the boys that put it over."

He said, "If I'd known that, I would've given it to you. Have you got it here?"

I said, "No, I haven't got it now, but I'll get it and give it to you tomorrow."

So I brought it to him. I met him on the corner of Fifth and Main streets and I gave it to him, and, you know, that character, when I handed it to him, he took it and tore it up and threw it in the trashcan on the street. He walked away and said, "I'll be seein' you later on."

It went on a while, and we run into him again, and it kind'a died on out. He finally came out of it, and then he gave me "Jelly Roll Blues." It must'a been quite a favorite of his, 'cause he put his name on it. Then we lost track of him.

So he finally come up to San Francisco. I met him standin' on the corner talkin' to Bowman and a bunch of fellas.

He yelled, "Hello there, LeProtti!"

I said, "Hello, Jelly! What are you doin' up here?"

He said, "Man, I'm gonn'a go to town!"

I said, "What are you gonn'a do now?"

He said, "I'm gonn'a open a joint right over there. I'm gonn'a close you up, you and Mapp."

I said, "You're not gonn'a close me up." I said, "You're closin' Mapp up."

He said, "I'm gonn'a close him up. I'm gonn'a really put on a show!"

The place he had was right on Columbus Avenue, downstairs in a cellar; you went downstairs to get in it. Well, he had a bad spot because everything was on Pacific Street. We had moved and was at the corner of Columbus Avenue and Jackson Street, and we were downstairs, but we carried the name Purcell's with us. So Jelly went on over there and got him a little band there, and he started out pretty good. My boys used to slip over there at night to hear them. Jelly started with three pieces; he had a clarinet and cornet.

I met him on the street one day and said, "How're you doin', Jelly?"

He said, "All right! I'm doin' all right!" And then he asked, "How much do they pay your men over there?"

I said, "Why do you want'a know?"

He said, "Because I'm gonn'a give them fifty dollars a week. I'm gonn'a take all your men."

That's kind of how he was, kind'a boastful, and then, on the other hand, you'd catch him in just the right mood, and he was a swell guy. Looked like sometimes he had something that was itching him all the time. It was like an irritation that he'd have to get out'a his system; he'd have to scratch it. He had no right to tell me he was gonn'a take my band, but sure enough, the boys came back to me and said Jelly had offered them fifty dollars a week to go over there and play.

One of the boys said, "I wouldn't work with that character for anything."

I said, "What's the matter?"

He said, "There'd be a fight right there!"

Then he told me how they worked over there. Jelly would be playin', then they'd play a chorus together, and Jelly would say, "All right, lay down there and let me have it." Then he'd play a solo—of course, he could play; there was no gettin' away from it. Then the clarinet would be playin' a solo—and didn't play to suit Jelly—and he'd holler for him to quit, and he'd take it. If you didn't play it accordin' to Jelly's idea, he was just liable to bawl you out right there. My boys and me, we always played like a family together, and it was what you call Dixieland-style today. We had our rehearsals together, and I'd take a chorus, another guy would take two choruses, you take a chorus, and that's the way it went on.

Finally, they had a big fight over there. I won't say for sure this is authentic, but I heard it, and then I heard different. They were havin' a big fight, and Jelly is right in the middle of it. He pulled his pistol out, and the police caught him. The captain of the district told him he was a newcomer, and he'd better take some air before he got in any trouble. Anyhow, Jelly disappeared, and I never seen him no more. That's the last I heard of him until I heard the poor fella was sick, and next I heard, he'd died. He's a character, that guy.

Jelly Roll Morton

THE JUPITER

Mr. Jelly Roll Morton rolled into San Francisco in late 1916 or early 1917. He was unusually quiet about chewing up the local talent and, even by his own admission, left under less than triumphant circumstances. After 1913, the Barbary Coast was under a fairly constant siege from reformer types, and he was caught up in one of the waves. His own story is presented here, as a contrast with those of Sid LeProtti and Reb Spikes, through the courtesy of Mr. Alan Lomax, who wrote Mr. Jelly Roll.

I didn't want to lose Anita, and I went with her [to Arizona]. But that restaurant business didn't last her long. She got fooling around with some phony gold stock and lost everything she had made, and in a few months we moved to Frisco, where we opened The Jupiter.

I ran the entertainment with a ten-piece band and ten entertainers, and Anita handled the bar with ten waitresses, and we did great business. It was *too* good. Soon the manager of the place across the street had us in trouble with the police. He had it fixed so we couldn't get hold of a license for dancing. I fooled around and spent a lot of money. Then I wrote a letter to the police department and showed them my open mind. In a couple of days, Anita and I followed that letter to headquarters.

They kept us waiting for a couple of hours, and by then our Creole was up. They didn't know Anita had a pistol in her pocketbook when they called us in. The police chief slapped the letter down on the table. "Do you know this hand?"

"Yes, it's mine," Anita said.

"Who dictated it?"

"Me," I said.

"You haven't the intelligence to write a letter like this."

"Say, I was going to school before you left Ireland," I told him, and he began to rave. He touched a button under his desk, and you never saw so many six-footers in your life, popping though all the doors. I began to get scared, but still thought I'd better keep talking. "Looks like you plan to mob somebody."

"Shut up before you get your head knocked off. You're too smart. That's why you're in trouble."

"We're not in trouble. We're being molested, and we're going to fight for our rights." That's what Anita told him, sitting there cool with that gun in her pocketbook. She was a wonderful woman. But it didn't do any good. Nothing helped.

We spent fifteen hundred dollars for an attorney who wasn't worth a dime. He told the commissioner, "Now, Mr. Commissioner, this is a nice boy, and I want you to give him a chance."

"I don't want no sympathy," I said. "I demand my rights."

The commissioner looked at me. "You heard what the captain said, boy. We'll close you down if you allow dancing." I guess what worried them was that my place was black and tan—for colored and white alike.

The night Prohibition came in, the police told me it was the penitentiary for me if I sold liquor. From then on the police would hang around the door of The Jupiter and annoy the patrons with uncalled-for remarks. "Why do you come here? What's your name? Don't you know this place is likely to be raided any time?"

I finally told them they would have to get on away from my premises, and I was so angry, they moved on. Then that doggone captain made a stoolie out of one of my waiters, named Frenchy; paid him to plant a bottle of whiskey in the slop barrel, but that fool went and got drunk at a bar owned by a friend, told this friend I was going to be raided, and the friend tipped Anita off.

Anita found the whiskey and hid it. Just about that time, in came the police captain and said, "You're under arrest because you're breaking the law."

Now I was getting so hot that I was just about ready to shoot somebody with that left-hand-wheeler of mine, and I told that police captain, "Who said so?"

"I said so."

"Well, your word's no prayer book," I said and began to feel for my gun, because I had decided to go down fighting. Just then Anita kicked me under the table.

I hollered, "Why are you kicking me under the table?"

Anita began to laugh, and I began to laugh, and that policeman must have thought we were both crazy. He said, "Boy, they're going to find you in a ditch dead some day," and he dashed to the place where he thought the liquor was hidden, and when he didn't find it, he began to raise hell. He asked all the customers why they came to a place that was raided all the time. Anita just laughed at him, gave him a drink, and asked him to come back anytime.

Business got bad then, and Anita wanted to forget The Jupiter. But I got mad and insisted we hold onto the place. I even arranged for John Taylor, the toughest guy in Frisco, to hang around and protect us. He had beat up the police chief, so I figured he could help us. But Anita managed me, the way she always did.

She left Frisco one night and went to Seattle without telling me that she was leaving. Then she wired me to come on and join her, or she would go onto Alaska without me. That scared me. I was afraid I could never find her in Alaska, so I left The Jupiter just as it was and caught the next train for the state of Washington. Anita met me with a smile, "I didn't want to go to Alaska, baby, just wanted you here."

Sid LeProtti

THE BARBARY COAST IS FINALLY FADIN' AWAY

So then come King Oliver and his band about 1921. They went around from place to place with bass fiddle, guitar, a fiddle, cornet, clarinet, and trombone. King Oliver played the cornet and taught Louis Armstrong how to play. He had a terrific band. The band played at The Pagola on Market Street. They came down to Purcell's place to play, and the bass player chewed tobacco. They got to playin', and everything was gettin' hot and rompin'. I remember they was playin' a waltz—somebody asked them to play a waltz—and waltzes was very unusual for them fellas. It was "Sidewalks of New York"; it was just gettin' popular in those days. I was watchin' the bass player and I seen him go "sissst, sissst," and I wondered what he was doin'. He's turn his head and kept goin' "sissst, sissst." Pretty soon, I looked over and saw some brown spots on the wall.

After they got done playin' and went, I went over and looked at the wall. That character had spit all over the wall.

So I says to the boys, "Come here and look what that tobacco-chewin', wall-spittin' band did over here."

One fella said, "What?"

I said, "I said that character spit all over our wall here."

Another fella said, "I don't think they'd do that."

I said, "Come on over here and look."

They came over and looked and seen I was right. It wasn't chewin' tobacco though; it was that old Southern stuff, snooze. After that, we usually called them "the tobacco-chewin', wall-spittin' band."

Some of the people around Purcell's kind'a made fun of their Louisiana-style music. And some of my fellas that had learned music and was playin' with me, they got kind'a hinkty because they could read music. We was playin' stock orchestrations, "Dill Pickles" and all that commercial stuff. I told them fellas we was playin' the junk and didn't have much of the original stuff like King Oliver and his boys did. I told them I come through the same category, and it's just like I've learned since, you can play all the music and all the notes and everything, and you're not playin' nothin'. I told them the story of my meeting with old Henry Stewart and what he'd taught me.

King Oliver used to come down to Purcell's and sit in with us and play after he got done playin' down at The Pagola. King Oliver had one bad eye. It had a kind'a blue cast, and there was a blemish on the eye. The position he was playin' in, you couldn't tell what he was lookin' at. He didn't need no music because he was really wonderful the way he played. A funny thing about him, he was the only one in his band, out'a six pieces, that would come in and sit in with us. The rest of the fellas wouldn't even come in.

I don't blame King Oliver's trombone player for not comin' in there. I had a fella just workin' extra, playin' trombone, named Russ Morgan, same name as the bandleader. He was a cow-puncher from up in Montana and was a kind'a light Negro. He had a ruddy complexion; it looked like a little Indian mixture had gotten in there somewhere. The peculiar thing about the way he played the trombone was he didn't play no trombone parts; he played the lead, and, what I mean, he played it. And the way he played the old tune, "Rubber Plant Rag!" It has nothin' but sixteenth notes all the way through, and he'd play it on that trombone just as clean as a whistle. He

Sheet music cover of Charles Johnson's 1906 rag, "Dill Pickles"

was terrific, and, as I say, I don't blame Oliver's trombone player for not comin' down there.

Russ is the fella who broke up the show with the entertainers stealin' the tip money. The band was supposed to get half the tips the entertainers got, and we'd split the tips every night at one o'clock. Then the band and the entertainers would go on home, and I'd go on and play the piano until three, or four, five, six o'clock in the morning, as long as the crowd stayed. I kept the tips I made after one o'clock. The entertainers were palming the dimes they got. If they'd get a half a dollar, they'd give you a dime instead of a quarter; they'd get a dollar, and they'd give you a quarter.

So Russ says to me, "That Mabel and the rest of that bunch out there is killin' us. If we had the money that belonged to us, we could have quite a time. Practically all of them is killin' us except Mitch and Nettie."

Willie "Strut" Mitchell, who is in Los Angeles, and Nettie, they didn't come any cleaner than those two; but the rest of them characters was somethin'.

The entertainers all sat over in one corner on chairs. One night, there we were, all playin' along, and the place was full'a people; Mabel got a two dollar bill for a tip from this man, and she come up and give us four bits. Russ dropped that trombone and reached out there and grabbed her. He batted her beside the head and made her nose bleed. Then he took her apart and grabbed that two dollar bill and made her give us the rest of our share.

Then he turned around to the rest of the entertainers in the corner and said, "Now that ought'a be a lesson to the rest of you, 'cause I'm gonn'a do the rest of you like that if you aren't honest. We're all clean here. You forget when Vincent Rose come in here and give us twenty dollars to play, we put five dollars in with tips you people got. You don't think of that. You just play fair and square after this."

Mabel went downstairs holdin' her bleedin' nose, and to make a long story short, the tips commenced to increase right away.

One of the fights we had at Purcell's was between a sailor—who was the old man of one of the girls who worked there—and a civilian. They started inside and come outside on the sidewalk, and the sailor was gettin' beat up. His girlfriend, on the second floor, had the winda' open watchin'. When she saw what was happenin' to her old man, she got one of these small Filipino mahogany cedar chests and threw it out the winda' on the civilian's head. I wished you'd seen the cedar chest after it hit his head; I wished you'd seen his head after it hit it. That girl was always gettin' in some kind'a trouble, and then she got killed.

I was sittin' there one night playin' and all; everything was just goin' fine. The dance floor was crowded, and everybody was just havin' a good time. This girl who threw the chest was dancin' there with her sailor. Then a soldier come in from Vallejo. This sailor had run off with this girl that the soldier thought was his lady friend, and there they were dancin'. This soldier opens up with a Colt .45 six-shooter in that place. Purcell's was on the north side of Pacific Street facin' south toward the business district. The bandstand was on the west side of the buildin' with the piano against the wall. When the shootin' started, the drummer got in behind the wall and the piano, and I got underneath the piano. There was a back door that led out to the restrooms. When I went to look for the other fellas, that's where they was. Everybody else had stampeded out'a there the best way they could. Well, nobody got hit, and how, in a crowded place like that, anybody didn't get killed, I don't know. He emptied that six-shooter in that place. The only thing we figure today—that nobody got killed because the boy was drunk, or maybe he just wasn't shootin' down. There was several people got scratched up and hurt because of the stampede.

We had orders from Sam King, when I played his place first, then Lou Purcell, when he was alive, anytime there was a fight, keep the music goin'. You'd catch hell if you stopped the music; make no difference what happened, just keep it goin'. If the music was goin', somebody'd be dancin'. The times the shootin' started, there was nobody kept any music goin' with the lead flyin' around there.

The soldier that come in Purcell's and done the shootin' come back to finish the job about a week later. Purcell's was about thirty-five foot long building and narrow. You went upstairs to the second floor where the girls done their business and lived. There was a bannister goin' up the stairs, then a bannister rail at the top. In front were two rooms, then along one side to the back was all rooms and a hall. That soldier come back and went upstairs. When he got to the top of the stairs and stood up on the bannister, he took his gun and knocked the transom out of the girl's room. The sailor was sittin' in a chair asleep, and she was layin' on the bed asleep. He went "Dung," "Dung," with that pistol, just two shots, and he got both of them.

Entertainers at Purcell's, c. 1934

The porter was swamping the floors, and he was a little dingy. He started runnin' and hollerin' because that gun went off, and he was scared. He didn't show up for work for a week after that.

There's been a lot of excitement around the Barbary Coast. Even at that, it didn't happen every day. It happened over a period of years. Sure, we had the gaudy houses and dance halls, and the sailors used to come in, and if they were simple enough, somebody would take their money away freely like they've always done from biblical times on down. People that's the prey of wolves, they just get ate up. I still think until today that people in them days was livin' better than they do today because we didn't have such vicious people that would kill people for nothin'. We had fellas that they'd hold people up, and break in and burglarize the stores, and once in a while, a policeman would get shot or something like that, but they weren't as vicious as they are today.

Instead of havin' them full of marijuana, in those days we had what they called the hop fiends; they was on opium. I've been up in Chinatown and seen them take that stuff. Course the bad part about it was after they use opium for a while, and then they don't get much of a kick out of it, and they went to the snow in them days and started blowin' it up their nose. They called cocaine the snow back then. You'd see them blow snow up their nose, and it would eat all the mucous membrane out'a the nose, and then that'd be the end of them. The hop fiends would do little petty stuff to get money for their hop. I only know of one hold-up of any consequence then. It's nothin' like today, walkin' in and shootin' people and killin' people for no reason. They just wasn't that vicious in them days.

I knew a girl, a very beautiful Irish girl; oh, she was really pretty. She was born and raised in San Jose and worked in the sportin' house where I played at before I went to the Barbary Coast. What happened to her was pitiful then, but it's not pitiful now. After I left the sportin' house and went to Purcell's, I run into her one evening in Caligaris's Drug store on the corner of Kearny and Pacific. She was still a really beautiful black-haired Irish girl. The minute I looked at her though, Jesus, I seen the eyes was leapin', and she was full'a dope.

I said to her, "How did you get here?"

She said, "Whatever you do, don't tell my brother."

She knew I knew her brother.

I said, "That's just what I'm goin' to do."

She said, "If you do, I'll choke you."

I was small then but pretty husky, and I said, "No, you're not gonn'a choke me."

And then I asked, "How did you get into this, Vivian?"

She said, "Al."

Al was a fiend.

I went to the police department, and they picked her up, and they sent her to the farm. I told her brother about it. I'm relatin' how there can be some good come out of it. She come out'a there cleaned up. I met her on the street once, down by the Emporium on Market Street. I never will forget how she thanked me and how she went on. She knew that between me and her brother she'd gotten off dope. The last time I saw her brother was in 1930. He told me that she'd stayed off dope and married a lumberman in Santa Barbara and was the mother of four fine kids. She got away from it and stayed away from it; there's been so many that, once it gets a hold of them, it's kind'a tough to get rid of it.

Out'a the twenty years I played the Barbary Coast, fourteen years of it was all night. The last place I was in, after Purcell's moved off Pacific Street, was on Jackson Street just west of Kearny. There was glass mirrors all around the place, and the piano was right up against the wall at the back of the building. The customers, they'd throw money up there, and I'd just keep the left hand goin' and grab the halves and dollars with the right hand; it was quite a trick. If somebody would throw a dollar and say, "Give me a half change," I'd just keep goin' and reach in my pocket for it and throw the change back. It was mostly all silver in them days; there was very little paper money. Ordinary pockets in the pants wouldn't last no time at all, just wear right out. About every month or six weeks, my wife would have to take lightweight canvas and sew in new pockets. I kept my wife busy sewin' them pockets.

In them days, my salary was thirty-five dollars a week for playin' with the band and then playin' all night on the piano. The men in the band got twenty-five dollars a week because they cut out at one o'clock. Imagine, I averaged $465.33 a month over a period of twenty years. That's good money in them days, and that includes the seventy-five dollars—which was the most I made in one night—on that one song.

Editorial cartoon, part of the San Francisco Examiner's *1913 campaign to close down the Barbary Coast*

The beginning of the decline of the Barbary Coast was a crusade started by the Reverend Paul Smith when he exposed all the doings that was goin' on. At that time, my band was playin' at the Porta La Louvre [circa 1916]. On the Barbary Coast they had to cut out the afternoon dancin'—we used to play in the afternoon, too—and then there was nothin' but evenin' dancin'. Then finally in our travels around we finally come back to Purcell's. It started to get rough in 1915, it started gettin' rougher in 1916, and it got worse in 1917. It got to the place where they ruled out all of the sportin' houses. Then they got kind of rigid with us. They stopped all the dancin' in the boundary of the Barbary Coast. They let the dancin' go on across town in what they called the high-class tenderloin around O'Farrell Street where the Black Cat and Coffee Dan's were.

Then Captain Arthur Layne come in and took charge of the station house for the area. Captain Arthur Layne had just come from the Harbor District and he'd cleaned up the waterfront.

I said to Lester Mapp, "Look what we've got!"

He said, "Oh, we'll handle him. We'll take care of him, and he'll be all right."

In our place particularly they'd get tighter and tighter and tighter, and the Barbary Coast is finally fadin' away. They stopped the dancin' again, but it went on in the places the policeman winked his eye at. That's when we had "Old Folks" out watchin' the door. The girls were there, but they didn't allow them to dance, and that was the only way they had of makin' a livin'. To get around the dancin', the men would come in and buy them a bottle of beer or a drink, and then they'd sit and drink it, and the girls got the checks just like the dancin' girls did. When it was free and easy, they'd dance and get checks like girls done before.

We lost some of the girls because some them really had to go back to work. We cut down to just a few girls, and we kept the nicest lookin' girls. The place kind of reorganized from the old-time dance hall to the cafe. In Purcell's and a lot of other places, they had to put in entertainers; it was the same way as in white places.

They got rough and they'd raid the places. We went on to play all summer, and they'd stopped the music at one o'clock, and in October we started all night playin' again. Every Christmas Eve, we used to go out at the LaHonda Home in San

Another in a series of editorial cartoons featured in the San Francisco Examiner, *September 1913*

Francisco for the old people and play for them. There was a terrific windstorm that day, and Golden Gate Park was all strewed with branches, and when we got back, we went to work. There was quite a crowd, the place was packed, and about a quarter to one o'clock I happen to look out. I'm sittin' with my back to the door and way down at the other end of the place, but when I turned around, I could look straight out the front door. The tables was on both sides, and the dance floor was in the middle. Nobody was dancin'.

After I looked, I said to Slocum, "Look what jumped up at the door; there's the devil."

It was Corporal Alperts and another policeman again.

Slocum said, "Oh, don't pay no attention to them!"

Corporal Alperts stood on one side, and the other fella stood on the other side, for a while, and waited until five minutes after one o'clock. I was playin' "Baby, Won't You Please Come Home."*

Then he raised his hand and said, "All right Sidney, stop the music! The house is pinched!"

There was a rathskeller downstairs and two floors of rooms upstairs in the Olympic, the last place we was in. Another policeman had gone down through the rathskeller, and up he come from behind the bandstand. He come in the back door and had all the doors blocked and everything.

Corporal Alperts said to all the patrons, "Just get your hats and coats and file out. But you girls and musicians, stay over there!"

In the meantime, they'd raided other places down on Pacific Street, and we all went over to the Hall of Justice. That wasn't the closin' of the Barbary Coast entirely, but that was a raid, and you could see it comin'.

Then Captain Layne sent for Lester Mapp to come and see him about what's goin' on.

He says to Lester, "Lester, you, and all the rest of them characters down there, if you'll play ball with me and run them places right, I'll leave you alone. If you don't, I'll close you up. You absolutely got to stop that gamblin', and you'll have to cut that music out." That's what Lester told me.

We had gamblin' right in the joint, right downstairs in a room. I seen the policeman gamblin' as well as anybody else, and that ain't lettin' the cat out of the bag—that was a known fact. One policeman, Woodpile, used to be in there a lot. We had all night music goin' again. They'd also stopped the sale of hard liquor, and they'd raided a lot of places and found hard liquor and closed them up. The cafe era was comin' in those days, and the great thing of southern baked ham and southern fried chicken was comin' in.

I said to Lester, "Why don't you put in southern baked ham and fried chicken?"

He said, "I'm gonn'a gamble just as long as I've got a joint!"

It just got worse and worse and tighter and tighter. Then come your Red Light Abatement Law; then they just practically locked it up. A lot of joints

---

*Some recent research reveals this tune was copyrighted in 1926, a date later than the closing. This might have been a memory lapse, or the tune could have been "Bill Bailey, Won't You Please Come Home."

Sid LeProtti's Jazz Orchestra, Persian Gardens, Oakland, c. 1930 (L to R: Sid LeProtti, piano/leader; Marcellus Levy, drums; Bob White, reeds; Sax Sexius, reeds; Londrus Roy, banjo; Danny Webster, trumpet; Roy Keyes, guitar; Elliott Worth (?), trumpet)

went of business, because if you owned property and I was runnin' a house of prostitution, or somethin' was goin' on wrong, and they caught me—the way the law reads, they close your property up for one year. You can't rent it for one year, and, naturally, you have to pay taxes, so that just automatically closed things down.

In March 1921, Corporal Alperts, and I can't think of the other man's name, walked in and stopped the music at one o'clock. I was playin' "Four O'Clock," one of my own tunes. It's peculiar how I run onto it. I had some exercise scale books, and I was runnin' over the scales practicin' thirds. So it sounded good, and I made a tune out of it, and that's where it started. I been playin' it about forty years since I composed it about 1912.

So we all went over to the Hall of Justice again, and I says to my clarinet player, Slocum, "That's the last note you'll play in that place."

He said, "Oh! You're always hangin' crepe."

I said, "Well, all right, but they closed us before."

Lester Mapp said, "It's all right. Come back to work Monday night!"

When we got back to work Monday night, they didn't allow no women in the place.

We wasn't runnin' no stag joint, and at eleven o'clock, Lester says to me, "Sidney, what boat can you catch to go home?"

I lived in Berkeley then, and I said, "I can catch the 11:20."

He said, "All right. Come back Wednesday night."

I seen the papers that Captain Layne said that Purcell's was closed and would stay closed. He designated the places that would stay closed. That was the last of Purcell's. When we come in that Wednesday, Lester told us we were closed for good. That was the end of the Barbary Coast. Two or three times they said the Coast was gonn'a open up, but it never did.

After the Barbary Coast closed down, we went out and played special dances and for entertainment we used to call gigs. We played out at the Presidio, at the hotels, and different stuff and another. I kept the band together for a while; the clarinet, the flute, and the piccolo player went north, and Reb Spikes went to Los Angeles, and Roy Tayborn left. Reb Spikes and Roy Tayborn come back. I organized a band to play Saturday night dances, and I done very well. I traveled all up and down the Sacramento Valley. I played Williams for eight years at a Saturday night dance.

Right after the Barbary Coast closed, we was doin' casual work, and me and the boys were hired for Prince George of England. He was on a British battleship and stayed at Del Monte Lodge. We was hired to play for a party that included Prince George, Samuel F.B. Morse, the President of Del Monte Properties, and a lot of other important people. Nothin' but champagne was served. After the party, Prince George walked across to the bandstand and I had the pleasure of shaking hands with the man who was to be King of England. He shook hands with all the boys and myself, and gave us his personal card and said, if we ever got to England, to look him up. But we

Sid LeProtti at his cigar and shoe-shine shop in Berkeley, c. 1925. The sign on the wall reads: "Sheet music, records, orchestra music furnished for dances."

never got to England. He was a very fine fella; he didn't have to put himself out to speak to us.

In 1918, the band went out to Honolulu to play at the Alexander Young Hotel, and we was the first Negro band to play there. We went across the Pacific as musicians and come back as soldiers. We had a six-month contract at the hotel, and about a month before it was up, we was drafted in the army. The colonel and first sergeant at the headquarters company had soldiered with my wife's father in the Philippines, and they gave us permission to finish our engagement at the Alexander Young Hotel. After we finished, we was drafted in mass. We was allowed to go into the Twenty-fifth Infantry, stationed at Scofield Barracks there, instead of bein' sent back to draftee camp.

In the twenties, I bought a shoe-shine parlor in Berkeley for something to do durin' the week. I got a chance to play with Louis Armstrong a few times when he was here. In the early thirties, they reopened the Barbary

Coast and named it the International Settlement. They tell me it was pretty tame compared to what it used to be. It even had a new place named Purcell's. In the late thirties, I moved out here in Walnut Creek.

I still tell the kids today [1952] I think the old musicians were outstanding because they were creative. They must'a been because you hear so many of the old tunes now. First we played the polkas, mazurkas, and a few songs, then along come the first jazz musicians and made those songs. Bands those days had fellas that made the arrangement from memory. They'd look at a sheet, go over it a couple of times, throw it away, and that was it. We'd take a piano script and made our own arrangement. Now, without arrangement, the musician is lost; but nowadays, there are more musicians qualified to write, so maybe that accounts for it.

Out here in Walnut Creek, I sweep the Walnut Creek City Hall and Library every day. I still play on weekends and for the service clubs, like the Kiwanis and Lions, at weekday luncheon meetings. I usually get two Berkeley boys, sax and drums, when I need a band. I'm still poundin' the piano, and just as long as I can keep foolin' the public, I'll keep goin'.

Sid LeProtti's Early Life

Recalled by Mamie LeProtti, told to Tom Stoddard

Sid's Father was an Italian, and his mother was a Negro, and he was an illegitimate child. His mother was working in an Oakland rooming house when this episode happened, and Sid was the fruit of it. The father was a merchant in Oakland, I think his first name was Francis, and he was a harpist. The parents never married, but the father gave Sid his last name and christened him. Sid's grandparents on his father's side were born in Alsace-Lorraine, and they came from there. They owned property near the Tech. High School, and his grandmother ran a laundry.

Amanda Marsdon was the first Negro to sing in the Opera House in San Francisco, and she was Sid's grandmother. She had come from Virginia and was born a slave. I think she came out around the gold rush. She came through the underground and finally came to California. Sid had an aunt who was an ear piano player, and she could go to an opera and come back and play the whole opera. His grandfather was from the West Indie Islands.

Sid was born on November 25, 1886, in his grandmother's house. His mother left a few weeks later, and his grandmother raised him after that. Sid's real name is Louis Sidney LeProtti, and his mother's name was Hettie Marsdon. She was born in Vallejo and didn't have any musical training. Sid only went as far as the sixth grade. His grandmother put him that far, and his mother wouldn't help, so his grandmother took him out. His grandmother also gave him music lessons for eleven months under a young German girl. That was before his feet could touch the pedals. Sid just made himself after that eleven months. He could read anything you put in front of him, opera or anything. Sid and his mother didn't get along well together. She lived with a Swede around there for a long time.

Grandmother Marsdon died when Sid was eighteen; that was in 1904. He and his grandfather didn't get along too well together, and he put his trunk in a wheelbarrow and took it to this lady's house, where he started boarding. After his grandmother died, Sid just bummed for himself.

In World War I, they took the whole band in the army. They got permission to enlist in the Second Hawaiian Regiment after they got called. After they were in for a while, they decided they wanted to go into an all-colored regiment and the colonel put them in the Twenty-fourth Infantry. Sid took the whole orchestra with him. They got orders to sail for San Francisco because the Mexicans were shooting up Nogales, Arizona, at the time. When we got to Fort Mason, San Francisco, on the transport, they left the women standing on the pier and took the men down to Nogales. They were at Camp Stephen D. Little near Nogales, Arizona, and Nogales, Sonora.

The colonel allowed Sid's band to play off the reservation for money, and they were the first enlisted men who were allowed to do that. The wives lived in Nogales, Arizona, and they played for a picture show there. The other soldiers just got their thirty dollars a month, and that was it. They were in the army just a few months when the Armistice was signed on November 11, 1918, and they were still in training. Leon Herriford was in the army band with Sid in Arizona. While they were there, the colonel had them play a concert in Nogales; it was very popular.

Sid could make up any number of pieces but never had any copyrighted. He was the only one I ever knew who could play his own "Canadian

Capers." He taught it to a fellow, and he had it copyrighted and published. There was one part the fellow could never get.

When musicians would come to town, I'd ask Sid, "Aren't you goin' to see so and so?"

He'd say, "Hell, no! I saw him enough when I played with him."

Sid worked with a lot of fellows, but he was like a lone wolf; he never brought them home with him or anything like that. The ones he used to work with he'd bring home to rehearse, but that was it. Sid and Roy Tayborn, the trombone player, were buddies; I think Sid thought more of him than anybody he played with. Roy was also a barber and was the first person to cut my son's hair. Roy was in the army when Sid's band was.

Right after Sid started on his own, he started to play piano professionally. His first job was at the Keyboo Inn at San Pablo and Fortieth streets in Oakland. It was a small club. After that, Sid went to playing a sporting house at Angel's Camp. About 1907, he finally went to San Francisco's Barbary Coast and played a nightclub over there. Wesley Fields was a piano player about ten years older than Sid, and he kind of took Sid under his arm and helped him to keep out of mischief.

First, Sid played for Lew Purcell, who had a dance hall on the Barbary Coast, then he played for Sam King. Sam King's place was named Sam King's. They were both colored places and were in competition. Lew Purcell had a son, George Purcell, who helped him manage, but George died young and never married. They catered to whites and colored. Sid led a band at Purcell's, and Wesley Fields led one at Sam King's. Purcell's was on Pacific Street and they moved to Jackson Street after Lester Mapp took over Purcell's. The whole area was the San Francisco sporting district of the time. Purcell's and Sam King's places were dancing places where the girls danced on a percentage basis. If you bought champagne or beer, they got so much of it. The girls were also prostitutes who were available to take to their rooms.

About 1915, they began to close up the Barbary Coast. By then, Lew Purcell and Sam King were both dead; they were rivals and died within a few weeks of each other. Lester Mapp was running Purcell's on Jackson. I remember "Bab" Franks played with Sid there. They caught the band playing after hours, which was after 2 a.m. They'd played after hours for years and had a man to look out for them. There was a mean old policeman who was out to get them, and he did and closed them down.

After they closed down Purcell's, Sid got a job at the Porta La Louvre. The white musicians were having a dispute with the owners, and they hired Sid's band. On that job, Sid was the first Negro to play in San Francisco under a contract. That was in 1915 or 1916. The Porta La Louvre was in the basement at Market and Powell streets. When they played there, they tried to join the union, but Number 6 in San Francisco wouldn't pass them; they said Sid and the drummer couldn't read. The picture they took of the band was when they were at the Porta La Louvre. They called the band Sid LeProtti's So Different Orchestra and had Clarence Williams on string bass, Benjamin "Reb" Spikes on saxophone, Slocum Mitchell on clarinet, Sid played piano and was the leader, Gerald Wells played flute, and a little crippled fellow played drums. While Sid was at the Porta La Louvre, Rudolf Valentino got his start there. He came there to get his first job dancing, and my husband started him off.

From the Porta La Louvre job, the band went to Los Angeles to play Byron Long's Tavern in Watts. That's where they joined the union, and when they got back Sid started the Negro local for the boys in Oakland. Sid and I married in Los Angeles, November 28, 1916. It was the second marriage for both of us. My name is Mame Louise and I was born November 23, 1889. I took piano lessons when I was a kid, but I never made anything out of it. I first knew about Sid when I was sixteen and still in school. He wasn't in school then. We had a daughter and a son who are both dead now.

Right after we married, we went to Honolulu, Hawaii, and played on the Alexander Roof Garden. They were sent over by a booking agent in San Francisco and had a contract to play. The whole band went over; there was Reb Spikes, he was born in Los Angeles; Clarence Williams, who was a Southern boy; Slocum Mitchell from the West Indie Islands; Gerald Wells, who was from Seattle, he's passed away since Sid died; and Sid and the drummer. Sid, Slocum Mitchell, and Clarence Williams took their wives. When I first heard about their music, they called it ragtime. In Honolulu, Sid's band was called the So Different Jazz Band. The whole band could play jazz and classical music. At the Alexander Roof Garden, they played classical music on Sunday nights. All the patrons there were whites. We were in Honolulu six months when fellows got called in the draft.

After World War I, Sid never had a regular full-time musical job. The original band kind of broke up. The band had a chance to go east, and Gerald Wells wanted to go, but Sid wouldn't go. Gerald left the band over

The newer, larger Sid LeProtti's Band, San Francisco, c. 1923 (L to R: Roy Tayborn, trombone/baritone euphonium; Elliott Worth (?), trumpet; John Terrell, tuba; unknown on banjo; Harry Pierson, drums; Lottie Brown, singer/dancer; unknown on violin; George Heard, clarinet; Sid LeProtti, piano/leader; Norris Hester, alto sax)

it, and it kind of broke up. Gerald didn't go east and finally went back to Seattle. Sid opened a shoe-shine parlor and cigar store right after World War I. They had a piano in there, and when the band had a job, they used to rehearse in there. It was on University Avenue and Grove in Berkeley. The people who lived in North Berkeley who had their shoes cleaned there would go by at night to hear them rehearsing.

About this time, the membership of the band changed. Roy Tayborn played trombone, Harry Pierson was on drums, John Terrell played tuba, George Hearn played clarinet, Lottie Brown sang and danced, Norris Hester played saxophone, and a fellow named Graves was the trumpet player. A fellow named Henderson played with them sometimes. He was older than I am, around Sid's age. He drank a lot and used to come to rehearse sometimes. Some other fellows were Charles Striker, Herb Clark, and "Ham" Hamilton; they played some kind of horn, and "Ham" chauffeured for some very wealthy man in Berkeley. Herb Clark and his brother were from the West Indie Islands, and both of them died about forty years ago. They started going to all the country towns like Fort Bragg, Williams, and all up in there. They played for house parties, dances, and other occasions. They played for dances quite a bit.

Sid and Clem Raymond played together once in a while, but Sid didn't care much for Clem, not that Clem wasn't a good musician; it was that he pulled things Sid didn't like. One of the things Sid didn't like about Clem was he cut prices. He was great on undermining you on a job by cutting the union price.

Reb Spikes

I'VE SEEN TOM TURPIN
PLAY THE BARBARY COAST

My life on the Barbary Coast wasn't so long because I went there in 1907
and 1908. I went to visit my brother Tom. I was only there two or three
months, that's all. I did meet Lew Purcell and a lot of them people because
they came in Tom's barber shop. His shop was right there on the Barbary
Coast. Then I come back home to Los Angeles, and when I went back in
1914, the Fair was on.

Tom's barber shop was about three doors from Purcell's, and I hung
around there all day durin' my visit. Purcell's was at 520 Pacific, and it was
called The So Different. Tom and Lew were good friends; he'd come in
Tom's shop and get shaved every day. Lew was well-liked and generous.
All the guys just hanging around—he used to give them all change. He
lived in Oakland, but I don't know where he was from. I never knew his

Pacific Street, c. 1910. Note "The So D" on the building next to the Hippodrome, indicating the home of The So Different.

wife or seen her. In 1907, Lester Mapp and Lew's son, George Purcell, tended bar in The So Different. When I went back in 1914, Mapp owned the place after Purcell died, and the boy was bartendin' there for Mapp. I don't know how Mapp got it. The place might'a closed and Mapp took it over, or maybe he bought the wid'a out. I know George Purcell didn't own any part of it.

I met Wesley Fields when I was in Frisco after the 'quake. I was just a young kid then, only eighteen or nineteen years old. Wesley was playin' in Purcell's then, and I met him for a long time around there. When I went back in 1914, Wes was still around there playin' somewhere, but Sid LeProtti had the job at Purcell's. Wesley couldn't read, but he was a devil of a piano player. He was from Des Moines, Iowa, and his sister was a concert pianist. Wesley was the only one I ever heard that was close to Jelly Roll on ragtime. He also played boogie woogie but they didn't call it boogie woogie then; it was all that runnin' bass and everything. Everybody used to play that, even before the teens, all through them early years. The blues players, that's all they needed was that runnin' bass. "Twelfth Street Rag" was an outcome of that runnin' bass.

Wesley played blues or anything; anything he ever heard he could play. If someone came in and sang opera, they'd hum it over to him and he'd play it. I don't know how many keys he played in; most of them he could fake in. Most of them ear guys got two or three keys they're the devil in; the others they stay out of them. Most of them play in E-flat, C-sharp, and F-sharp; they play a lot in the black keys. Wesley was a great piano player.

The gals used to come in Purcell's and sing a song over to him once, and that's all he'd need; he'd play it back as an accompaniment for them. But when the singers commenced to come in with their sheet music, they had to get someone who could read it, so they got Sid LeProtti. Fields was better than Sid on ragtime and that stuff. If you learn musically, you don't have the feelings of the guys that's playin' nothin' but feelin', that's all he goes on. I've always had that experience. You take some guy that's a devil of a good faker and can play anything he hears and do all kinds of improvisations, and take another man that's a musician, and he sticks to a lot of things that the ear player don't stick to because he goes on over it and don't pay no attention to it. Wesley was an awfully good piano player who played something like Jelly Roll. Of course, he played before Jelly, and I don't think he played as much as Jelly, but he might have. The two of them come along at two different times. Fields was mostly popular before 1910, and Jelly Roll was popular up to when he died.

My oldest brother was Tom. He always stayed in Frisco, and ran a barber shop until he died. Tom was twenty-five or thirty years older than me, and I was the baby of the whole family. My father had a boy before he and my mother married and that was Tom. Tom was a pretty good-sized boy when my father married my mother. So Tom was a half-brother, but you'd never know the difference. Hangin' around Tom's shop all day, I got to know all the guys on the Barbary Coast, because they came around to his shop. Then, after I got to know them, I'd stop by sometimes and hear their music.

Red Kelly's was across the street from my brother's shop, and I met him several times. When I visited Tom in Frisco, I lived at Tom's house.

Sam King's place was in the next block down from Purcell's. Freddie Vaughn played piano in Sam's place. He was a whole lot older than I was, and he'd been playin' in all those places for years. Freddie played ragtime and could remember any piece he heard. He was mister five by five—he was about five feet high and five feet wide. He had about the same shape as Jimmy Rushing. I only met Freddie when I was in Frisco in 1907.

There was a singer named Romeo, who was a very nice singer, who sang all around on the Barbary Coast and out at the beach. He was about six-foot-nine or ten, and was around before the earthquake and fire of 1906. He had a fine baritone voice.

Los Angeles had mostly just piano players in the early days before 1913. I know when I used to go to dances here they just had a piano player. He had all the dance jobs and his name was Sam McVea. He finally got up to three pieces: piano, mandolin, and drums. That's the only Negro I remember around here, and you couldn't have a dance unless you had McVea. We didn't have any dance halls in Los Angeles, so there weren't any places for musicians to play. San Francisco had the dance halls for the bands.

The Negro Ninth Cavalry came through Purcell's in 1907. They were going to the Philippines. While they were there they had a helluva lot of fights out in Pacific Street. Nina Jones was there about that time. She came out there with a show and left the show. Her husband was a drummer for the show; I don't remember his name. They separated in Frisco, and he went on back East. She was a good singer, very good, and she sang at Purcell's. She eventually got killed in San Francisco and was dead when I went back in 1914.

When I visited San Francisco I think they just called the music ragtime. I wasn't playin' music then; I learned later from my brother Johnny that I'll tell you about. They could have called their music jazz. It was called jazz music 1914 when I came back to San Francisco, because we were called a jazz band then. I don't now how the name originated.

The best jazz trombone player I ever heard in my life was in Frisco in 1907. He was a little dark fella, short and thin, named Frank Withers. Oh, he was great, really great. He played slide trombone, and he played in Wesley Fields's band at Purcell's. He and Fields were the whole band. I know they had a drummer, but I'm not sure there was anyone else. Frank would play all of the melody and variations and all that stuff on his trombone in 1907. He played everything that Fields played, and that was continuously all night. They played everything that was popular, and everything that wasn't published, and everything that everybody else played. I used to go listen to them whenever I could. I didn't meet either of them personally to know them. Frank lived in Oakland when he played the Barbary Coast, and that's what little I knew of him. Frank came in Tom's barber shop and talked to Tom. Later on, I met Frank just before he went to Europe, or when he'd come back from Europe. He came in my store in Los Angeles, and I remembered him. We had a long talk. In Los Angeles, if a musician didn't know where the Spikes Brothers Music Store was, he hadn't been to Los Angeles. Frank went all over Europe and Paris, and all around. He was a sensation; he went over to Europe on his own, but he played over there with all the French bands and other guys. He was great.

I don't know anything about Scott Joplin playin' the Barbary Coast, but I've seen Tom Turpin there. Tom Turpin was from St. Louis, and, when I saw him there, he was only in town for two or three days. I heard him play. He'd just come in Purcell's, sit down and play a few tunes, and then take off. That was in 1907. Turpin died in 1911 or 1912. When we went to St. Louis in 1912 with the Won't You Please Come Home Bill Bailey Troubadors, Tom was dead. His brother, Charlie, was there and had a saloon, and, across the street from the saloon, he had a theater in a tent. Charlie Turpin was also a deputy sheriff and lived for years and years after we was there. Tom and Charlie's sister come out here to Los Angeles and married a friend of mine, Wilberforce Thomas.

A couple of other early guys were Dick Robertson, the singer, and Henry Stewart, the piano player. Robertson later got into comedy like Bert Williams. Henry I met before I went to Frisco; he was here in Los Angeles way back in 1905 and 1906. He was a pretty good ragtime player, but he was more of a concert pianist. At least, he played the classics, and he used to give concerts and recitals. He was a pretty good concert piano player. Henry died in Salt Lake City.

Adam Mitchell was kind'a the king of clarinet jazz. He's the first I ever heard playin' that way and the best I ever heard. We all called him Slocum, and I don't know where or how he got that nickname. I don't know if he's the originator of jazz clarinet, but I heard Slocum playin' jazz in 1907. He was doin' all the stuff that you hear Benny Goodman and all those guys doin', but he was doin' it back then. Slocum could whine and cry on that thing and do all that blues stuff; he was a sensation, that's all. He came to Frisco with the minstrel show, and Purcell hired him and took him off the minstrels. I think he was with Busby's Minstrels when he came to San Francisco. He set San Francisco wild, and he was talked about all over town. He played there all those years between 1907 and was there when I went back in 1914. I went there and went with Sid's band; he was still there, and we played together for a number of years. Everywhere we'd play, people would admire him. He was a stick-out jazzman.

I was born in Dallas, Texas, on October 31, 1888. We came to Los Angeles in 1897. I had a medical examination last week, and the doctor said I was in great shape for my age. My father was a businessman in Dallas, and we were in nice circumstances. We lived in a neighborhood of fairly wealthy people, mostly white. Our home and all of our businesses were set afire and was destroyed, all in one night. They never knew who did it. My father was so disgusted, he put me and my mother on the train and sent us to Los Angeles. The rest of the children was in school and college. They came out later, and my father came later after disposing of what little there was left.

My father was born around Dallas, Texas, somewhere, and my mother was born in St. Charles, Louisiana. My mother was eighty-eight when she died in 1938, so she was born in 1850. Her name was Madora Spikes; I don't know her maiden name. My grandmother on my mother's side was named Curry; I don't know whether she married again or not, but my mother's father was a Frenchman who was born in France. Grandmother Curry lived to be a hundred and eleven years old. My father's first name was Monroe; his father was Irish and Norwegian, and he was part Indian. They say that when he was a young man, he played the old-fashioned violin, all that Southern stuff. I was the baby of the family and only eight or nine when we left, and I never heard him play. After my brothers and sisters got to be old enough to take lessons, about seven or eight years old, my mother had them all take piano lessons. Mother went to classes with them and took piano lessons with them. They're all piano players but me and my older brother Tom. Him and me are musicians, but we don't play the piano. The only little piano playing I do is if I want to compose something.

I sit down and pick it out. After I get it on paper, I can't play it—at least, not like someone else can play it. I can just pick 'em out and get 'em down. Sometimes, I don't even touch the piano for a year or two. I didn't want to be a musician; I wanted to be an artist. I used to could draw good with either hand.

Practically everybody in my family lived a long time. I lost a sister and brother some time ago. My sister was ninety and my brother, eighty-seven.

In 1793, the Mexican priest Don Neverro came here from Monterey, Mexico to start Los Angeles. He had fourteen families with him, and nine of that fourteen families were Negroes, and they settled in Los Angeles. They were all integrated, and there was only one white man in the whole bunch, and they was forty-two people. That was the beginning of Los Angeles, and then, in 1860, the state passed a law that no Negroes, or Indians, or Mexicans, or Chinese, or Orientals could go to a mixed school. They had to have a segregated school of their own. Then they went to court in 1880 and broke that law up; then they had desegregation. Here a hundred years later you're fightin' the same thing; it's a helluva thing.

When I was a baby, and my father used to play with me around the house, he used to call me Rebel. I guess I was mean or nasty or something. That stuck on me, and I've always been know as Rebel. Of course, they always cut it down since I was a baby and called me Reb.

I never was raised in prejudice. I went to school here in Los Angeles all my life and lived with everybody. I don't get into this black movement. If you're livin' in this country, you've got to be an American. There's no use havin' a Mexican over here, a Negro over there, and a Japanese there. It's just got to be a cosmopolitan town like Frisco was when I was there. No one paid no attention to color. As long as you had your money and paid, you were a lady and a gentleman; that's all that was necessary. I don't understand this stuff, demandin' this and demandin' that and can't stand on their own.

There wasn't much music in Los Angeles, I remember, before I went to Frisco in 1907. I saw Blind Tom here in 1903 or 1904, but I never knew him. I saw him once or twice. He'd come out and clap for himself, then he'd play.

Will Johnson came here in 1907, playin' bass with his Creole Band. He had Ernest Coycault with him on trumpet. Coycault called himself Johnson because Will and him looked so much alike everybody thought they were brothers. Will later went to Chicago, but Ernest stayed here 'til he died. Dink Johnson came out later on, and he was Will's brother. I remember Will had a guitar player named Williams, because he later opened up a hotel just a few doors from my music store, and was there for years and years and years. They had a valve trombone player named Padio, and he came from New Orleans with them. He went to Vancouver, British Columbia, and I heard he died there. A lot of those New Orleans fellas, you never knew nothin' but one name. He's still around here if he's alive. The band kind'a broke up, and I only knew the ones that stayed around here. Some of them went back to New Orleans, and some, I understand, went up to Seattle.

Reb Spikes

MINSTRELS, MEDICINE SHOWS, AND ON THE ROAD

My brother Johnny was a finished musician. So was my sister; she was a concert pianist. I never wanted to play music because everyone in my family played it. Around Los Angeles I was tryin' to do everything, cleanin' bricks, and tryin' to learn how to plaster and how to roof. Johnny came home in 1907, and he went downtown and bought me a set of drums. That's when I started in music. I learned how to play them, and Johnny just took me with him to Arizona, and that's where I started to play professionally. We formed a team: he played piano, and I played drums. We were a sensation around Arizona. They'd never heard drums and piano, but that's what they used to have in dance halls in Frisco. So, all the dances, black and white, and saloons and everything they had around there, we played. All we had was drums and piano. Then Johnny started me off on wind instruments, and I'd go from one to another. I used to practice them in my room when we wasn't workin'.

We played in Bisbee, Prescott, Douglas, and Globe in Arizona; in Albuquerque and Santa Fe, New Mexico; and El Paso, Texas. Later on I quit two or three shows in El Paso; I just never would go south. They tell me it's not so bad down there any more. We even went down and played Nogales, Mexico. We played a saloon and dance halls down there. We put on a show at the Dream On Theater in Globe, Arizona, called *Coon Nights*. It was January 27, 1910. There were a few Negroes in each town in Arizona. There were blues players with guitars and quite a few piano players around Arizona. I can see a lot of them in my mind, but I can't think of their names.

They all played that old ragtime and blues style. It was original stuff they played. Most of them were ear players, and they didn't write them down. They didn't know anything about writin' in those days, but they composed them tunes themselves. Gene Thomas was one of them. He was a piano player and played in all of the sporting houses. Tom Shepard was another; he was a piano player. Jockey Bill played piano and guitar and sang. He was a nice singer for those days, and he had a lovely voice. He was kind'a in demand around there. I don't know whether he was an ex-jockey or not. He was a little bit'a fella. They had a lot of Negro jockeys those days. These guys were around Arizona and El Paso, Texas. Around Prescott, Arizona, there were quite a few blues players with guitars.

Johnny's eyes went bad in 1906. He had rheumatism, and he was drawn up in a ball-like. They took him to Hot Springs and they buried him in that hot mud. It drove that misery all up into his head and closed the pupils in his eyes up; that's what the doctor said. Then they took him to San Francisco for an eye operation in 1907. They cut a hole right straight through his eyes so he could see in the back. After that, one eye was no good and one was fair. That's what he had until about 1936 when he lost the other eye.

Johnny's main instruments were piano and trumpet, but he could play a lot of other ones. He played the piano good, and he was a good trumpet player; he had college trainin' in them. After his eyes failed him, he had to hold his music right up to his eyes to read it. We traveled for four or five years doin' a musical act after he got in that condition. We had chimes, marimbas, harps, saxophones, piano, trumpets, and we'd go from one instrument to another. It was the old-fashioned musical act where we'd play about seven different instruments.

After Johnny went blind in 1936, he practically give up the trumpet. He could still pick it up and play if he wanted to. He went mostly to teachin' piano. He even got married after he was blind. His wife was nice to him; he was the happiest man. He knew all of the programs on the radio that he listened to every day, and he knew what time they come on, and he'd listen to them. He even wrote a lot of music after that, but he'd have to have someone take it down for him. He'd tell a joke and laugh harder and longer than some guy that was perfect. He said it wasn't nobody's fault he was blind, so why have ill feelings. I don't know if I could do it or not.

Johnny never played the Barbary Coast. He played in Oakland at a joint that Cliff Ritchie, the singer, had called Cliff's Place. That was about 1920, and they had a three- or four-piece band. He played there six or seven months. Johnny died in 1955 when he was eighty-seven, so all those years he was blind like that. He was a very happy man.

I didn't meet any other Negro musicians in Albuquerque or Santa Fe, New Mexico. Johnny and I played the theater in Albuquerque. We played different places in Santa Fe. Johnny played piano at the Elks Opera House in Santa Fe for the motion pictures. Those days you had a piano player, and when the horses come on, or there were chariot races, you played a whole lot'a fast music. Then, when it was a love scene, you played hearts and flowers. All theaters for motion pictures was that way. There were all Mexican musicians around New Mexico. They played Mexican music, and it was good. They had guitars, violins, string bass, and trombones; mostly they were string bands. There were some good ones.

There was a baritone euphonium player I met while Johnny and I were travelin' that was great; oh, he was great. He could make that thing sound like a human voice and just like a cello. You'd swear it was a cello if you stood outside to hear it. His name was Roy Tayborn, and later on, I took his job when they fired him out of Sid's band. He came to San Francisco with Dr. Ferdon's Medicine Show, playin' in the band. I met him the first time when he was on the road with Dr. Ferdon.

Ferdon had this medicine show that traveled around, and Johnny and I were with Ferdon for a couple of seasons. They'd go into these little towns and set up. When he'd come in a town, he'd rent an office or a storefront downtown and made a medical office out of it. Then he'd have his tent-show out in a big tent as close to town as he could find a good-sized vacant lot. Ferdon wasn't even a doctor; he was spieler. He always carried a doctor with him, and he'd have the medical doctor in the office downtown. His name was Dr. Wells. When he'd go in a little town, he'd remove tapeworms in two or three hours from people. They'd put the tapeworms in jars and things and put them on exhibition. I often wonder if people still have tapeworms; I haven't heard of them in years.

They had stuff for asthma, diabetes, and anything else. It was powders and soap and stuff you drank. Dr. Ferdon was a good talker and he claimed his medicines would cure anything. He could sell anything. He could talk anybody into buyin' anything. You'd walk right up and buy that stuff when he'd get through talkin'. Ferdon and Dr. Wells used to make all that stuff in the back end of the tent where the show was. Ferdon and Dr. Wells were white. I used to have a little sugar-diabetes, and I drank it by the bottle to help it. It didn't do me no good, but, to hear him tell it, it was awful good.

We put on a big show out in the tent to draw the people for Dr. Ferdon to sell medicine to. We had about a ten- or twelve-piece band or orchestra, six or seven entertainers, comedians, a quartet, a magician, dancers, or whatever he could pick up. It was always changin'. The show was free, and afterwards he'd get up and sell the medicine. They'd take in two, three, four hundred dollars a night that way. They used to have a lot of doctors out with that patent medicine; that used to be a big thing before the teens and all through the teens, too.

It seems like every show we traveled with they picked me to be on the door because I didn't do nothin' but the musical line. Usually I didn't go on until the middle of the show, so they'd say, "Reb, you take the tickets and check out." I got so that if you said you've got a hundred and twelve tickets at thirty-five cents, I'd just snap and tell you it was thirty-nine dollars and twenty cents. I knew the total; I didn't need a pencil or nothin'. Those guys at the theater would say, "How'd you do that so fast?" All they ever had to tell me was how many tickets and the price, and I could tell you how much it was.

Some of the shows you traveled with those days was Negro-owned and the owner was the comedian or something. Family-owned shows they used to call them; they had ten, twelve, or fourteen people. Several of the shows, the owner would say to me, "You take the tickets." I'd work that till I went on, and then afterwards, he'd say "You go check up the box office while I wash up." Then he'd go back and wash the blackface off his face while I'd check the ticket wind'a. Three or four shows they had me do that, and then I got the reputation and couldn't get out'a it. I guess that's why I later got more in the business end of music than the playin' end. After you take the tickets and count the wind'a afterwards, you don't go on to much of the show.

In those family shows, you had to count the wind'a in a hurry to get out'a town. They were generally one-night stands, and you had to pack up and head for the next town. It was a lot'a fun for a young fella and a lot of hardships that you laugh at afterwards. Bein' Negro, it was tough. We spent about four months in Kansas in 1912, and I don't think I slept in a bed over three or four nights in durin' the whole time. None of the hotels and white rooming houses would let you stay there. In a lot'a towns, you couldn't go into a restaurant. You'd have to go eat cheese and crackers, sandwiches, and things. We carried a little hot stove to warm your coffee and some food on. You'd have to carry bedclothes so you could sit up and cover yourself in the opera house or theater or wherever you were playin'. The only place you'd get to stay in a bed was when you'd run into a town where there's some colored people here and there, and you could put a couple over at this house and a couple over at that house.

One of the bands that got together in the early days down here in Los Angeles was led by Wood Wilson. He came from Dallas, Texas, and plays all kinds of stringed instruments. We played a picnic about 1913 that I've got a picture of. That was durin' one of the times I was home between travelin'.

I first met Jelly Roll Morton in 1911. I was managin' a theater in Tulsa, Oklahoma, and he come through there. Jelly Roll was the greatest piano player I ever heard. Jelly's best I ever heard in that Louisiana-style or ragtime or jazz or whatever you want to call it. The first time I heard him in Tulsa, I knew he was great.

In 1912, my brother and I were with a show called McCabe's Troubadors. I told McCabe about Jelly Roll, and McCabe sent for him. He came over and joined the show. I didn't know he was a comedian, but he told me he did that. I was gonna get him for a piano player, but when he come there he brought some little dark woman with him. They had a comedy team, and

Wood Wilson Band in Los Angeles, 1913 (L to R: Benjamin "Reb" Spikes, baritone sax; Charlie Wilson, drums; Mathews, promoter; Wood Wilson, banjo, mandolin, and leader; Harry Southard, trombone; Curry, piano)

that's what they said they'd do. Jelly could play so much piano that after he'd black up—he was much lighter than I am—he'd go out in front and play two or three tunes as an overture before the curtain went up. After they heard him play, they insisted on it. The girl that was playin' for the show was just a strict legit player and would just play note for note. The whole orchestra was just piano and drums. Jelly would go out there and everybody would be stompin' and goin' on, they liked him so much. Then he'd come back and do his blackface act with the little dark woman.

We were travelin' all over Kansas and Missouri and Illinois with McCabe. Jelly and his woman used to squabble all the time. Jelly squabbled with anybody; he was always in a squabble. Anyway, they had an argument and fight there in the show, and they left. They only didn't stay but a couple of months. I don't know where he went after that. I told him about Los Angeles, and he came out here in 1914.

Kid Ory with his 1922 Los Angeles band (L to R: Kid Ory, trombone; Papa Mutt Carey, trumpet; Fred Washington, piano; Bud Scott, banjo; Boner, sax; Billy Butter, tenor sax; "Pops" Foster, bass)

The only Negro-owned place in Los Angeles was the Dreamland at Fourth and Standard, and a fella named Hite ran it. That was before Les Hite ever came out here, and they weren't any relation. That was back in 1913. I brought Lionel Hampton and Les Hite here together in 1925 from Chicago, and they played with me. Hampton was supposed to be just out'a school then. The famous picture of Ory's Band, with Ory, Papa Mutt, Pops Foster, and Leon White was taken at the Dreamland. We played there later on in 1916.

Durin' the war, from 1914 on, there was four or five Negro-owned places. The next time I saw Jelly, he was playin' one of them called The Cadillac. That was across from the old Southern Pacific depot on Central. A Negro fella named Murray owned it. He had two or three places around Los Angeles. Another place he had was Murray's Cafe at Fifty-Sixth on Central. My brother and I did about three tunes with Jelly later on. One of them was "Wolverine Blues."

In 1919, Jelly Roll was playin' with me in a place over in Oakland. It was a white dance hall downtown in a basement; it was a hofbrau or somethin' like that. That job was after we come out of the army and I'd left Sid. Jelly's wife was Anita, who was Dink Johnson's sister. She run off and left him one night. She sent him a telegram and told him not to follow; she said when you get this telegram I'll be movin'. Anyway, that was about nine or ten o'clock at night, and that guy quit right then and left to follow her. We'd heard about Henry Starr, who was playin' out there in Oakland at some little theater, but we'd never met him. So we sent out there, and he come down and took the job, and that's how I come to meet Henry. I've got a record that Henry made for me on Vocalion. This was the first record he ever made. The song is called "Maybe Some Day."

Jelly went back East and had them standin' on their ears back there. Jelly talked so much that most of the time you couldn't tell what he was talkin' about. He was just constantly jabbering. When he went back East, he wanted to sue Duke Ellington and ASCAP and all them because, he said, they were stealin' his stuff. He had some great ideas; that's the reason they've got him in the Hall of Fame. He is the greatest jazz piano player. These guys now—they call them great jazz piano players—but they're just playin' a bunch of riffs. You don't hear no melody; it's just boo doo doo, boo doo doo doo. You don't know where they're gonna hit the piano. But Jelly, he's got a melody, and he's playin' the hell out'a the piano.

Jelly was likable, but you couldn't win an argument with him. He'd just keep talkin' 'til he won. Jelly always said everybody was stealin' his stuff. Don't care who they are, they're stealin' it. Just before he died, him and I were gettin' ready to open a publishin' house. We went out and talked to BMI, and they wanted us to come over with them, but we're both ASCAP, and we told them we couldn't do it. So we were to open our own publishin' house, and, doggone, about three weeks after that, Jelly died.

I remember one day in 1914 when some movie people called me up one day for me to get a band to go out to Celic Zoo to play for a picture. This was before I opened my store or went back to the Barbary Coast. I hustled around Los Angeles for nearly a day gettin' six fellas together. I had to hustle up guys that worked at night and couldn't find some guys who were off with their sweetheart or gal or somethin'. I finally rounded up six musicians and took them out there. When we got there the next day, there wasn't any strings on the piano; it was a silent picture and they didn't care if we could play anything. I could'a just picked up anybody on the street and took them out there. We only got three dollars for the day, and we stayed there all day.

Freddie Keppard and his Creole Band came to Los Angeles in 1914. I don't remember much about the band. I remember the trombone player because he played a valve trombone. Freddie stayed around here for a while. I thought Freddie was a better trumpet player than Armstrong. I've heard Freddie so much in person, and I've heard Armstrong, too; I just think he was better than Louis, and he was playin' long before Louis. I always heard that Buddy Petit was ahead of all of them. Freddie was one of the first ones to come out here.

Reb Spikes

BACK TO
THE BARBARY COAST

I don't know anyone alive who played the Barbary Coast when I did. When I went back to Frisco in 1914, Lew Purcell and Sam King were dead. Lester Mapp owned King's place and Purcell's place. So he had bands at both places. Mapp also owned the spot in the ground that Charlie Uter ran, that people want to as an after-hours spot. It was called The Squeeze Inn, and Sid LeProtti played there too. Uter was one of those West Indians; they was all well-liked, and everybody liked Uter. Lester Mapp is West Indian—he's from Barbados. He came there on a boat and was the only West Indian sailor on it.

When I arrived in San Francisco, Mapp hired me and put me down at Sam King's, playin' with Juicey Payne. Juicey wasn't no great ragtime player. He was a trained musician and strict musical. All the singers that he played for had to have their music, or he couldn't play. There was a big light yella fella that played with us; he was a good trumpet player. I can't remember his name, but I think he worked in the post office durin' the day. I think he played trumpet with Sid at Purcell's before Gerald Wells came. Wells took his job, and they put him back at Sam King's. Purcell's was the big place, and the best musicians was there.

Across the street from Sam King's was Louie Gomez's place that we called the West Indian Club. All the West Indians went there. There were quite a few West Indians around there from Barbados, Trinidad, and all down in there.

Old Fong, the Chinaman, used to do the Chinese lottery. He would come around durin' the day and evenin' and write tickets. You'd tell him how you were playin', and he'd write it for you and take it in. There's certain ways you can play. You can play a five-spot to a twenty-spot, or anyway you want'a in between, but you have to know the combination. Guys generally played a dollar five cents or a dollar thirty-five cent tickets. The dollar thirty-five cent ticket was what was called a nine-spot ticket. That'd give you pretty good money if you won. The drawin' was at ten o'clock, and if you won anything, Old Fong would bring it around at eleven or twelve o'clock at night.

They had Roy Tayborn playin' baritone euphonium in front of me at Purcell's. Roy won $1,500 or something on the Chinese lottery. He liked to drink, and he started gettin' drunk and layin' off two or three nights a week. Mapp got tired of that and fired Roy. He brought me up and put me down in Purcell's in Roy's place. That's the way Sid's band got together. It wasn't no band to start with, just each one was hired individually by Mapp. In those days, if a good musician come to town, they'd just hire you and put in a dance hall with whoever's playin' there. Old Pete was in Purcell's before Sid was. Then Slocum come to town, and they didn't have nothin' but three pieces there for a while. Then Gerald Wells come in town and got a job.

Roy Tayborn was the best I heard in my life on baritone euphonium. He had to be one of the greatest baritone players in the world. He was a good jazzman. He played right along with the rest of them. He didn't do all that stuff that they do on the trumpet. He played variations and country melodies and all that stuff. He could fake just like Slocum could on the clarinet. I never did see Roy play anything but baritone, and, as I told you, I first met

Patrons dancing inside Spider Kelly's, c. 1911

him when he was playin' with Dr. Ferdon. When he went to Frisco, he played with Sid for several years before I went back. Roy was a very, very nice man and a fine guy. He was born in Ohio, and he was a college-graduate musician. Roy went to Oberlin College in Oberlin, Ohio; we talked about it many times. He was just a fine guy. He didn't mind nobody's business, he just liked to drink, that's all. After many years, he moved down here to Los Angeles and finally died here.

Old Folks used to stand out in front of Purcell's spielin'. He'd say, "Go right in! The show's comin' on. We got entertainment!" It was just like a spieler in a circus tryin' to entice people to come in. He was out there to get the white people slummin'. He didn't do any dancin' when I was there.

In Frisco in those days, if you had money you could do anything you wanted to do. You could walk right up to those hop joints and go in, sit down, and watch the people smokin' opium. You could smoke it too, if you wanted to. It was all open, and that was one of the tourist things. Mapp had all the protection for the places he was runnin' and doin' things that was against the law. Policemen would pass right on by in their uniforms. Mapp stood right out in front at night, and he say, "Hello, Sergeant! Hello, Captain! Nice to see you out this evenin'." They'd say, "Hello," and pass right on by. He was payin' off, all of them places were.

The tourists would come down and go up to Chinatown and go through the opium dens. They'd come down to Purcell's, Red Kelly's, and them other places. That was part of the tour. When a party of slummers would come in, the girls would all get up and give them their benches. Sid Grauman, who owned Grauman's Chinese Theater later on, used to bring down gangs of people. At that time, he owned a little theater down on Market Street. Sid used to bring in a lot of wealthy people. He came in Purcell's two or three times a week.

The inside of Purcell's was just four walls with the bandstand at the back. The band was on a platform they built, and the bar sat in front. Along the sides they just had benches, and the dance floor wasn't bigger than a small livin' room. The place was narrow and very long. That's all there was to it. King's place had the bandstand on the side. All those places were about the same. There wasn't nothin' fancy about them. Of course, some of those white places was all fixed-up fancy. In Purcell's, we didn't have any special area for the tourists and slummers to sit in.

When all the girls were workin' on drinks, the guys would come and just sit down. The element and trade they had down there didn't call for anything fancy. When the rich people came down slummin', if they wanted something ritz, they'd go uptown to the St. Francis, and around they come down there slummin', and they wanted to see the worst. That might'a been the psychology of it.

The band in Purcell's started playin' at eight o'clock and we quit playin' at one o'clock. The customers just got entertainment after that, no dancin'. Sid used to make good money because, after one o'clock, he'd stay and play for the entertainers. He wasn't gettin' no salary, and he was doin' it all as a favor for the entertainers while they were singin' and dancin'. So all of the entertainers had to split their tips with him, and if you've got five or six entertainers splittin' with you, and you're one person, you make four or five times as much as the rest of them. Sid used to make good. Sometimes, on Saturday nights and such, Sid would make forty or fifty dollars.

Entertainers and musicians at Purcell's, c. 1934 (L to R: Billy Davis, dancer;
Elmer Claiborne, sax; Wes Peoples, piano; Helen Ross, dancer; Bob Barfield, sax;
Eddie Alley, drums; unknown dancer; Jimmie Brownley, trumpet; unknown
dancer; Belvin, trumpet)

Sid and the entertainers would stay there as long as the crowd came in.
Then at four or five o'clock in the mornin', when the crowd died down, all
the women that was half-drunk and finishin' up the night, they'd go down
in this little hole under the ground called The Squeeze Inn. It had a piano
and tables in there like a nightclub. That boy named Uter ran it. It was
popular with all the women on the street, and there was four or five hundred
of them, both black and white. They'd go down there from four o'clock to
eight o'clock in the mornin'. Sid would go down there and play after he

finished at Purcell's. I wasn't in there but once or twice. Sid didn't get away from the Barbary Coast sometimes 'til seven or eight o'clock in the mornin'.

All those places had a liquor odor. None of them was closed long; it was almost continuous twenty-four hours. If there was any cleanin' up at Purcell's, they did it between four or five o'clock in the mornin' and noon. They had guys comin' and goin' all the time.

In our band in the picture, there's Clarence Williams on string bass, me on sax, Slocum on clarinet, Sid on piano, Gerald Wells on flute, and Old Pete the drummer. Pete was about seventy years old when the picture was taken. He was a real old minstrel drummer that just played "boot, dit dee dat, boot, dit dee dat." Pete had been with the Georgia Minstrels, and when he come, there wasn't many drummers, so they hired him and put him in the band. He was an old-fashioned drummer that just played bass drum and snare drum. I don't remember whether Pete got sick or whether we decided between us to make a change when we got downtown. Everything we done, we talked it over.

After Pete left, we got a little snaggle-toothed kid whose head went up. He was about the same as Old Pete. Then we got Huddleson; I think we sent to Philadelphia to get Georgie Huddleson. Wells found him, and I know we sent back East for him. Little Huddleson played the xylophone and drums. I know he read for drums, but I don't know how fast he read on that xylophone. He had a rack, and there was everything on it; he had horns, rattles, cymbals, blocks, and all that stuff. Anything we played, he'd play it a second time, and he could get up and take him a solo on it. He'd stand on that xylophone and play anything we'd play too. Huddleson was a little crippled boy. He was only about four-feet high and had a short leg and a bad limp. When we went in the army in World War I, they wouldn't take him, and we didn't have a regular drummer in the army. We just picked one up that was in the army. The last time I heard about Huddleson, he was livin' in Montreal.

Gerald Wells was a West Indian too; he's from Port of Spain. He was just an average musician. Slocum was from Martinique in the West Indie Islands, where they had that big disaster. His real name was Adam Mitchell. He spelled it Mitchell, but he pronounce it "Mishell." Slocum was the daddy of all the clarinet players. They claimed that Slocum went east and all those guys back there stole his stuff. That's the word that was out in the twenties.

I used to hear Jimmie Noone on records—I never did meet him—and he was near Slocum. We'd play behind Slocum, and sometimes we'd have to stop and laugh ourselves at the passages he'd make. He could play a piece fifty times and never play it the same way; he'd play different variations all the time. The other guys, they get a style, and they play in that style all the time. Just like Benny Goodman: he was good, but he'd get his big kicks when he'd squeal on the clarinet—maybe hold four or five bars. But Slocum would be all over the place in that time with variations and jazz and whinin', all the same time. He was great. After Slocum left Sid, about 1920, he went back East for a while. Then he came down to Los Angeles in the early twenties. I put him to work playin' tenor sax and clarinet in my band at the Follies Theater.

I liked Wade Whaley's style of clarinet playin'. Whaley come here playin' that New Orleans style of jazz. He come out here in 1919 or 1920 with Kid Ory and Papa Mutt Carey, and they had Eddie "Montudi" Garland on bass. They also had a piano player with them, and I know they hired Ben Borders on drums.

Clem Raymond was from New Orleans and played around here. He played with Jelly Roll here a long time, and I think he learned a lot of stuff from him. Clem wasn't up in Wade's class in those days, but he was a pretty good player. After he went up to Oakland, they tell me he improved quite a bit.

Pop Humphrey was like all the New Orleans players. All of them played that Creole jazz like Wade. They all knew the same thing and played about the same. All of those guys tried to imitate Slocum—all but Whaley—but none of them was as good as Slocum. Slocum was better than Whaley, and there was no comparison with the rest of them.

I was never much of a jazzman. I played baritone sax, and I never could play a lot of hot jazz. I played a lot of counterpoint like cello parts. That's what made our music good and different from anybody else. All them other guys was jammin' and jammin', but when we'd play, I'd be carryin' a counter-melody, and I always tried to play two melodies. Sometimes, I'd play behind Slocum's variations.

There was a young kid around there named Earl Whaley, who also played sax. He wasn't no relation to Wade, and he later took a band to China. His mother was killed up there in North Beach in Frisco by some soldier. It was all over town about the murder in 1915. That left him an orphan, and I don't think Earl was over seventeen or eighteen then.

I started playin' with Sid in 1915 durin' the Fair. Sid had been playin' the Coast for several years and took Wesley Fields's job from him. Wesley was still playin' in Frisco in 1915. I think Fields's wife was named Jean, but I never seen her. They lived up in North Beach, just above Broadway. It was the first or second street up where me and my brother Tom lived. I never knew of any songs Wes composed, but he could play anything anybody wanted by ear. He was a real player.

I lived with my brother Tom all the time I was in Frisco. One time we lived out west of Fillmore Street, and then we lived in North Beach, and then we lived awhile up above Chinatown, a couple of blocks up the hill on Pacific Street. That was up past the Dixie Hotel. Tom always had him an apartment where we lived.

Clarence Williams would play nearly all cello parts on his bass. He wouldn't just play "zup, zup, zup, zup"; he'd play counter-melodies like I'd play on the saxophone. Williams was a trained bass player, not like those guys that beat the bass together, those guys who'd just pick it up and don't know what they're doin'. Williams was a great bass player; he could play anything. Later on, he came to Los Angeles and opened a music store. His brother went with him. In those days, you had a lot of phonographs to repair. People had those old wind-up things, and the springs always broke. His brother took up repairing them. I used to do it in our store. Williams died here in the later part of the twenties.

There were two sisters around Purcell's named Mabel and Maud Turner. Maud was Lester Mapp's girl, and Mabel was an entertainer. Maud came there as an entertainer, and, after she got in with Mapp, she just stood around mostly as the proprietress, unless someone asked her to sing.

Mabel was a hard hustler; she was hustlin' all the time. The entertainers would sit and wait for a customer to come over and ask them to sing or dance. Mabel, she'd go over and ask you, "Wouldn't you like to hear a song?" The rest of the entertainers would take their turn, and they didn't like the way she had of hustlin'. It was just her natural disposition that people didn't care for; it was just her nature: greedy. She had a hot temper, too. The band didn't get none of the entertainers' tips. If someone gave them two or three dollars, they'd give fifty cents to the band. It didn't amount to nothin', maybe two or three dollars a night for all the band.

A lot of the white musicians and entertainers from other places would come in Purcell's after they got off work at one o'clock. They'd come in 'til three or four in the mornin', slummin'. I came in at ten minutes to eight and got my instrument out, and at one o'clock, I'd pack my instrument back up, and I left at five minutes after one. When the band quit, I went home. I just didn't like that element of people and things, and I was glad to get out of there. I thought five or six hours of that kind'a jive a night was enough. I wasn't married then, and I didn't smoke, and I didn't drink. I never did call the employees by their first names. I never got that familiar with them; I called them Mr. and Mrs. I respected them and they respected me. They called me Mr. Spikes, and I called them Miss Dora, or whatever her name was. It didn't make me no difference if I knew she just got through turnin' a trick with a man upstairs; I still called them Miss and Mrs. Sid was pretty much the same way, but he had to stay, because that's where he made his money, after one o'clock.

I guess the reason I feel and look so good today is I'd go home and get in bed and get a good night's sleep. Most musicians start out and get drunk and eat a big steak and couldn't sleep. A lot of times, I'd get up at two or three o'clock in the afternoon and meet the musicians goin' home to bed. They'd been up all night runnin' around. I've had bands where we were due on the job at eight o'clock at night, and guys would show up that hadn't been to bed all night, and come in half-drunk and try to sit up there on the stage. I've had them to make some bad mistakes in that condition. Some musicians even got it in their minds they can play better when they're half-drunk. No man can do that.

George Bryant moved to San Francisco after he'd been with the Georgia Minstrels for twenty years or more. The old minstrels used to go out at twelve o'clock in the day in the small towns and get on the main corner and they'd play a regular concert. They'd play four or five overtures like the *William Tell Overture* and all the light flashy stuff like that. Then they'd play a lot of what they called ragtime then. And that was their ballyhoo for the crowd at night. They did that every day. George was the musical director for the Georgia Minstrels for years and years, and traveled all over with them. They had a wonderful band and could play anything. When he'd come to Frisco, he'd play the nightclubs, and he played piano in them. His home was in Omaha, Nebraska, but when I came back in 1914, he had moved to Frisco and was playin' out at the beach. George was a nice trumpet player, but he wasn't a jazzman; he was legit. He wrote all the arrangements for the Georgia Minstrels, and any arrangin' around Frisco, he did. He was a wonderful arranger. He came down to Los Angeles in 1927 and played a trumpet for me in the band I had at the Follies Theater. I used him as second trumpet. He was a good musician, but I'd always let my first trumpet player take the hot solos.

Jack Ross played violin out at the beach somewhere. He might'a played with Bryant. He was a left-handed violin player but he strung it up right-handed and played it left-handed. Jack was on the Coast years before I was there in 1914. I saw and heard him play several times. He was just an ordinary violin player. Most of the places out at the beach had two or

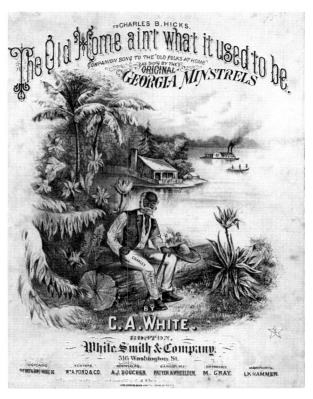

Sheet music cover featuring the Original Georgia Minstrels, one of the first all-black minstrel groups, 1875

three musicians, mostly guitars and violins. There was a boy around there named Johnny Long who was pretty good on guitar and banjo. He played with Bryant.

We used to play all of the popular tunes of those days at Purcell's. We played all of Scott Joplin's rags. They were popular for dancin'—and Sid knew all of them—and some of Tom Turpin's rags and other tunes we'd hear other guys play, and then we played the popular tunes that were out them days, like "St. Louis Blues." I don't remember the names of any of them—hell, that's been over fifty years ago. There were very few tunes we had the music to. Sid would get the piano sheet, and that's all we had. He'd play it on the piano, and we'd try to follow. Until we learned it, we were all fakin' our parts.

Kid North was a great racehorse man who used to come around. He played one or two tunes on piano. I heard them talk about it, but I never heard him play. They said his greatest tune was "Ace In The Hole." I think that's where he got his reputation as a piano player. What I knew of him, he was a racehorse man. I don't know what Kid's job was, but he was always dressed up immaculately all the time in the latest style. Kid North worked for a man named Howard for forty or fifty years. Howard owned all those racehorses. Kid went everywhere the racehorses and Howard went. We always thought he was a big man in racehorses. He always had lots'a money.

We had a lot of characters around Purcell's. There was Big Boy, our floor manager. The floor manager like that would get in a fight every night. In a place like that, you've got fifteen or twenty girls dancin', and the floor manager goes up to them and asks them what they want'a drink. Then he hollers out to the bartender "Wine," "Whiskey," "Whiskey and rye," "Ginger ale and whiskey," or whatever it is. Then the bartender sets them all up and mixes them. The floor manager gets the tray and brings them back to serve the party. When the guy pays, he gives the girl the check. Those dance hall girls are supposed to be workin' on drinks. They got 50 percent of the drinks they sold and they got one of those checks every time they sold a drink. They weren't supposed to be prostitutes, but they had their rooms upstairs. If they'd catch a live one, they'd slip upstairs and turn a trick. They made eight, ten, twelve dollars a night dancin' and sellin' drinks, sometimes more than that if they caught a real live one and he starts buyin' champagne. They'd catch those drunken soldiers and sailors comin' in there that have been out four or five months. Big Boy eventually got killed. I understand some guy shot him. Lew Purcell's son, George, got killed about the same time. It was a girl he was goin' with that shot him.

There was a guy around there named John Davis. He might have had a nickname of "Hod." Anything to be done around there, Davis done it. He used to put on dances like the Texas Tommy and the dirty dances shakin' his behind when people wanted to see that. He did all kinds of those dances with the women there. He used to dress up like Bert Williams and do comedy songs like Bert. He done the pantomime like he was playin' cards, and he'd put his pants up to his chest and have a short coat. He sang all the old Bert Williams songs. Then, Davis could sing a pretty good ballad; he had a nice voice. You'd come in another night, and Davis would be tendin' bar. Another night, he'd be the floor manager, takin' orders and servin' drinks. Another night, he'd throw you out, he's the bouncer. He was a big tall guy, about six-four. There was always three or four bouncers standin' around there in case somebody started somethin'. There was always plenty of them. If you'd come in there the next mornin', Davis would be there, with his pants rolled up to his knees and some old shoes on, scourin' the floor, cleanin' the bar, and washin' the walls. Anything to be done, Davis did it. He was dancer, singer, entertainer, bartender, floor manager, bouncer, janitor, and whatever else was to be done around there.

I met Johnny Peters when I was in Frisco right after the 'quake. He's the one who originated the Texas Tommy, and then he had the Johnny Peters Dancers that went all over the country doin' it. Johnny wasn't too tall and was a light brown Negro. When I came back in 1915, Dutch Mike and Pet Bob were doin' the Texas Tommy. It was quite a bit like the Jitterbug.

Dutch Mike looked like a big Irishman. He was tall and slim and had a broken nose. Pet Bob was just a tall dark Negro boy and a good dancer. They learned to do the Texas Tommy from Johnny Peters. Dutch Mike and Pet Bob would come in and dance for the entertainment of the people. They weren't hired there; they'd just come in and got a reputation, and sometimes people would ask them to dance. Other times, the girls would just feel like dancin', and they'd dance. I don't think I said ten words to either of them, even though they come in every night, and I played there.

Willie "Strut" Mitchell was a singer and dancer there at Purcell's. He was a good hustler too; he'd make a lot of money. He died down here in Los Angeles in the early thirties. Cliff Ritchie was another singer there. They'd both just step around and dance a little bit, not a regular Buck and Wing or anything like that.

I remember seein' Irwin Jones. I only saw him sing and dance on the stage; he never played banjo when I saw him. He used to dress up in a perfect green coat made up the color of a pool table. He was as black as you could be. He used to sing some kind of song about St. Patrick's day, and he pretended he was an Irishman.

Whiney was a guy who was always around the Coast. He was kind of a message-boy for everybody. If any of the women wanted someone to run an errand or anything, they'd get Whiney.

Giles County was a banjo player around Frisco. He wasn't much good; he only knew four or five chords. The song he did most was about "Way

Back In Giles County." It had a lot of verses and always ended with someone eatin' cornbread and beans, hoein' corn, and pickin' cotton down in Giles County. The whole song was about what was goin' on in Giles County. He used to get down and screw his banjo, like he was friggin' it, while he was playin' it. He'd start right in on a corner or anywhere doin' it. People would give him money because they thought it was funny and crazy. It was a hustle that made him money. He went all over the world playin' that fool thing. I don't know if he was from Giles County or not.

Harry Couch was a Negro who played piano around the Coast a little bit. He was an ear player, and I met him at the Fair in 1915. I don't think he ever had a regular piano job. A lot of those guys that knew some tunes would come in sometimes, and Sid would let them play a couple or three tunes. He'd get down and take a little rest while they played. Sometimes I'd talk to them on the bandstand.

They used to call Frank Shievers "Mr. Jazz." He played piano and drums. He was more of a comedy piano player than anything. He used to dress funny, and he had a little act he put on in cabarets. I think that's where he got his name "Mr. Jazz." He went to China and never did come back.

I met Bill Powers at the Fair in Frisco. He was playin' around the Fair, and he used to play out on the beach. Durin' the Fair, they had four or five little places out there where Negro musicians played with three or four pieces. I never heard Powers play but used to see him nearly everyday. They said he was a pretty good piano player.

Back in those days, if you played a lot of music, the average person didn't think you was good. You take most of those guys they were crazy about up there, like Wesley Fields and Freddie Vaughn, everything they played was by ear, and people thought they was great. If you put music in front of them, it slowed them down quite a bit.

Tom Pitts was a good ear piano player around there. He was in Frisco durin' the Fair, and I think he had an uncle who lived in Oakland. He wasn't a professional musician, but he wrote a tune that became famous, "I Never Knew." After I moved back to Los Angeles and opened the music store, Tom came down here in the twenties. He came in the store with this song, and we liked it. He let us have it on consignment. We had a contract and agreement on it, and we give him fifty or a hundred dollars advance for it. Then he went to Phoenix, Arizona, and one of McDonald Publishing

House's agents heard it and bought it. They published it, and Paul Whiteman made the first record of it. It was a sensation. That made two people have contracts on it, and when we went to send it in to be published, they told us it had already been published. We brought a suit against McDonald Publishing Company. We had a lawyer up there in Frisco we got to sue them. I think his name was Griffith, and the day the trial comes up, he was out fishin'. We lost by default. Pitts was a hop-head, and he moved all over. He had a gal, and wherever she went hustlin' tricks, he went. He was just a pimp. I never hung around the Coast and with the other musicians. Most of those guys were a bunch of pimps and things. When I got off work, I went home.

Nettie Lewis was just an ordinary singer and dancer; she had a nice little voice. She was a favorite amongst all the slummin' people because she kept herself clean and neat and nice. She could sing about as many dirty songs as she could nice songs. "Room 202" was one of the favorites of the dirty songs, and they had all kinds of verses to it. It was all about the things that went on in Room 202. All the singers had their own verses, and they could sing it all day long. Some of them knew fifty verses, and as long as someone would keep givin' them a dollar once in a while, they'd keep singin' it. Most of the people come in a place like that want dirty verses.

Glover Compton was a piano player and Nettie Lewis's husband. I only heard Glover play once or twice, and I didn't think he was a great piano player. Glover is the guy that took Sid's song and sold it. The copies of it was made by George Bryant. George did all the writin' and arrangin' around there. We played it three or four years around and just called it "Sid's Rag." Sid gave Glover a copy of it, and, when he got back to Chicago, this fella Cohen got a hold of it. Cohen called it "Canadian Capers." We always suspected Glover got somethin' out of it. The tune became a bit hit. Sid was very easy-goin', and he let it slide by.

The funny thing was, when we come down here to Los Angeles to work for Byron Long, we took Cohen's job. I jumped Cohen one night when he was in there.

I said, "What are you doin' takin' that boy's song?"

He wouldn't even talk to me, and Sid was just standin' there, and he never said a word. I'd had the guy arrested right there, and, if it had been me, I'd have been suing that guy yet. He just looked at me and walked away.

Reb Spikes

LEAVIN' THE COAST

After the Fair in 1916, we wanted to get out'a that dump at Purcell's. We decided amongst all of us, we wanted to get out. We wasn't makin' no money; two and a half a night was all. Sid was makin' more, but I think he was tired of it too. I didn't drink and smoke, and Sid didn't drink and he didn't smoke. Wells didn't drink. Slocum and Williams didn't either. We just didn't have any drinkers in the band.

Wells went downtown and contacted old man Swanberg of The Porta La Louvre. He come down and heard us.

He said, "Yeah, yeah, I want your band."

Old man Swanberg had a union place, so we had to be union. We went down and took the union examination, and they said three of us could read and the other three couldn't read. They said Sidney, Williams, and Slocum couldn't read, but we could all read. If we'd taken the job that way, that would'a broken up our combination. So old man Swanberg telephoned his friend Al Levy in Los Angeles and asked him to put us to work for a while. He said he was gonna let Levy use us until he could get us in the union or something. He said, "Yeah, I want them." So old man Swanberg sent us down here. We come down and played Levy's Tavern. When Sid started, he was playin' at The So Different Place, so after we left there, we called ourselves The So Different Jazz Band.

We came down to Los Angeles and played Levy's Tavern for about six weeks, and the white boys in San Francisco went on strike. Old man Swanberg came down here, and, in two days, took us back to Frisco and put us in there as non-union. We played the Porta La Louvre eight or nine months. When we worked there, we had to play the lunch hour every day and the evenin' shows. Only three of us played the lunch hour. We'd take turns, but Sid had to play every day. Wells and I would play a week, then Slocum and Williams would play a week. We all played in the evenin', and they had shows there. They had ballet dancers and all kinds of special music, and we played all of it.

After we left The Porta La Louvre, we came down here to play Byron Long's Tavern at 108th and Central Avenue in Watts. It was later called The Plantation and Jazzland. While we were playin' there, we played several nights a week at Dreamland in town before we went to work at Long's. That was the later part of 1916. At Byron Long's Tavern, Rudolf Valentino was hired to exhibition-dance, and we were the musicians. A lot of famous people like Wally Reed, Charlie Chaplin, Lottie Pickford, Jack Pickford, Blanche Reed, Fatty Arbuckle were frequently at Byron Long's. Usually, they'd come two or three nights a week. A guy named Jones was the host, and him and Byron Long were very popular men. We had Harry Richman and Cliff Friend singin' with us. Cliff Friend is the boy who wrote "Just a Little Cry at Twilight," "Baby's Prayer at Twilight," and a lot of good songs. Al Jolson come out there one night and bought one of them. It was "Oh, How She Can Dance." He bought it the way we played it. We played it Hootchy-Kootchy style, and that's what attracted him. Slocum was doin' a lot of whinin' in it and doin' all kinds of things.

We went to Honolulu, Hawaii, after we left Long's. The people over there heard about us, and they contacted a bookin' agency in San Francisco, and

The Twenty-fifth U.S. Infantry Regiment Band on parade, Nogales, Arizona, 1917

they sent for us. We left for Honolulu in February 1917 for a six-month engagement to play the Alexander Young Hotel. Sid LeProtti and me was on the same boat. I wasn't married when we went there, but Sid was. He brought his wife, Mamie, with us. I haven't seen Mamie since I left Frisco in 1919. She used to be a pretty girl. We got mixed up on the boats, and Wells, Mitchell, Williams, and Huddleson went on the boat ahead of us or behind us. They either came a day ahead of us or arrived the next day. The Alexander Young Hotel was right on the main street of Honolulu, whatever that is. All I know is how to get there. The only street I know in Honolulu is School Street, where I stayed.

We finished our six-month engagement at the hotel, and we were drafted in July or August 1917. Three of us was drafted, and so the other two enlisted. I think it was me, Sid, and Williams were drafted. They wouldn't take Huddleson because he was so crippled up. We were supposed to come back to the States to go in the army, but Colonel Callahan over there got permission to take us in the Twenty-fifth Infantry right there in the Islands. Sid was a piano player, and there wasn't anything to do, so they put him on trumpet. The reason they took us was because old Callahan wanted us because we were very popular. The Twenty-fifth had the best baseball players, the best runners, and the best football team, and Callahan wanted the best jazz band. They'd never had a jazz band in the army before.

We went in the army, and, after thirty days, they brought us to Nogales, Arizona. Sid played fourth or fifth trumpet in the army band. Every once in a while, he'd go "toot, toot." He was in there three or four months and never did much more than go "toot, toot"; he'd never played one before. When we got to Nogales, we got a job playin' downtown at the theater. We didn't get through work until about eleven at night. I don't think we was ever on curfew in the army. Half the time, we never did go back to the camp;

Sid LeProtti, Twenty-fifth Infantry, Honolulu, 1917

we'd stay around downtown. We used to play for all the dances in the army. You're not allowed to charge for dances on the camp, so the colonel gave us permission to sell the drinks. We'd make a tub of lemonade. We let everybody in the dance free, but we sold them lemonade. We got fifty cents or a dollar servin' the lemonade. There'd be three or four hundred people at the dance, and when the lemonade ran out, that was it, no seconds. We'd make ten or twelve dollars a night out'a that.

After the war and the armistice, they released a soldier if he could prove he had a job. They especially let a draftee out if he had somebody sponsor him on a job. That was the only way you could get out'a the army. Gerald Wells wrote to somebody he knew and told them if they could find a job for us, we could get out. They told this boy that run the Canary Cottage. It wasn't but a few days, we got a letter guaranteeing us a job and a contract. We signed the contract, and they let us out'a the army. We got out and went right on out to the beach to work at the Canary Cottage. Our whole band was intact in the army, only we didn't have a drummer. I never did know nothin' about the beach out there; I went out at night and left at night. I never did go to the beach durin' the day.

After we finished the Canary Cottage, I went over to Oakland and worked there four or five months in 1919. That was where I played with Jelly Roll. When I was playin' there, I lived down in one of the white hotels over the Orpheum Theater. There was a place over there named the Oak Leaf that was an after-hours spot run by Henry Hastings.

Then I came home in December 1919 and opened a music store with Johnny. I never went back up to San Francisco to stay. After that, I got into the business end of music more. One time, Johnny and I used to have a musical meat market, and another time, Curtis Mosby and I used to be partners in a music store.

My musical career was a funny situation after I left Purcell's and LeProtti. I was always in the managerial end of things. When I had bands or anything, I always had to take care of the business and all like that. In the music store and playin' with Johnny, he was almost blind and couldn't do things. I had to keep the stock up, make the repairs of the instruments and phonographs, go get stock, check it, and that would take up nearly all of my day. Then I'd go out and play at night if we had a job.

I was doin' giggin' mostly after I opened the store. I was runnin' night clubs too; I had two or three clubs. The only real band I had after 1919 was when I went in the Follies and when I went into the dance hall in Redondo Beach. We stayed there five or six months. The American Legion Band, and those bands like that, those were boys that I played with when I had a gig. We worked about three nights a week at the American Legion dance, and then we'd pick up other jobs. We worked three to five nights a week, which was pretty steady. That went on six or seven years. I'd just call them when I had jobs. In the picture of the band, there's Ellsworth, he played drums and danced; Gene Wright was on piano; the next guy is Edgar Williams (he was just standin' in to indicate we had a vocalist); then me; Max Shaw was on the tuba; Russell Massengale, trumpet; Leon White, trombone; and a guy named Perkins on banjo. The band is what I'd call a gig band. There just wasn't a whole lot of places for Negroes to play steady in those days. You didn't have any Coconut Grove that they'd let you play in. White bands was in all of those places. Outside of that, I run the store and nightclubs.

When I came home from Frisco, I opened a nightclub and got a five-piece band to play for me. I was in the army with Leon Herriford, and he was lookin' for work. I wanted to put him in there with them as a friend and a good musician too. They just wouldn't let him play with them. They said they didn't want a noisy band, and it was just right the way it was. Those boys were doin' good anyway. They played at a dance hall and made pretty good—they ran it themselves. After they finished the dance hall, they'd come to my nightclub around twelve o'clock. It didn't hurt me none, because everybody would follow the band down to my nightclub. I got more business that way than if I had been runnin' all night. Maybe 250 people would come in and load the place up.

They wouldn't let Herriford play with them, so I had to use him on the floor. Leon was from Kansas City. His father was principal of our school

"It Must Have Been a Dream" sheet music cover, c. 1920, featuring Les Hite

here in Los Angeles. Leon eventually got a band that was playin' for Frank Sebastian out at the Cotton Club in Culver City. He was called The Whisperin' Saxophonist because he had such a sweet whisperin' voice on the sax. He'd come on every night at twelve o'clock, and the people would just go nuts. They called the band The Quality Five. He died in the twenties; Les Hite was one of his saxophonists, and Hite got right in there and got the band. After that, it was the Les Hite band.

Evelyn Joyner used to sing in one of my nightclubs down here. He used to sing all of those comedy songs—he had a gang of them.

There's an interestin' story about how they got the name for the Cotton Club in Culver City. Frank Sebastian didn't open the Cotton Club; it was his uncle, who'd been a waiter out in Culver City for years, and another fella. When they were gettin' ready to open, the uncle and this other fella come down to my place for a band, and while they were there, they saw a big pictorial sheet for records on the wall of McKinney's Cotton Pickers, and it said, "McKinney's Cotton Pickers of the Cotton Club, New York." The uncle said, let's call our place the Cotton Club, and that's how they named it. When they were there, I also got the band job for Leon Herriford. Frank Sebastian wasn't even in it then. Frank was such a handsome guy—oh, he was handsome—and he come along, and I think they made him host. Then his uncle died, and he got the place.

We started a Negro union in my music store. The store was at Twelfth and Central and was the headquarters for all the Negro musicians. I supplied Negro musicians for all the Hollywood parties and motion pictures. Anytime they wanted to make a picture and needed Negro musicians, they'd call me because we was the headquarters. We made a little change bookin' bands for those things. With all the boys comin' in here, we got to talkin' about a union, so some of them got together here, and we started one.

My brother was at the store, too, and he was active in music. He had a little band around here with a guy named Henderson on clarinet and tenor sax. Bill Hegamin—he was Lucille Hegamin's husband before they broke up—played piano. Frank Watts was the drummer, and Johnny played the sax and marimbas. Johnny could play nearly all the instruments. He did all the arrangin' and orchestration of music we published and played, while I tended to business. Henderson was older than I am, about twenty years older; he was about the same age as Johnny. He played with me once in a while, too. He was a good jazzman for the times of jazz. He played all the old Dixieland things like Ory and Papa Mutt and all of them. I don't know where he was from, but he could read. All we ever called him was Henderson. Bill Hegamin went on to Shanghai, China, and I guess he died over there.

I remember when Jack Carter came through here. They were talkin' about a great pianist they had named Teddy Weatherford. I heard him a few times, and he was great. The band went on over to Shanghai, China. Teddy Weatherford stayed over there, and the rest of the boys came back.

With my Legion Band, one time I had a contract to go out to a recordin' studio in Hollywood to make a record with the band. When we got out there, we had rehearsed and rehearsed, and had a lot of special stuff on a tune. After we got there, we had to wait for this white band to finish their recordin'. The white band was playin' Catalina Island and had a big band of about eighteen pieces. While we were sittin' in the waitin' room, they start recordin' the tune we'd been rehearsin'. It was one of the popular tunes of the day. So, we only had a six-piece band, and we're sayin' what in the hell are we gonna do now. When they came out and we went in, we played one side, and I had an idea.

There was a policeman here named Sheffield, who had a reputation for bein' a bad cop and always gettin' after bootleggers. When he'd arrest them, he'd always say, "It had to be you." He was a great friend of mine because he was crazy about music and musicians. I said we'll play some blues, and we'll call them "Sheffield Blues." Then I said to the band, while you're makin' the vamp for the introduction, you knock on the door.

So when we started the vamp, one of the boys went "Bam, Bam, Bam," like he's knockin' on the door.

Another one yells, "Who's there?"

I yell, "Sheffield! Open the door!"

He yells, "Throw it in the sink! Throw it in the sink!"

Then you heard the door open and we started playin' blues.

After we played the blues quite awhile, we ended by all singin', "It had to be you."

I've played drums, trombone, saxophone, clarinet, and a little piano. Mostly, I played sax. I like Coleman Hawkins and that boy Johnny Hodges that plays alto with Duke. Benny Carter of course I liked and a guy here named Bump Meyers. They're the best sax men I knew. There were a lot'a fellas back East playin' that I never knew. In the early days, it used to be that you could tell the white musicians' playin' from the Negro musicians. The Negro bands had more feelin' in their music, especially on that hot stuff or jazz. The white guys played the notes, but they didn't have the feelin'. Now, some of the white bands have gotten it down to the point where you can't tell whether it's white or Negro.

I met King Oliver when he came through Los Angeles after he left San Francisco. He played for Lucius Lomax up there in Oakland at the Creole Cafe. The Creole Cafe opened about 1920; it wasn't opened when I was playin' downtown Oakland in 1919. Oliver came by the store before he went back to Chicago. He didn't play in Los Angeles.

I made records with Kid Ory in 1922 and went back East with them in 1923. I met King Oliver again in Chicago. He was playin' the Royal Gardens, and I heard him play four or five times. I also met Armstrong there, playin' with Oliver. They both played the same type of trumpet; it was the New Orleans gutbucket style. When I was back there, I also met Fletcher Henderson, and he made some records for me back there.

Another guy I met at the Royal Gardens was Bo Diddly, who was singin' there. He was the first scat singer I ever heard. He was scat singin' before Armstrong was singin' anything. He came through Los Angeles a year or so later, goin' to Japan and on out through there. Then he came back and stayed here a year or two. When he came back, he sang with my American Legion Band. The American Legion boys hired him as the entertainer and singer.

Solomon's Penny Dance Hall was at Tenth and Grand Avenue, and Curtis Mosby played there. It was frequented by all the sailors—just hundreds of sailors went there—and it was a large place. They got such a crowd, they had to have afternoon and evenin' dances. Solomon made lots of money. They called it Penny Dance, but it cost you a nickel or a dime to dance.

Harry Southard was another guy around here; I don't know where he came from. He was the leader of the Black and Tan for years. Several of them left and organized The Quality Five. There was Paul Howard, Leon Herriford, and they got Lawrence Brown, who was just out of school. Their first job was at the Cotton Club, and they eventually got up to eight pieces. Southard played after that but never had another band. He had a barber shop, and when anyone wanted a trombone player, they'd call Southard. He was a good trombone player, musically or fakin'. Southard died in the 1960s, and he was a pretty old guy then.

In later years, I wrote a couple of musicals with Johnny. One was *Steppin' High*. It ran for about a year and went all the way back to New York. The last show I wrote was *Rhythm Town*. It opened just as the Los Angeles streetcars went on strike. The strike was on for about a month, and the people didn't have no transportation to get to it. We had to pay the cast for a month, and after that we were broke because there was no money comin' in, and we closed it up.

Curtis Mosby's Dixieland Blues Blowers on a float advertising Solomon's Penny Dance De-Luxe, Los Angeles, 1923 (L to R: Henry Starr, piano; unidentified child with toy trombone; Bob Brassfield, sax; Freddie Vaughn, banjo; Harry Barker, trumpet; Lloyd "Country" Allen, trombone; Curtis Mosby, drums/leader)

Wesley Fields, jazz pianist, c. 1920

WESLEY FIELDS—
THE KING OF THEM ALL

by Harry Mereness

Numerous attempts were made to locate Mr. Mereness, who was finally found in Denver, Colorado. He has kindly given permission to reprint this article he did for the Hot Music Society of San Francisco in 1940. It is one of the few attempts, if not the only one, to tell the story of black jazz on the Barbary Coast up to that time. Mr. Mereness vaguely recalls writing the article, but can shed no further light on the subject. The article is reprinted with a minimum of editing.

Wesley "Fess" Fields is likely one of the oldest living jazz musicians in the United States, and the most important in historical interest connected with San Francisco. Armstrong is forty; Johnny Dodds died last year, aged forty-five. But Fields, who had a band at "Nigger Mike" Purcell's on the Barbary

Coast around 1910, and until lately played a brand of piano remembered with relish by such fine local practitioners as Bill Laub and Paul Lingle, commenced his keyboard studies in 1896 and will one day this year celebrate his sixtieth birthday. It is on the authority and testimony of Bill Laub that I have headed this article: "Wesley Fields—The King of Them All." Fess undoubtedly was one of the greats of the Barbary Coast piano players, which is saying quite a bit since many of the "professors," such as Morton, Scott Joplin, and Tom Turpin, regularly made that good-time district.

It was one of our rainy Monday nights of a couple of months back that I dropped in on Fess in his Stockton Street room. I was in the mood for some tall talk about the days when a musician was a musical entertainer. Where Fess makes his home these days is not far from the scene of his early exploits, in a Chinese-operated rooming house that must make a point of the "rooming." As you climb the first flight of wooden stairs, broad and gleaming, the eye catches the very definitely-worded sign—"No Girls Here." For the benefit of the incurable optimist and drunks with ocular deficiencies, this warning is repeated at the head of the first-floor landing.

Fess failed to remember me when he opened the door, a common failing of Negroes who find that all whites look very much alike. However, after I had refreshed his memory, he invited me in with much warmth. Fess is one of those fortunate human beings who had the character of well-aged whiskey, of medium height but royally built with a big frame, wide shoulders, and all well-upholstered. He has a happy, big-jowled face, all-in-all a figure of power and self-assurance that springs from years of happy, energetic life.

Just finishing dinner, the remains of a banquet showed good reason for his Falstaffian figure, with pounds of cheese, remains of a whole chicken, loaves of bread, and sundry other evidences of powerful eating spread around the room. On the wall, Fields has a historical photograph that immediately catches the visitor's eye. This, it turns out, is his band that played at Nigger Mike's—as well as at the Creole Cafe in West Oakland— and at Tait's, one of the famous restaurants of old San Francisco. This photo is one of the few pictures of a Negro jazz band that contains the traditional violin, added, of course, to the otherwise familiar Dixieland setup. The drummer, of course, plays a marching drum. One of the first things Fess told me about this 1908 band concerned the trombone, Frank Withers, whom he claims was the first to play a modern style. "He played cello parts," Fess explained it, "when other men was playin' an oompah, oompah style." The oompah was accompanied by signs that left no doubt of his meaning.

The list of the great in the musical and outside world that Fess has known is endless. While I smoked, listened, and made mental notes, he reeled off "Original Creole"; Bacquet (Becket he pronounced it to my surprise); Whiteman, who he knew as one of the violinists of the S.F. Symphony which he heard regularly for at least ten years; and Sarah Bernhardt and William Randolph Hearst, both among the scores of celebrities at Nigger Mike's. One of the interesting and perhaps hitherto unknown facts regarding the "Original Creole" Band, first to leave New Orleans and which toured the Pantages West Coast circuit around 1913, was that, according to Fess, they brought with them a woman pianist. Her name was Mrs. Prince and she must have had the "stuff" to meet the requirements of those exacting pioneers.

Bill Laub can tell you quite a bit about Fess since he was one of Laub's first teachers. Bill loves to relate how, as a lad in short pants, he would creep into whatever horrible sink of iniquity Fields was playing and listen fascinated by the hour. He was particularly impressed by Fields's mastery of trills, which at the time was known as the "meadowlark" style of rag playing. "Maps," (sic) he relates, was the jazz center of that era.

The Peacock Melody Strutters, Oakland, 1922 (L to R: Alfred Levy, banjo; Alexander Levy, sax; Marcellus Levy, drums; Leroy Houston, trumpet; Alvan Howard, banjo; Alvin Slater, trombone)

Alfred Levy

HOT LICKS
AND SWEET THINGS

I was born on May 9, 1904, in Oakland, California. There wasn't nothin' I ever wanted to be except a musician, after I started playin' it. I'm just crazy about it, and I've had lots of good times at it. I ain't made a lot'a money, though.

When Momma used to see any of us with our instrument case goin' on a gig, she'd say, "That starvation box ain't gonna take care of you."

I'd say something like, "Momma, I love you, but I love music too. Tonight, I'll blow a tune for you."

There were three of us kids, my twin brother, Alexander, and myself, and one older brother, Marcellus. He was three years older than Alexander and me. Momma was born in Washington, D.C., and she came to California on her own. She got a job out here, and then she come. Momma's father's name was Alfred Slaughter and her mother's name was Sarah. Momma took us back to Washington, D.C., on the train, when we were small, to see her parents, but I don't remember nothin' about it except ridin' on the train.

Pa's name is Edgar Wilford Levy, and he's ninety-five years old and livin' in Berkeley. It broke Pa's heart here a few months past to go to his oldest son's funeral. Papa was born in San Francisco and was a shipping clerk in the printing company of Althorp and Balls there for thirty-three years. His father came from the West Indies and his name was Alexander Levy. My twin brother was named after him, and I was named after Momma's daddy.

My grandmother on my daddy's side was named Maria and I don't know where she was from. I don't really remember any of my grandfolks except that Mamma had this much written in the Bible. My other brother, Marcellus, who just passed, got his name from the book *The Robe*. Momma liked the book so much, she named him that. Momma bought this place here at 2426 Market Street, Oakland, in 1924, and I've been livin' here since.

Jesus, thinkin' back to early days sure does scratch my brain. Our first band was started from us kids gettin' together and wantin' to play our instruments. When I was about seventeen years old, I took up the banjo, and my twin brother was on banjo, too. After we had just been playin' a year or so, we started taking our instruments to parties. We were kind'a bashful and shy with the girls and all that.

Momma used to say, "You've got to get out to some of these parties."

So, in order not to be embarrassed, we'd take our instruments and go down to the party, and, naturally, they'd want us to play. They liked us, and that was the start of it all. Pretty soon, we were on the payroll, gettin' four or five dollars apiece, and the word got out the Levy boys have a band. We named ourselves The Peacock Melody Strutters, and we painted it on the front of Marcellus's drum.

The cats said you ought to switch from two banjos to something else; two banjos are too much for a four- or five-piece group. Alexander switched to C-melody saxophone to make us more compatible. Elmer Claiborne taught my brother a lot of stuff on the sax. Elmer was about three years older than me, and he was a wonderful musician. He played trumpet with Wade Whaley's Black and Tan Syncopators. They're the ones that inspired us to have our little group. We used to go down to Webb's Hall, against Momma's permission, and listen to their jazz. Elmer lost his lip early and switched to saxophone just before he started helpin' Alexander.

We had our picture taken, but several of the group were just standin' in. Our regular guys were me on banjo, Alexander on saxophone, Marcellus on drums, and Gene Richard on piano. Sometimes, we also had Elmer Claiborne on saxophone, Sonny Craven on trombone, and Clem Raymond on his clarinet when he first came here. The Peacock Melody Strutters— sometimes we used Peacock Melody Syncopators instead—was a Dixieland-type band. We played with two beats and two back beats. On banjo, I did mostly rhythm and a little improvising, but not much solo work. Alexander was a pretty good sax man, but he didn't live long enough to perfect it. Marcellus was a pretty fair drummer, and he learned to read later on. Gene Richard was an ordinary piano player who could read, but he wasn't any solo man. He saw what he played and played what he saw. We used to get a little criticism about him, but we kept him because he could read, and he was the only piano player we ever had. He wasn't really interested in music, I guess, and never applied himself. He just quit music after The Peacock Melody Strutters broke up. Gene still lives in Berkeley, and I saw him in church last Sunday. Sonny Craven was a very good trombone player. He was with Wade Whaley before he gigged with us, and later on he was with Lionel Hampton. Clem Raymond came here in 1923 with some combo and defuncted (sic) from them and came over here to Oakland. He used to play college dates with me and my brother. He was beautiful guy, and he could play variations. Later on, I played with him several years.

We started gettin' good jobs around, at parties, dance halls, and clubs. We tried to copy all them pieces off the records, all them old pieces I call Dixieland pieces, like "Darktown Strutters Ball," "St. Louis Blues," "Tin Roof Blues," and "Margie." We play some of the same tunes today. We got some of the stuff from the old-timers around here who played the Dixieland beat.

We got a job playin' a dance hall over in San Francisco around Geary and Van Ness streets, and got in trouble with the union. Harry Pierson and some of the old guys were gettin' a colored union started, and we got in a little hassle with them. Pa Levy, who was a mogul in the lodge, had to come in the picture to help us, and we joined the union.

We all had regular jobs during these times. I was runnin' a mimeograph machine for J.B.F. Davis Insurance Co.; Marcellus worked at American Insurance Company as a supply-man and ran the elevator. Music was just a sideline business, where we played gigs during the weekends.

It's funny how we got started in music just goin' to kid parties. We got to be crazy about the music game, and Marcellus and I became professionals. The Peacock Melody Strutters lasted about five years until my twin brother passed in 1926. That broke our combo up.

There were a bunch of old guys playing around here, even before we started. The first ones I remember were, Sid LeProtti—he was one of them good readers and steady and not what you'd call a take-off man; Henry Starr was what you call a get-off man and one of the early guys; Charlie Strather played saxophone and got to be president of colored local 669. Charlie was crazy about music; he used to just hold the saxophone and play the violin in church. He wasn't any good; he just never could play.

A guy named Henderson—that's what everybody called him, and I never knew his other name—was one of the old-timers and played saxophone. He was about twenty-five years older than me and played baritone and tenor. He played the style of that time and was considered a hot man at his age and tough to keep up with. He might have played the Barbary Coast. Henderson had a music store up here and then he went to Los Angeles to live.

Henry Starr was one of the main ones on the Barbary Coast. I don't know if he headed a band, but he stayed at the Coast for a long time. I never saw the Coast, but people would say Henry's over there on the Barbary Coast when I was nothin' but a kid. Henderson and some of the old guys may have been with Henry; I knew his personnel, but it loses me now.

Harry Pierson was a drummer, and Old Man John Terrell played bass. Herb Clark was another old-time drummer, and he got to be president of the colored local before we amalgamated with the white union. He was a beautiful guy.

Clarence "Fess" Banks was about the same age as Henderson. He liked to play sousaphone most, but he could play violin, piano, and all the other instruments. He was kind'a an instructor of music, kind'a a teacher, and I played a few casuals with one of his bands early. Fess was an ordinary player, not too hot, but in those days, if you could blow your axe and read, you were considered a good musician.

Al Stewart, the sax man, was an old-timer. He was pretty good for the time and played a tenor. Al used to play some of those places out by the beach. My brother Marcellus played with him. He came from the South somewhere—Texas or Louisiana, I think.

Roy Tayborn was a really good trombone player and an old-timer. I played with most of the old-timers around but they never talked about the old days; they just went on and played. Those were most of the old guys and, as far as I know, they're the ones who set up the colored local.

Henry Starr was around from before I started playin' and just died eight or nine years ago. He was about ten years older than me, and he was fast. Henry used to get after me and my brothers because he wanted us to learn how to read. Henry had his own style, and he would get up and play anything. He was a musician and modern. After you do the thing written down, then you tell your story. The rest of the guys would just go along with the rest of the band. Not Henry, he wasn't just gonna sit in the alley, he would do his thing. When I got to play with him, I remember him doing "Sweet Little You," and he'd have the people cryin', and then he'd do "Old Man River," and make the people scream. Henry was a good singer, too, and he played that beat that was in.

I never noticed any difference between the New Orleans musicians and any others. A musician is just a musician. In the early days, you might'a noticed a little something. Like Red Cayou's style, he had a Louisiana style. It was a more distinct rhythm or beat. Henry was way over Red. Henry used to admire Red though, and he'd show Red some things on the piano, and Red used to appreciate them. Red wasn't a perfectionist as a reader, as Sid LeProtti was, but little Red, with them little short fingers, he could tell his story. Henry was the best get-off man around though.

After I lost my twin brother, I took a coffee break and went to Los Angeles. I bummed around the beach at Santa Monica for almost two years. Once in a while, I'd play with some of the local guys. Mostly I played with Jack McVea's father's group. Jack was my buddy and played much stick (clarinet). Isaac McVea, Jack's father, had a great big band, and they used to play some hotels down there. Isaac was a hustler and had plenty of jobs. Jack would always tell me to bring my axe, and the guys would say here's a musician from San Francisco and ask me to play. I was just recuperatin' down there, and when I'd get broke, I'd wire Momma to send me some more money, so I was just playin' casuals. Marcellus had got married and moved to Sacramento durin' this time.

The guys in Los Angeles I remember hearin' were "Tin Can" Henry Allen on drums; Les Hite on sax—Les was playing with Leon Herriford's band,

Red Cayou, known for his Louisiana-style piano playing, pictured with The Three Sharps, c. 1930 (L to R: "Red" Cayou, piano; "Spoons," drums; Bill Blocker, sax)

and later on, he got his own; "Montudi" Eddie Garland was playing bass; and old man Henderson was down there.

I heard Slocum Mitchell down there, but I never conversed with him. He was good enough in them days to still be playin' in these days, wherever he is. He was that good a player. He was very well thought of and spoke of as a musician by everybody. I can still hear some of his tunes now.

Curtis Mosby, the drummer, and Henry Starr were playin' The Hummingbird at Twelfth and Central when I got to L.A. Gloria Swanson used to come in there. Curtis came a little later than the old-timers in San Francisco. I played his San Francisco club in the thirties, and he used to have a music store over here in Oakland. In the twenties, Los Angeles was a toddlin' town compared to San Francisco. San Francisco was tamed down.

After about two years bummin' around, I came back here and studied my instrument on down and got back with the guys. I just love music; that's my first love. I went with Hill's Vaudeville Band. That was the first steady gig I went on after I lost my twin brother. We had Bob Hill on trumpet, "Shiek" on drums, Fess Banks on sousaphone, Elmer Claiborne on sax, me on banjo, Tony Rodgers on trombone, and Frank Shievers on piano. Tony was a comedian trombone player, and not what you'd call a trombone player that played trombone. But all the rest of the boys were hot. We played a little hotter than the Dixieland stuff. It was hot jazz and had a little different kind of beat to it. We played right up on the stage and we had to make up an act. Our band traveled all over Northern California on the Hippodrome circuit, playin' towns like Fresno, Monterey, Sacramento, Marysville, and so on. Frank Shievers was a helluva good piano player, and he was good enough to be a stage act by himself. He could blow his axe and take off. He could read what the man said and then blow his own soul and tell you what he wanted to say.

After Hill's band, I went with Clem Raymond's Black Peppers and Wade Whaley's Black and Tan Syncopators. They had different styles. I was with Clem first and the longest. Our first job was at the Balconades Ballroom at Eighth and Market streets in San Francisco, and we had that job for eight months. We used to play opposite a white band, Walter Cosgrill and His Band. Cosgrill was a white banjo player. When they'd go off, we'd go on. Cosgrill had a wonderful band, and they'd play some tough things. Their band could read and played what they seen and played mostly sweet music.

Bob Hill's Vaudeville Band, Hippodrome Theatre, Oakland, c. 1927 (L to R: Tony Rodgers, trombone; Al Levy, banjo; Bob Hill, trumpet/leader; Frank Shievers, piano; Elmer Clayborne, sax; "Sheik," drums; Clarence "Fess" Banks, brass bass)

They could improvise in their way. When they did, they'd make us sit up and take notice. We had kind'a a competition thing, and competition does make you better.

Clem's band was the hot band, and when we'd go on, Clem would say, "Those guys think we're gonna get up here and play nothin' but Dixieland all night long. We're gonna play some sweet things first. Those guys think we're gonna start out stompin', and we're gonna fool them. Let them guys start out with some hot licks, then we'll show them."

They'd do some hot things, and then we'd start to stomp and run them out of gas. Once in a while, they'd fool us and play some new tunes. Clem

Clem Raymond Orchestra, Balconades Ballroom, San Francisco, 1930 (L to R: Ben Watkins (?), tenor sax; Wade Whaley, sax; Charles Robinson (?), banjo; Elmer Fain, brass sax; Charles Jackson (?), piano; Danny Webster (?), trumpet; Brock (?), trumpet; unknown; Edward "Kid" Ory, trombone; unidentified on drums)

would get hot and say, "They think we can't read. Tomorrow, we'll go down and get that music and learn it. Then we'll show them I got readers in my band."

Some nights, if we played too many sweet things waitin' for them to start playin' hot licks, the manager, Packett, would come up to the bandstand and hang around, as if to say, you all are supposed to be doin' the jazz part of the deal, so get goin'. We'd play hot after that. Clem was particular about his music; he wanted to do more than go "toot, toot, toot" all night.

All the band had to wear tuxes, and we all had single pictures took, and they put them up in the lobby. They paid us top money. All the musicians in the band were wonderful. Eddie Liggins was our piano player. He was a very good piano player, and he used to demonstrate sheet music at Sherman Clay. Harry Barker played trumpet, and he's passed; Baron Morehead on trombone; a guy named Oscar on another trumpet; James Payne on drums, me on banjo; and Clem on clarinet. Clem wasn't a great reader, but he was makin' an attempt, and he had the readin' guys backin' him up. Clem was a musician who was really good, and he kept trying' to improve. Clem used to have rehearsals. He would get us in and lock the doors and bring us orchestrations up there, then say, "Take it from the left-hand corner and bring it all the way down." Clem said his guys were gonna read and see what the man said. Even if you knew the stuff, you had to get together on it by rehearsing. All the boys could read, and the whole band could get off a bunch of hot licks.

The Balconades Ballroom wasn't no bar or jook joint. It was a beautiful crystal ballroom. They used to have a streamer from one side of Market Street to the other with its name and the "Walter Cosgrill and His Band– Clem Raymond's Black Peppers." At night, we'd start about nine o'clock and we played 'til one o'clock; that's dance hall time, not nightclub time. (Nightclubs close at two.) We'd start out with a tough number like "Louisiana Bo Bo." Then we'd shoot in some dance numbers and a couple of hot ones to feel out the crowd—each night the crowd's different—and then try to play accordin' to the crowd. You'd get requests, and we tried to take care of all the requests.

Later in the evening, Clem would say, "Let's play a coupl'a those new numbers in here," and we would try them out.

That's the way an evenin' would go.

I always remember Clem sayin', "My guys are beautiful, but I don't want you all gamblin' backstage durin' intermission."

We'd get backstage and be shootin' dice while the other band was playin'.

After we left the Balconades, we went over to Ripper Dan's Ballroom. Ripper Dan's was on Market Street, about Sixth, right down from the Balconades. Ripper Dan thought we could help his place, so he said for us to come on down. He had a Walkathon goin' there and we played there a long time. The musicians changed quite a bit at Ripper Dan's, and in the pictures we had taken there was "Happy" Johnson on trombone, Jimmy Regland on trumpet, "Chink" Snowden on piano, Charlie Turner on drums,

Walkathon at Ripper Dan's Ballroom, c. 1927. The Clem Raymond Band is on the stage behind the contestants.

and me, and Clem. After we left Ripper Dan's, we went to Monterey and played for a while.

In the late twenties, I got to know another old-timer named Bill Powers; he was a piano player. Him and his son used to play casual gigs around here. His son, Gene, was a stick [clarinet] player. The old man took his son and Buck Campbell to Japan. His son came back, but I lost track of the old man. Buck Campbell is back around here. Buck was a beautiful musician. He could see around the corner and see what the man said. Then he could improvise. He could get in his head what was wrote down and then go on and fake on his own wonderful.

After Clem's jobs gave out, I went with Wade Whaley for a couple of years. Wade was different than Clem. He kept stickin' to the Louisiana beat. He never did delve into the music part of the playin'. I never knew whether Wade was readin' or spellin' the music. Wade used to kind'a stick with his

Californians in Yokohama, Japan, c. 1928 (L to R: Gene Powers, reeds; Bill Powers (Gene's father), piano/leader; Buck Campbell, reeds)

little Louisiana bunch. He had Sonny Craven and all them guys that could play that good old New Orleans stuff, but that was all; they didn't play nothin' else.

When I played with Wade, we had Sonny on trombone, Gene Allen on piano, Elmer Claiborne on sax, Little Walker on drums, Wade on clarinet, and me on banjo. There were a couple of other cats we added to the group when we needed them. We did have rehearsals once in a while to get together on the music. We played a nice club in Monterey for a long time. We lived down there and worked every night. The gigs were good then, and you wouldn't think about no other work. If you'd talk about a paintbrush, I'd look at you like you're crazy. I was with Wade a couple of years in the early thirties.

Fess Duncan, the piano player, was with Wade before Gene Allen. After I left Wade, I went with Fess, and we played a whole year at the El Nido Cafe in El Cerrito. The band's name was Fess Duncan and His El Nido Cafe Band. Chester Wells was on saxophone, Danny Webster on trumpet, Buster

Wysinger on drums, and me on banjo. Fess sang scat songs and played kazoo, besides playin' piano. Fess was just okay on the piano; he could get by. His singin' was ordinary; he wasn't no great vocalist. Henry Starr used to like Fess, and he would stop by as we were gettin' off work at the El Nido to get us to go play for all those rich folks down on the Peninsula [San Mateo Peninsula].

Henry'd say, "Okay, Fess, get the guys together and let's come on down the Peninsula," and we'd take off.

That's when I used to hear Henry sing "Old Man River," and we'd play for George Hirsh and his family at all them great big private parties. That was in the early thirties, and we used to broadcast over KRE during that time with Fess's band. Fess Duncan died in 1938.

In 1934, I was bummin' around home, and Marcellus was in Sacramento, playin' in a band led by Jack Boone, the piano player. Marcellus sent me a telegram sayin', "Jack wants you to play up here; we're openin' up the New Pantoy Club, but don't bring no banjo, they've gone out of style." All I had was an old tenor guitar with four strings, so I wasn't gonna go, but Momma said to go on anyway, and I went on. When I got there, they took me down to the music store—they were big shots up there—to get me a guitar. So I defuncted on the banjo and started playin' the guitar. The job was a good one, but I didn't know nothin' from nothin' on that guitar; all I was doing was fakin' the whole time I was in Sacramento. I leaned how to play the thing after I got back to Oakland.

The New Pantoy was a nightclub out on Franklin Boulevard that ran all night long. It was a fabulous place, with a floor show that we used to play for. They had entertainers and dancin' too. Sacramento was a wide openin' town, with gamblin' and girls and no curfew. We played from nine o'clock until six the mornin', then we'd go down to the radio station and broadcast. Sacramento was jumpin' a lot more than San Francisco was in those days.

The New Pantoy bein' so new and so beautiful, it made Charlie Derrick to build him a new club. He had the old Jitterbug Club over the Nippon Theater in downtown Sacramento. Charlie built a very nice place called the Eureka Club. Ike Bell and a bunch of guys came up from the Bay Area to open it, and we played there later on.

Another place we played was the Harlem Club. That was owned by Billy Dansby. There were quite a few cat houses around there like Lee Rooms

The interior of the Eureka Club, Sacramento, 1930. For a time, Sacramento displaced San Francisco as the liveliest musical hotbed in Northern California.

and the Lindy Rooms. We used to hang around the cat houses and the madams would be always tellin' us to go to work so their girls could go to work. The girls normally quit at two or three in the mornin', and they'd come down to the Harlem Club until we got off at six. The girls would bring their great big tick and throw money in the kitty for us.

Dansby was a funny guy; he used to tell us, "You musicians, you got to rassle with the drunks when they cause trouble."

That was a hassle. We had to put our instruments down and go out and be part-time bouncers. Mostly we tried to sweet talk the drunks because we had some big, tough babies come in there.

Dansby also tried to play the drums, and he was always comin' up to Marcellus and sayin', "Let me drum a set, and you go down and rassle with the drunks."

I got married to Wilma Lefridge, from Seattle, in Sacramento in 1936. She was a dancer, and it didn't last.

About 1936, I came back to Oakland, where I've been livin' and playin' since. That covers my early years in music and the guys I met, and it's caused me to scratch my brain a lot. I've had a lot of fun in music, meetin' different guys and playin' different gigs. I remember a chick told me once: "There's one thing different about you musicians from other people, you're always so happy to see each other. You always yell 'Hi, guy!' and are the happiest bunch." That's true. Even if you said somethin' like, "I ain't gonna blow with that cat, he can't blow nothin'," the next time you see him, the malice is gone. You ask about what he's doin' and tell him how great he looks and how great it is to see him. I love musicians, and I love music. That's my first love. I love to see the changes in music and gettin' to be your own critic. I still love to woodshed with the new musicians.

*Charlie "Duke" Turner
at his drum set, c. 1930*

Charlie "Duke" Turner

I Never Played
The Creole Cafe

I never played the Creole Cafe; it closed in 1925 or 1926. I shined shoes in the barber shop across the street and used to hang around outside listening to the music. Wade Whaley, Clem Raymond, Papa Mutt (Carey), Kid Ory, and Slocum (Mitchell) played there. Wade Whaley came out to take Slocum's place. I don't think Ory had his own band; he either played with Wade or Papa Mutt. Ory was big stuff when he was playing trombone at the Creole Cafe. Later on, Ory went to Los Angeles and played there a long while. Freddie Washington played piano at the Creole Cafe with Wade, and he was around here for a long time. He's in the picture of Kid Ory's band in L.A., and he finally went back East. They brought some old guy out on the Flip Wilson show by the same name. He played string bass on Flip's show, but he said he used to play piano. I think it's the same guy. The Creole

Cafe opened about 1918 or 1919 and, at the time, was supposed to be one of the prettiest places this side of the Rockies. King Oliver played the Creole, but I can't remember who he was with.

I scratched around Oakland Tech. High, playing music for several years. I gigged around with different kid bands; we had a few guys who'd get together and play for parties and dances and things. The Levy brothers also had a band in the early days at Tech. High, and they got around a lot more in those early days. Marcellus Levy played drums with their band, so I only played with them a couple of times when he couldn't make it. Al Slater was their trombone player. The last I heard of him, he was over in Honolulu.

Alva Howard, who's in the picture of the Peacock Melody Strutters, didn't play with them. They didn't need two banjos. He lived right around the corner from me. I lived on Nineteenth and Adeline. He was pretty close to my age.

Leroy Houston played trumpet with the Levy's, and he was a very, very good friend of mine. He was a very good musician and could play almost anything; he was a real trumpet player. He started off with the Salvation Army. His dad had passed away, and he was playing with one of the school bands—Lockwood School, I think—and from there he got a chance to play with the Salvation Army band. They made it possible for him to learn the trumpet and take lessons. After that, he felt pretty close to them. I recall on several occasions when their band was to appear, he wouldn't take other engagements so he could play with them. As he grew older, he realized what they had done for him, and he appreciated it more and more.

At the time I was getting started, I didn't get around as much as some of the guys because there were so many good drummers here. Edward "Little" Walker came up with the real old-timers and was a very good one; he had a brother named Mitch Walker. There was Marcellus Levy, "Spade" Hall, "Tin Can" Henry Allen, James Payne, Buster Wysinger, Al Stewart, and Curtis Mosby. I played for Curtis when he had the cafe over in San Francisco. It seems like Curtis was from New Orleans; I'm not sure, but I don't believe he's a native. I think that Leon Herriford came to the Bay Area with Mosby. Harry Pierson was another drummer. He was also a vocalist, like me, and was here very early. Harry played mostly with Sid LeProtti, Norris Hester, Elmer Claiborne, Roy Tayborn, and Will Graves. Harry's wife's name is Grace, and he had a couple of boys named Harry and Gwinn.

Clarence Banks' Syncopaters, Lakeside Gardens, Oakland, c. 1922–23 (L to R: Clarence Banks, brass bass; Charlie Turner, drums; Elmer Claiborne, reeds; Sydney Stayton, reeds; (?); Winslow Allen, trumpet; Bob Hill, trumpet; Al Levy, banjo/guitar)

My first organized band was Clarence Banks' Serenaders or Syncopators, about 1922 or 1923. Clarence "Fess" Banks was a music teacher around here for many years. Fess played piano, reeds, brass, and percussion, and was quite talented. He died about twenty years ago. We had our picture made at the Lakeside Gardens. It was upstairs on the Twelfth Street in Oakland and was a very pretty place. We had Fess on tuba, me on drums, and Elmer Claiborne on reeds. Elmer started playing trumpet as a little guy and then switched to reeds. He lived on Center Street in Oakland. Sidney Stayton was also on reeds, and Winslow Allen and Bob Hill were the trumpet players. Bob Hill was about my age, and he and Frank Shievers, the piano player, went to the Far East. Frank got this little band together to go. He wanted me to come, but I couldn't make it. A drummer named "Shiek" went instead of me. They never came back. We played mostly weekend affairs and dances, and middle-of-the-week parties. I was with the band two or three years, off and on, but, even at that, we'd take a fill-in gig with this or that group.

I was born here in Berkeley, California, March 14, 1904. I'm the baby of eight. All of my family is from New Orleans except me. My dad, whose name was Lawrence, died when I was two or three years old, and I don't remember much about him. One thing I remember is he had a banjo around the house at one time, but I don't know whether he played the bloomin' thing or not. One of my three brothers used to play the mandolin pretty good, and two of my four sisters played piano. My mother didn't play anything. Her name was Rose and her maiden name was Clark. The family came out to California in 1900 or 1901. They were having it pretty tough in New Orleans, and the railroad was moving people out here pretty fast to work as cooks and waiters, so my dad came out here to work for the Southern Pacific.

After I left Fess Banks's band, I started playing with Clem Raymond's band. Clem started playing clarinet around here shortly after World War I. He came out from New Orleans to play with Sid LeProtti. Sid was playing piano over on the Barbary Coast, and he was quite a pianist. Sid was playing Purcell's, I think, and anyone who came to San Francisco had to go to Purcell's where Sid played. After they left there, they went into a hofbrau on Market Street.

When I was playing at the Walkathon with Elmer Fain's band, we had a woman piano player we called "Princess Bell," and she had the original manuscript to Sid's "Canadian Capers." She was a very good pianist.

Another gal we had around was Helen Fletcher, who played trombone, and she was as good as anybody around. Trombone players were hard to find here for a time. She played with a lot of the bands. She'd put her hair up and wear men's clothes, and most people didn't notice the difference.

The personnel of Clem's band changed a lot over the years I played with him. Of course, I played with other bands, too, and I played with Wade Whaley quite a bit before I finally led my own band. Some of the guys I remember with Clem were "Country" Allen, trombone; Ben Watkins, trumpet; "Chink" Snowden, piano; "Happy" Johnson, trombone; Jimmy Ragland, trumpet; Al Levy, guitar; Marcellus Levy, drums; Dean Orland, piano; and

George Hurd, saxophone. Hurd is a dentist in Long Beach, California, now. Ben Watkins played trumpet; there were two Ben Watkinses who played trumpet, and both of them played trumpet for Clem. One was a little short fella, and we called him "Little Ben"; the other one led a band around here for a while. I imagine that Clem played with nearly everybody around here at one time or another.

I played with Clem quite a time at Webb's Hall in Oakland. It was on Eighth Street at Pine or Wood—the last street down on Eighth Street. We played Sunday night dances there and any other dances they might have. We usually played a Saturday night dance somewhere else. Webb's Hall was a big barn of a place, and they used it for a roller-skating rink, too. Sometimes they had skating and dancing at the same time.

I played lots of other gigs with Clem. We'd play up in the country sometimes, like Fort Bragg, Sacramento, Marysville, down the Peninsula, and we even played way up in Dunsmuir one or two times. I went on one country dance job with Clem, and the song and dance man didn't make it, so he used me as the song and dance man. After that, if they wanted a song, I'd sing, and if they wanted a dance, I'd dance. We played San Francisco quite a bit. In San Francisco, we played the Balconades Ballroom at Twelfth and Market streets, on the southwest corner. The El Patio Ballroom was just a couple of yards on the other side of it.

Eddie Liggins was our piano player at the Balconades, and he played a handful of piano. I thought he was far superior to Red Cayou. Eddie was a finished player who could read anything; it was years before Red could read a little bit. Eddie was playing when he was knee-high to a duck. I remember his mother used to let his long black curls grow halfway down his back.

I played with Clem more than anyone, but in those days, things would change around pretty fast. One night you played with this bunch, and then you didn't play with them for a while. There were many out-of-town jobs I couldn't go on, and other guys who needed work would take them.

I got married in 1929, and we were really struggling after that. Since 1923, I had been working regular at a full-time job. I started out as a file clerk and worked into a supply man. I retired in 1969 after forty-six years with Continental Insurance Company in San Francisco.

We had a lot of guys who would come here from the East on their way to the Orient. They'd stick around for a while and play gigs, then take off for the Orient. Earl Whaley, one of my favorite sax-men, went to the Orient. He was from around here and was six or seven years older than me. He used to run around with my brothers and sisters. Earl played also at the Creole Cafe with Henry Starr and Wade Whaley when I shined shoes. He went north to Seattle and formed a band he took to China. Bill Powers, the piano player, and his son, Gene, the reed man, were from around here and went to the Orient.

I played a lot with Wade Whaley before I got my own band. He was from New Orleans and was a little short fella, about my height, or maybe an inch or two shorter. He played a lot of stick. Wade had Eddie Liggins on piano and sometimes Red Cayou; Elmer Claiborne on trumpet; a real old guy named Henderson on baritone sax—he was the only guy who played baritone for a long time; Sonny Craven played trombone; and Danny Webster on sax. Danny was a short guy and very thin. If you looked at him real quick, you could mistake him for Mexican. A guy named Butler, who played sax, came out from the East to play with Wade. He went on to China.

Back in the days of the Creole Cafe, Henry Starr and Wade used to play together. Henry was a very good piano player, and he was on radio and all over. He had three brothers: Bob, Luke, and Elmer. Wade and Henry also played the Iroquois in the early days. It was in uptown Oakland at about Eighth or Tenth Street near Broadway.

I played a few gigs with Bob Brassfield around here. His drummer was "Babe" Lewis, and he lived right around the corner from me. If he felt like taking the night off, he'd just get me to go in his place. Babe also played for Sonny Clay. Babe went to Los Angeles and then came back through here with Sonny, and left from here for Australia. Sonny had a fella named "Pus" Wade on sax and Russell Massingale on trumpet. Russell is from around here, and his brother, Wesley, the drummer, runs a restaurant on San Pablo Avenue in Oakland. When they got back from Australia, they played the Kentucky Stables in East Oakland. It was up the street from the Toyon Inn where I played with "Sax" Sexius. Brassfield and Clay were mainly Los Angeles guys. Another L.A. group was led by the McVea brothers. They were very popular in L.A. and came up here a couple of times to play, and I met them.

Wings over the Pacific: publicity photo for Earl Whaley's Orchestra, Shanghai,
China, 1937 (L to R: Pomping Villa, piano; Reginald Jones, bass, soprano sax;
Ernest Clark, trombone; Calvin Temple, trumpet; Earl Whaley, reeds/leader; Wayne
Adams, reeds; Henry Allen, reeds; Earl West, guitar; G.A. Austin, drums/violin)

Al Pierre was a guy from Portland, Oregon, who came down here for a
while, and I played a few gigs with. Him, Elmer Claiborne, and I played a
little spot down in Palo Alto. Al was a very good pianist. Al was like Eddie
Liggins; you put a piece of sheet music in front of them, and they could
play it. They both played a dance style and improvised quite a bit. It's tough
to compare guys like Al and Eddie with guys like Red Cayou. Red was from

Wes Peoples Orchestra, San Francisco, c. 1935 (L to R: Cameron Brown, trombone; Jake Porter, trumpet; Jimmy Brownly, trumpet; Clive Martin, drums; Freddie McWilliams, vocal/leader; Wes Peoples, piano/leader; Al Levy, banjo/guitar; Blakely, tenor sax; stand-ins for string bass and last tenor sax)

New Orleans and was an excellent player for his style. I played with Red in Clem Raymond's band, and then Red and I and Freddie McWilliams, the dancer, used to play a show every Sunday afternoon for a while. Red knew Louis Armstrong, and he knew all the old tunes, like "Muskrat Ramble." Red was a small guy and played with a lot of flash.

Lester Mapp, who used to run places on the Barbary Coast, had a place on Seventh Street in Oakland during the twenties and a lot of the old guys used to come in there. Some of the old-timers were Ham Hamilton, the trombonist, and Herb Clark, the drummer, who played with Fess Banks and Sid LeProtti. Herb worked at a bank on a regular job, and he's dead now.

Roy Tayborn, the trombonist that I played with in Sax Sexius' band, played the Barbary Coast with Sid and was a very good musician. Charles Strather played violin and saxophone, and played with Will Graves, Norris Hester, and Sid LeProtti. He was a court crier or bailiff or something like that. Norris Hester was with one of Sid's later bands, and he has a printing shop on Alcatraz Street in Berkeley. Claude Davis was an old-timer and one of the first guys in the colored musicians' union. Bab Frank was an old guy who used to carry a piccolo around in his pocket and would come up and sit in with us once in a while. I don't know what ever happened to him and don't know where he's from.

"Sax" Sexius led a band around here that I played with. His real name was Justin Sexius and he was from Bakersfield, California, down in the San Joaquin Valley. Sax is only a year or two older than I am, and, of course, he played saxophone. I played with him from 1928 to around 1931, when I started my own band. We had Roy Tayborn on trombone; Sax; Grace Sexius, his wife, on piano and vocals; me on drums; Winslow Allen on trumpet; and Roy Keyes on banjo and guitar. Grace was a very good pianist and had a beautiful voice. Sax and Grace are divorced now, and Sax is living in Mexico. The picture of the band we had taken about 1929 was at the Toyon Inn on East Fourteenth Street right at Junction. It was a great, big, beautiful place.

In 1931, I played the Walkathon with Clem Raymond. It was at Ripper Dan's at Market and McAllister Streets in San Francisco. The Walkathon was where they would get out and dance or walk until they fell. The last one standing wins a prize. On that job, we had Clem and me, Al Levy on guitar and banjo, and Chink Snowden on piano. Chink was a nice guy and a good piano player. His sister, Calvin Snowden, was one of the entertainers at the Cotton Club in Los Angeles. Happy Johnson played piano with us. He was pretty good and a lot of fun, a very lively guy. We had a very good trumpet player named Jimmy Ragland.

The first all-colored Walkathon was at Sixteenth and Mission streets in San Francisco. I played it with Elmer Fain and his band. I was working in an office, and Winslow Allen came and got me and asked me if I wanted to play, and I said, "Hell, yes!"

Prejudice wasn't as bad here in California as it was in other places. Of course, any prejudice is bad. It got worse during the Depression years. Most of the prejudice was a squeeze play to get jobs. We played many places

Sax Sexius Band, Oakland, c. 1928–29 (L to R: Charlie Turner, drums; Roy Tayborn, trombone; Grace Sexius, piano/vocal; Sax Sexius, reeds/leader; Winslow Allen, trumpet; Roy Keyes, banjo/guitar)

where the whites mingled with the colored. It was very difficult for a colored band to get a steady job, even though we had a colored local, local 6. They didn't give a damn whether we had a second- or a third-class rating; nevertheless, I guess it's better than nothing. I had a job, working with Sax Sexius at the New Republic of China Cafe at Twelfth and Broadway in Oakland. We worked there quite a while until things were looking good;

then the union found out there was something wrong with the place, and we had to get out of there and give up a good job.

I formed my band about 1931 or 1932. It was more or less a little fill-in band. I took all the little scrap-ends that came along, Saturday and Sunday nights and Friday nights and weddings and things around here. I never went out of town because I never thought we were good enough. Then I took a job down in Watsonville, playing for the Watsonville firemen and policemen. They liked us and had us back. That's how I found out I was good enough. Another place we played was San Francisco, at a couple of West Indian cricket clubs. They were mostly colored but had a few white mixed in.

Once, at McFadden's Ballroom, we had what was supposed to be a battle of music with a white band. The white band was The Runnin' Wild Band and ours was Duke Turner's Hot Colored Band. It was continuous dancing, and the white group would play most of the sweet music, and we played the hot music of the time. It was some shindig, and I think we came off best.

I booked my own dates, and we played places like the Ross Country Club and the Laquintas Country Club in Marin County; the Riverside Inn, which was a dance pavilion in Stockton; and, for quite a while, we played the Guerneville Grove on the Russian River on Saturday nights.

In 1933 or 1934, we had our picture taken in Oakland at the Persian Gardens. We had that job a long time. In the picture, the bass player was a carnival guy who only stayed here two or three weeks and then went on with another show. You can tell he's different from his tunic. Sterling Wagner was our regular bass player, and he was with us for quite a while. He was from Sacramento and may be alive up there today. The first alto player is Elma Graves, who also played clarinet and baritone. The other alto player is Buck Campbell. He was a very good reed man and also played clarinet and baritone. Even though he was very good, after he took on so much weight, the guys didn't want to take him in the car on gigs because he took up so much room, so we let him out of the band. I last saw Buck in 1970, and he may still be alive. Alex Forbes was our banjo and guitar player. He was around the Bay Area a long time, and his regular day job was selling insurance. After our band broke up, he became a union official. Alex was about my age, and he's dead now. Jimmy Ragland, the first trumpet player, is from Spokane, Washington. He came down here to stay with an uncle

Duke Turner's Musical Cavaliers, Oakland, 1933 (L to R: James Vaughn, piano; unidentified, brass bass; Elma Graves, reeds; Charlie Turner, drums/leader; Buck Campbell, reeds; Alex Forbes, banjo/guitar; Jimmie Ragland, trumpet; Thornwall Kaiser, trumpet)

and was around a long time. He's not around the Bay Area anymore and may still be alive. Thornwall Kaiser is the other trumpet player. John Dean is on piano; he only played with us a couple of times, while he was trying to decide whether to stay with jazz or go back to the classics. He was very good and played mostly with other bands.

The most outstanding musicians around here, in my opinion, were Wilbert Barranco on piano—he still teaches and plays around here; Lawrence Brown on trombone, that's now with Duke Ellington; Jerome Richardson on sax, but he could play all the reeds, and he was with Quincy Jones recently; Freddie Washington on piano, that I mentioned as now playing string bass; Earl Whaley on sax was outstanding; and Oscar Hurt, the trumpet player, was outstanding.

PART II

BLACKS IN THE WEST

The diverse social, cultural, and racial background of New Orleans is usually given as part of the reason jazz was born there. Some of the characteristics mentioned are a free and loose social atmosphere in an area like the district, or Storyville; a fairly tolerant attitude toward blacks and their customs and rituals; a Latin-Catholic cultural background; a rapid increase in the number of Americans after the Louisiana Purchase of 1803; a port city serving a vast interior; a center for West Indian immigration; great racial and ethnic diversity; an entertainment center; a white Anglo-Saxon population superimposed on an olive Latin-Catholic foundation; a long history of a free black population; and at least a half-dozen others.

San Francisco and the Barbary Coast are in many respects similar to New Orleans and Storyville. It is important, if we believe that New Orleans is the

150

birthplace of jazz, to make some comparison between New Orleans and San Francisco. One of the ways we could do this would be to make a catalogue, similar to the list above, of the various characteristics, and then make a point by point comparison. This could lead to a number of errors, such as omitting important features of New Orleans, stretching our imaginations to make a San Francisco comparison, and overlooking important features of San Francisco because they were not observed in New Orleans. What I believe most New Orleans commentators to be saying is that New Orleans provided an atmosphere conducive to the birth of jazz. I believe that San Francisco and the Barbary Cost also provided this type of environment. These chapters aim to show the general atmosphere of San Francisco and the Barbary Coast, and how the black man fit into this environment. This method should provide an adequate basis for comparison with New Orleans and Storyville.

Aside from the need for comparison, it is important that we understand the social, cultural, racial, and musical milieu of San Francisco and the Barbary Coast. California's history is unique in the United States. Starting as a Spanish territory, California became a Mexican state, revolted to become an independent nation, joined the United States, and was then stormed by the greatest gold rush in history. Again, the factors which best illustrate the milieu in which San Francisco jazz was played are elucidated by a look at the black man in the West and on the Barbary Coast.

The first black man to enter the West was Estevancio (Little Steve) in 1538. He led the first expedition into the area which is now New Mexico and Arizona. Monroe N. Works describes the expedition: "A number of Negro slaves were in the expedition of Panfilo de Narvaez to conquer the Floridas (1528). Estevancio, a Negro, was a member of this expedition. This expedition was unsuccessful. In 1538 Estevancio led an expedition from Mexico in search of the fabled 'Seven Cities of Cibolia' and discovered Arizona and New Mexico. He was killed at Cibolia in what is now New Mexico. He was the first member of an alien race to visit the North Mexican pueblos. After a lapse of three and a half centuries the tradition of the killing of Estevancio still lingers in a Zuni Indian legend which says: It is to be believed that a long time ago when the roofs lay over the walls of Kya-Ki-Me, when smoke hung over the housetops, Mexicans came from their abodes in Everlasting Summerland. These Indians So-No-Li, set up a great howl and thus they and our ancients did much ill to one another. Then and thus was killed by our ancients right where the stone stands down by the arroyo of Kay-Ki-Me, one of the Black Mexicans, a large man with 'chili lips' (lips swelled from eating chili peppers)."[1]

Vizcaino made the first voyage of discovery to Alta (Northern) California in 1602, when he discovered and named Monterey Bay. One of Vizcaino's crew appeared before an investigative council in 1629 and told of the California Indians rubbing a black crewman who was with them to see if the color would come off, and they "gave the Negro a large pearl, but to the Spaniards, nothing."[2] According to most American histories, the first black person to arrive in what is now the United States landed at Jamestown, Virginia, in 1619.

Blacks were not generally mentioned as being black in Spanish and Mexican records. Where their color was mentioned, as with Estevancio and Vizcaino's crewman, the mention was an accident of circumstances. Estevancio, for example, was a slave who had been on a Florida expedition with eighty men and had ultimately led himself and three Spanish survivors back to Mexico City. There were probably other black slaves, but none are mentioned. There are a number of reasons why a black person would not be particularly noted in the Spanish-Mexican territories. The most important of these was the Catholic Church's doctrine of conversion of the heathen. Under this doctrine, all Indians and blacks living under the flag of Spain were to be brought into the faith. Thus, Indians and blacks were established as having souls and were, to some degree, brothers in the faith. This made possible upward mobility, such as Estevancio's transition from slave to expedition leader. White Protestant countries tended to believe that a good Indian was a dead Indian, and that blacks were good only as slaves and should be kept in absolute ignorance. Furthermore, Spaniards have a darker skin color. It fit in well with the Indians, and with blacks formed a subtle color tone change from olive to black. Finally, there were few barriers to mixed reproduction and marriage, especially among the lower classes. This tended to accelerate conversion to the faith and the breakdown in recognition by skin color. Today, many Mexicans are a mixture of Spaniard, Indian, and black heritage.

For the black man, the American West was depicted as an area of "individualism, economic equality, freedom to rise, and democracy." In 1833,

the Third Annual Convention for the Improvement of Free People of Color
met in Philadelphia and resolved that "Those who may be obliged to exchange
a cultivated region for a howling wilderness, we recommend, to retire into
the western wilds and fell the native forests of America, where the plough-
share of prejudice has as yet been unable to penetrate the soil."[3] This
assessment is borne out by some of the early success of western black men.

On September 4, 1781, Felipe de Neve, governor of California, led a group
of eleven families from San Gabriel to found El Pueblo de Nuestra Señora la
Reina de Los Angeles, better known as Los Angeles. Among the forty-four
people recruited to settle the colony, there were twenty-eight blacks, about
two-thirds of the total settlement. The Los Angeles County Museum of Natural
History features a diorama depicting this founding of Los Angeles. A black
family then owned the area now known as Beverly Hills.

In 1844, the first settlers in Washington state included a black person.
They went to Oregon to settle, but George Washington Bush, a black man,
was forbidden to settle there. They then migrated to Washington, where
Bush became a business and civic leader.

In 1841, William Liedesdorff, of black and Dutch parentage, left the Virgin
Islands and came to San Francisco, where he became the leading
businessman. He owned a 35,000 acre ranch, owned numerous businesses,
opened San Francisco's first hotel, and owned its first steamboat company.
He also served on San Francisco's city council and was the first black
American diplomat.

Biddie Mason was brought to Los Angeles in 1851 by a Georgia slave-
master. Through hard work, she saved enough money to free herself and
her three daughters. After that, she periodically bought fifty dollar parcels
of land in what is now downtown Los Angeles and made a fortune. She was
a woman of immense strength who was active in schools, churches, and
charitable work.

Pio Pico, governor of California in 1845 and 1846, had black parentage.

The West had its black cowboys and gunslingers. Nat Love, better known
as Deadwood Dick, helped Deadwood, South Dakota, achieve its gore and
glory reputation. Isom Dart, a noted cattle rustler, relieved many Colorado
and Wyoming ranchers of their cows. Bill Pickett and "Peerless" Jesse Stahl
were the best at bull-dogging and bronco-busting in the West. Cherokee
Bill, of mixed black and Indian parentage, was a psychopathic killer like

Billy the Kid and was hung at nineteen as a hardened murderer. Ben Hodges was a card shark, cattle thief, forger, and fast talker of Dodge City, Kansas. James Frances, George Moore, and William Robinson were riders and station keepers for the Pony Express and the Wells Fargo Express. George Moore was a black gold-miner in 1849 who became California's most famous stagecoach driver. William Robinson worked for Wells Fargo Express for over forty years, starting as a Pony Express rider.

The West had many black soldiers who fought and tamed it with distinction. They consisted of four black regiments, the Ninth and Tenth Cavalry, and the Twenty-fouth and Twenty-fifth Infantry. Black soldiers were called Buffalo Soldiers by everyone because the Indians likened their kinky hair to the buffalo's. They fought Indians and Mexicans, and created much of the western legend. The entire Sid LeProtti So Different Jazz Band served in the Twenty-fifth Infantry and added to their musical history.

One San Francisco black woman of great fame was Mary Ellen Pleasants, sometimes called Mammy Pleasants. Her exploits have been the subject of at least one book. She came to San Francisco in 1850 from New Orleans, with $50,000 and an outstanding reputation as a cook. Her greatest historical importance was her going to Chatham, Canada, in 1858 and meeting John Brown. There, she gave him $30,000 to finance his raid on Harper's Ferry. With the $30,000, Brown bought 15,000 condemned government rifles at two dollars each. Mary Ellen Pleasants remained a part of the plot and was to go into the South to prepare the slaves for the uprising. She was engaged in this work when word reached her that John Brown had jumped the gun, attacked before the agreed date, and was crushed. Mary Ellen fled to California where she lived the remainder of her life, socializing with San Francisco's most famous residents.

We have seen there were black gold-miners, merchants, millionaires, cooks, Pony Express riders, cowboys, and cutthroats in California from its beginnings. But how many blacks were in California?

In 1847, San Francisco's first census counted 459 persons: 247 white males and 128 white females, thirty-eight Indians, forty Sandwich Islanders (Hawaiians), and ten blacks (nine males and one female). In 1848, the count was 700 white persons (half of them Americans) and 150 Indians, blacks, and Sandwich Islanders. By 1850, California was a part of the United

States, and a constitutionally-required census was taken. Here are the California results continued up to 1970:

Year	Total Population	Black Population	Black percentage of State Total
1850	92,591	962	1.0
1860	379,994	4,086	1.1
1870	560,247	4,272	0.8
1880	864,694	6,018	0.7
1890	1,213,398	11,322	0.9
1900	1,485,053	11,045	0.7
1910	2,377,549	21,645	0.9
1920	3,426,861	38,763	1.1
1930	5,677,251	81,048	1.4
1940	6,907,387	124,306	1.8
1950	10,586,223	462,172	4.4
1960	15,717,204	883,861	5.6
1970	19,953,134	1,400,143	7.0

Note: The 1850 census figures for San Francisco, Contra Costa and Santa Clara counties were lost and are not included in the 1850 totals.

In 1970, blacks complained that census statistics were inaccurate regarding the black population and cited a number of reasons for this. If 1970 figures were inaccurate, 1850 figures can be no more than a guess at the black population. In 1850, there were 92,591 persons in a land area of 156,803 square miles—nearly two square miles for each man, woman, and child. In 1850 a large part of the population was at gold fields in remote mountain regions; the population was a highly mobile male population, scrambling from gold strike to gold strike, not waiting to be counted. Finally, in 1850 people were fired with gold fever, not census fever, and whatever calculations were made were probably sketchy.

As noted in the table of population statistics, some of the figures were even lost. Inaccuracies no doubt persisted for many decades, and some new problems have developed over the years. However, for the most part, the table does give us some idea of the population. Even a 100 percent miscalculation would change the quoted black population by only about 1 to 2 percent. This population was mostly centered in urban areas around San Francisco, Los Angeles, and Sacramento.

Prejudice against blacks in California was variable. From 1538 to 1850, when California became a state, no prejudice is noted. Slavery was permitted for a short time after 1850, and slave owners who bought slaves from the South were protected by law. Curiously, however, a number of blacks were freed from slavery by the courts, and several times locals raised funds to buy slaves' freedom from particularly vicious masters. On the other hand, with the gold rush, white Southerners came in great numbers. There were instances of racism, prejudice, inhumane treatment, and cruelty. Endless conflicting examples could be quoted. In most cases, blacks are barely mentioned in passing, and as we have seen, their numbers were not that great. There was, moreover, a mounting Chinese population that brought out the worst California prejudice, and there was the customary hostility to Mexicans that all conquerors have against the conquered.

In the mid-1850s, race laws were passed against blacks, Chinese, and Indians in which they were "denied the rights to testify for or against white persons in court, suffrage, jury participation, equal education, pursuit of certain trades, mobility and settlement in the state."[4] These were primarily aimed at and enforced against the Chinese. Blacks quickly and effectively organized against these laws through the Colored Conventions of 1855, 1865, 1873, and 1882. Through black political pressure, the right to testify against whites was won in 1863. In 1864, blacks won the right to public accommodations; in 1870, the right of franchise and jury service; and in 1880, the elimination of separate schools. It is curious that many of these reforms did not apply to Chinese and Indians. It is equally curious that such a small percentage of the population could wield such effective political power. In California, Chinese suffered more from racial prejudice than blacks until 1940, when prejudice against Chinese began tapering off and resurged against blacks, who arrived in substantial numbers after 1940 with their white Southern counterparts.

There are several conclusions we can draw about the Western black person. He (and she) was an individualistic, self-reliant person like the others who tamed the West. There is every indication that he was not forced to be included in or excluded from any activity. The olive Spanish-Mexican heritage in a Roman Catholic religious atmosphere provided for easier interaction and intermarriage between the races—as we have seen in Sid LeProtti's parentage. Blacks were a definite minority in the population and made up no more than 2 percent of the total population. This was a largely urban population that exercised political influence beyond its numbers. On the whole, blacks probably fared better in the West than in any other area of the United States.

Endnotes:
1. Monroe N. Works, *The Negro Year Book* (Tuskegee Institute), 263.
2. "Spanish Voyages to the Northwest," *California Historical Quarterly* 7 (1928): 381.
3. Herbert Aptheker, ed. *A Document History of the Negro in the United States* (Citadel Press), 141.
4. "The Black Community in California," *California Historical Quarterly* (September 1971): 259.

The population statistics are by courtesy of the Population Research section, Budget Division, Department of Finance, State of California, 1971.

The Barbary Coast

"Barbary Coast proper is in the northerly part of the city, comprising both sides of Broadway and Pacific streets, and the cross streets between them, from Stockton Street to the Waterfront (then Battery Street)...like the malaria arising from a stagnant swamp and poisoning the air for miles around, does this stagnant pool of human immorality and crime spread its contaminating vapors over the surrounding blocks on either side. Nay even the remotest parts of the city do not entirely escape its polluting influence.

"In the early days of San Francisco, Barbary Coast was the place of refuge and security for the hundreds of criminals that infested the city. In those days it was an easy matter for a stranger to enter this fortress of vice, but when once behind the walls he was extremely fortunate who had the opportunity to depart taking with him his life. Then the villains of every nationality held high carnival there. The jabber of the Orient, the soft-flowing tone of the South Sea Islander, the guttural gabbing of the Dutch, the Gaelic accent, the round full tone of the son of Africa, the melodious voice of the Mexicano, and the harsh, sharp utterance of the Yankee, all mingled in the boisterous revels.

"Barbary Coast is the haunt of the low and vile of every kind. The petty thief, the house burglar, the tramp, the whoremonger, lewd women, cutthroats and murderers, all are found there. Dance houses and concert saloons, where blear-eyed men and faded women drink vile liquor, smoke offensive tobacco, engage in vulgar conduct, sing obscene songs, and say and do everything to heap upon themselves more degradation, unrest, and misery, are numerous. Low gambling houses thronged with riot-loving rowdies in all stages of intoxication are there. Opium dens, where heathen Chinese and God-forsaken women and men are sprawled in miscellaneous confusion disgustingly drowsy or completely overcome by inhaling the vapors of the nauseous narcotic, are there. Licentiousness, debauchery, pollution, loathsome disease, insanity from dissipation, misery, poverty, wealth, profanity, blasphemy, and death are there. And Hell, yawning to receive the putrid mass, is there also."[1]

This was the thundering 1876 appraisal given by B.E. Lloyd.

This part of San Francisco called the Barbary Coast began with the gold rush. In January 1848, John Marshall discovered the magic metal at Coloma, California, and all hell broke loose. At the time of the discovery, fewer than 25,000 people populated California; by 1880 there were 864,694 people, an increase of 3,400 percent in thirty years. A population explosion of this size would cause its own natural upheavals, but in this case there were additional fuels for the fire. Nearly all the argonauts were tough males between twenty and forty years old. These new citizens were rarely the dry good clerk, doctor, preacher, blacksmith, miller, lawyer, or shopkeeper. Most were drifters, cutthroats, cowboys, sailors, swindlers, gunslingers, gamblers, and crooked politicians. They were rootless and thrill-seeking citizens who could leave at a moment's notice, and some who left did with a posse at their backs. Whatever they had been, they were all gold-crazed fortune seekers. The first forty-niners came from Mexico and South America where the news of gold first arrived. After that, they flooded in from France, Germany, England, Ireland, China, Holland, the South Seas, America, and Australia. They came

	Land Area	Population				
	(Sq. Miles)	1850	1860	1870	1880	1890
California	156,803	138,295*	379,994	560,247	864,694	1,213,398
Los Angeles	4,060	3,530	11,333	15,309	33,381	101,454
San Francisco	45	36,154*	56,802	149,473	233,959	298,997
Alameda	733	—†	8,927	24,237	62,976	93,864
Contra Costa	734	2,786	5,328	8,461	12,525	13,516
Marin	520	1,035	3,334	6,903	11,324	13,072
Solano	827	2,836	7,169	16,871	18,475	20,946
San Mateo	454	—†	3,214	6,635	8,669	10,087
Santa Clara	1,032	6,764	11,912	26,246	35,039	48,005
Total Bay Area	4,345	49,575	96,686	238,826	382,967	498,487

from everywhere to sift through the sands of the Sierras and give California its boisterous and gaudy history.

San Francisco was the gateway to El Dorado and the capital of commerce, transportation, the arts, vice, and crime. The importance of San Francisco and the Bay Area as the mainstream of early California is often underestimated by modern observers. Los Angeles is now California's most populous city, and it is natural to assume it has always held this position. This assumption is not true; the drama of early California was largely played out on the Northern California stage.

Any study of California history should include some survey of the population and geography. One important geographical fact is that San Francisco County has forty-five square miles of land area compared to 4,060 square miles for Los Angeles County. The massive land area of Los Angeles and its population sprawl led Alexander Wolcott to describe it as "seven suburbs in search of a city." San Francisco, on the other hand, is widely

---

*1850 population figures were lost for San Francisco, Contra Costa, and Santa Clara Counties; 1852 special census figures are substituted.

†These counties were formed between 1850 and 1860.

Statistics from Population, Population Research Section, Budget Division, Department of Finance, State of California, 1971.

1900	1910	1920	1930	1940	1950
1,485,053	2,377,549	3,426,861	5,677,251	6,907,387	10,586,223
170,298	504,131	936,456	2,208,492	2,785,643	4,151,687
342,782	416,912	506,676	634,394	634,536	775,357
130,197	246,131	344,177	474,883	513,011	740,315
18,046	31,674	53,889	78,608	100,450	298,984
15,702	25,114	27,342	41,648	52,907	85,619
24,143	27,559	40,602	40,834	49,118	104,833
12,094	26,585	36,781	77,405	111,782	235,659
60,216	83,539	100,676	145,118	174,949	290,547
603,180	857,514	1,110,143	1,492,890	1,636,753	2,531,314

known in California as "The City." The San Francisco Bay Area actually consists of seven counties which have a combined land area roughly comparable to that of Los Angeles, or, rephrasing Wolcott, seven suburbs with "The City." The chart has been prepared to show the comparative geography and population for Los Angeles and the San Francisco Bay Area from 1850 to 1950.

A review of the geography and population chart reveals several important points. The population growth of California as a whole has been spectacular. In a little over a century, it has come from an obscure territory in 1848 to the most populous of the fifty states in the mid-1960s, with over twenty million citizens. San Francisco grew from 459 people in 1847, to a hell-roaring, boot-stomping metropolis of 36,154, within five years. In 1852, when San Francisco was the largest city west of the Mississippi River, Los Angeles was a sprawled-out village with less than one person per square mile. Los Angeles began its phenomenal growth in the 1880s and passed the San Francisco Bay Area population total sometime in the 1920s. It was in the 1920s that Los Angeles began its rise as a jazz center and San Francisco's Barbary Coast was closed by the respectables. By 1940, Los Angeles had nearly twice the population of the San Francisco Bay Area. The most important fact for our study is that the San Francisco Bay Area was the major population center of California until the 1920s; San Francisco has always been the Bay Area focus of commerce, art, and vice. This position of leadership was also held over any city west of the Mississippi River until the early twentieth century. After that, San Francisco was outstripped in population by a number of cities but has remained the cultural and financial capital of the West.

Great numbers of the argonauts came from Britain's penal colony, Australia. Being in Australia to begin with meant they were the undesirables, misfits, and scum of Britain. Once they came to California, they bludgeoned out a more infamous history for themselves. They quickly became known as the Sydney Ducks, and the area they inhabited was called Sydney Town. The Sydney Ducks acquired the deserved reputation of being the most vicious criminals on earth. They pickpocketed, bullied, shanghaied, murdered, and terrorized the populace as everyday pastimes. One of their more notorious diversions was visiting the Chilean and Mexican settlements on Sunday afternoon outings where they burnt and destroyed the tents and shacks, murdered a few men, and raped the women. Another entertainment, during favorable winds, was to burn the rest of San Francisco down and loot the remains.

At least two new English words were added to our language by the Sydney Ducks. When strangers would venture into Sydney Town, the Sydney Ducks would often make gang attacks and rob them. When a victim was about to be set upon, the gang leader would yell "Huddle 'um!" as the signal to attack. "Huddle 'um" was contracted to "hoodlum" by San Franciscans and now has a well-known meaning. The word "shanghaiing" became familiar to every sailor in the world through the practices in early San Francisco. A hundred devices from trap-doors, women, liquor, and knock-out drugs to simple bludgeoning were used to deliver unconscious victims to ship captains in need of a crew. Some ships that left San Francisco had most of their crews lying unconscious on their decks as they sailed though the Golden Gate. Many of the unconscious never woke up and were dumped at sea. Early San Francisco's Sydney Ducks were responsible for the practice and popularization of the word "shanghai" throughout the world.

The municipal authorities of San Francisco were too corrupt to take any effective action against the Sydney Ducks. In many cases, the authorities were partners in their crimes and loot. In June 1851, the leading citizens became sufficiently enraged at their crime and violence that they organized the first San Francisco Vigilante Committee. The Committee hung a few of the more notorious Sydney Ducks and sent the rest fleeing from San Francisco. Some measure of control was exercised over Sydney Town for a short period, but the effect was not permanent, as the Sydney Ducks returned, and subsequent Vigilante Committees were formed. In the 1860s, Sydney Town lost its original name and became known throughout the world by the more familiar name of the Barbary Coast.

"The miners came in forty-nine, the whores in fifty-one, and together they produced the native son"—early ditty. Fast on the heels of the fast, loose men came the fast, loose women. Before the gold rush, the ratio of women to men was small. In 1847, there were 247 males in San Francisco and 128 females. After 1848, any sensible numerical relationship ceased to exist. In 1849, about 64,000 gold-seekers stormed California, and no more than 1,500 were females. In 1850, only one in every twelve new arrivals was female.

The first sisters of sin did not wait until "fifty-one" to board the ships of gold. In late 1848, a few probably arrived aboard ships from Peru and Chile. These ladies were recorded as being neither "wives, widows or maids."[2] It was only a matter of months before the fast women outnumbered the wives, widows, and maids. The record shows that the rewards of lying on one's back greatly exceeded those for standing at the washboard, and a number of wives exchanged their vertical washboard for the horizontal bedboard.

The effects of the disproportion of males to females were so great and enduring that it was not until 1960, 110 years after the gold rush, that females outnumbered males in California as they do in the other states.

In 1876, B.E. Lloyd said, "Someone has remarked that in the Eastern cities the prostitutes tried to imitate in manner and dress the fashionable respectable ladies, but in San Francisco the rule was reversed—the latter copying after the former."[3] There were so few respectable ladies and children that, once, a theatrical performance was stopped so everyone could listen to a baby crying in the audience.

San Francisco had every form of prostitution known to man; there were street walkers, saloon girls, dance hall girls, parlor house prostitutes, freelancers, crib girls, and even a Barbary Coast bar, The Dash, that served up drag queens, and an uptown bordello that featured men for the ladies' pleasure. Both of the latter types closed quickly, the first as an offense to public morals and the second from lack of interest. The male bordello was

Young prostitutes of the Barbary Coast, c. 1890

owned by a black woman. The saloon girls were sometimes known as "pretty waiter girls" and usually wore no underwear. An entire book has been devoted to a history of San Francisco's parlor houses.

It is not the purpose of this book to survey San Francisco's prostitution, a survey that could fill several volumes. Instead, a brief look at a few of the crib bordellos near the Barbary Coast will serve as representative of the various forms of prostitution. Some of the cribs were enormous and were usually called cow-yards by the locals. The Nymphia was a three-story U-shaped structure on Pacific Street near Stockton. It had 150 cribs and was the largest. The owner of the Nymphia was the Twinkling Star Corporation. The Marsicania had only thirty-three cribs and was located on Dupont Street (now Grant Avenue, the main street of Chinatown) near Broadway. It was known as the most depraved cow-yard. The most famous was at 620 Jackson Street. It opened in 1904 with 133 cribs. There were several unique features about it—one was that it was owned by the city fathers and quickly became known as the Municipal Crib. Another was that Mexican girls served themselves up in the basement at twenty-five cents, Americans and other nationalities were on the first and second floors at fifty cents, French girls worked the third floor at seventy-five cents, and black girls held the fourth at fifty cents. The girls rented cribs on an eight-hour basis and lived elsewhere because the rent, including protection, was sky-high. Chinese girls were available throughout the Chinatown-area cribs at the lowest rates. They were called "slave girls," but their condition of servitude was far worse than slavery and only a rare one survived past twenty-five years old. After they became badly diseased and worthless, they were forced to commit suicide.

In order to properly lubricate the citizen and traveler of San Francisco before, after, or during his visit to the girls, there were 3,117 licensed places that served beer, whiskey, or other intoxicating beverages in 1890. This works out at one licensed place for every ninety-six inhabitants. In addition to the licensed places, there were at least two thousand blind pigs or blind tigers, as speakeasies were called, that operated without a license. If children and teetotalers are deducted from the population, the serious drinking capacities of San Franciscans work out to gargantuan proportions.

In 1934, the *San Francisco News* ran articles on the old Barbary Coast:

> About the middle 1860s some imaginative sailor is said to have compared the unsavory quagmire of old Sydney Town to the piratical, lawless Barbary Coast of North Africa—and further than that nothing is known of the nomenclature which rendered the Barbary Coast of San Francisco synonymous with picturesque iniquity for more than sixty years.[4]

The Call newspaper (1869) wrote about the Barbary Coast and provided an imaginary tour:

> The Barbary Coast: that mysterious region so much talked of, so seldom visited—that sink of moral pollution—that stomping ground of the Ranger [dive operators, thieves, and swindlers were referred to as Rangers] the last resort of the ruined nymph du prave, the home of vice and harbor of destruction—where rages one wild cirocco in sin.
>
> Now we are on the flood-tide of the Barbary Coast, where noisome vapors, bellowing trombones and wailing violins make the night hideous. Here is Brook's melodeon typical of the city's free melodeons that pander to the tastes of the low and vitiated.

Bawdy songs and witticisms so obscene that they meet with the disapprobation of even a far from scrupulous audience, are in order. Behind boarded alcoves, orgies which may be imagined but not described, took place. These melodeons, while vicious enough, declined the use of knock-out drops and did not murder customers after robbing them. Such practices are reserved for the Thunderbolt Saloon, up the street, and the sawdust-sprinkled dance cellars of Pacific Street.

When a man with a roll entered a dive, word is flashed that "he's flush." Drinks are plied, he becomes reckless, and soon his "pile" evaporates on champagne. If a customer is "tight" with his money and female fingers do not pry it loose, the masculine muscularity of the establishment "puts a head" on him. "Putting a head" on anyone means slugging him with a blackjack or hickory stick. The drugging places work with more finesse.

Sometimes in these resorts you see a remnant of better days seated at a sorry piano. Fingers that once clambered though Mozart or Beethoven wander though "Katy My Darling" and "Lilly Dale." Sometimes a rich soprano note that all too soon relapses into dissipated hoarseness reveals what was once the pride and joy of some refined home circle.[5]

A look at the Bull Run gives us an idea of the action of the times. In this resort, the pretty waiter girls wore diapers. They were required to drink real liquor along with the men instead of the tea-colored water served in other resorts, and they were not permitted to leave the dance hall floor to relieve themselves. The liquor served to the girls was often spiked with "cantharides" to stimulate them. When one of the girls passed out, she was carried upstairs, stripped, and sexual privileges were sold to all comers. For an extra quarter, a customer was allowed to watch his predecessor perform.

One whoremonger on the Barbary Coast hung out his shingle which simply stated "Ye Olde Whore House."[6]

The Barbary Coast was not a white haven; a black person was as welcome as anyone. Herbert Asbury says, "of the bar-rooms, dance halls, concert saloons and brothels on the Barbary Cost, perhaps a score bent their energies to the amusement of the Negro." In 1917, he notes, "The House of All Nations was operated by a Portuguese named Louis Gomez, who boasted that among his dancing girls were to be found women of all civilized nations. Purcell's, The Dew Drop Inn, The Squeeze Inn, and The So Different were Negro places, employing Negro women, but catering to white men."[7]

Gunfire would occasionally rip through the walls separating Purcell's from Spider Kelly's, seen here in the early 1930s.

In the white dives, fights were sometimes faked to amuse the slummers, but Asbury says, "In many of the dives, of course, especially the Negro joints, it was necessary to fake a row, for plenty of real fracases (sic) occurred in the natural course of events. As far as indecent dancing was concerned, if a man bought a dance ticket and ventured upon the floor with one of the high yallers employed in these places, his conduct was determined only by his conscience and the amiability of his partner. The best-known of the Negro dance-halls, and the most turbulent, was Purcell's, which occupied a long, narrow room on the north side of Pacific Street between Montgomery and Kearny streets. It was furnished only with a bar, a few rough tables and chairs, and a score or more of wooden benches which faced a splintery dance floor. No nonsense about buying liquor was permitted in Purcell's; a visitor either drank, and drank frequently, or he was thrown into the street

Political cartoon from the San Francisco Examiner*'s 1913 crusade to close down the Barbary Coast*

by several husky bouncers who patrolled the dive. The bar in Purcell's was at the left of the entrance and was set against a thin wooden partition which separated the resort from the saloon and dance hall operated by Spider Kelly, who in his earlier years had acquired considerable renown as a lightweight prizefighter. Kelly's bar was also against the partition, at the right of his entrance. Shooting affrays were of frequent occurrence in Purcell's, and bullets often ripped though the flimsy wall and endangered Kelly's bartenders. To protect them Kelly lined his 'back-bar' and mirror with sheet-iron boiler plate."[8]

In the San Francisco city directory, Purcell's and King's first appears in 1901, located at 520 Pacific. Their establishment could have preceded this without their paying the cost of the listing in the city directory. According to Sid LeProtti, they were first located one block north on Broadway. It is also possible they operated as a blind pig. The WPA states: "No resort was better known then Lew Purcell's So Different Saloon (520 Pacific Street), a Negro dance hall, where the 'Turkey Trot' is said to have originated."[9]

Louis Gomez's is also listed in the 1901 directory at 403 Drumm Street. This would be a waterfront hangout and several blocks from the later location in the 400 block on Pacific Street. In 1935, the WPA project described an "Izzy Gomez in a black fedora...a coffee-colored fat man...painted, photographed, written and sung about. Since 1900 Izzy has been running his bar, since 1930 in its present location." Prior to 1930 it had been on the Barbary Coast. "Here sixty-three year-old Isadore greets his closest friends, tells tall witty tales of life in his native Portugal—or dances Portuguese folk dances with incredible grace despite his massive bulk."[10] Presumably, Louis and Izzy Gomez are the same person, and the black Portuguese saloon keeper referred to by Sid LeProtti and Reb Spikes.

There is only one known reference to racial prejudice on the Barbary Coast. The Cowboy's Rest was operated by a tough woman named Maggie Kelly who was also called Cowboy Mag and the Queen of the Barbary Coast. Asbury says, "Her greatest public renown came in 1898, when several Negro regiments were waiting in San Francisco for transports to take them to Manila. Other Barbary Coast dive-keepers welcomed the black soldiers, for they had money to spend, but Cowboy Mag remained true to her principles. Each morning until the regiments had embarked, she mounted guard at the door of her saloon with a revolver and remained there throughout the day, threatening to shoot every Negro who tried to enter. When a newspaper reporter suggested that she wasn't being very patriotic, she said, simply: 'I hate niggers! I'll blow the head off any nigger that comes into my place!'"[11]

The 1934 *San Francisco News* described the 1906 Barbary Coast:

> The layout of the post-fire Pacific Street as Police Lieutenant James Boland, who patrolled it, remembers, numbered (beginning on the south side of the street, east of Kearny) Caligaris' Drug Store, The Midway, U.S. Dance Hall, Bella Union (with the Montana Bar upstairs), The Owl (run by Black Tony Parmagini, recently convicted dope king), the Dragon, the OK, The Belvedere (dubbed The Old Ladies Home because its table girls were over 35) and The Oregon.
>
> On the north side, beginning at Kearny, were Louis Parenti's saloon, which, with its old-fashioned bar and amazing collection of prize fighter pictures, still stands; the Diana, Queen, Seattle, Hippodrome, Purcell's, the Golden City, Thalia, Mother Smith's Happy Valley, and the Club.
>
> By 1910 the 300 saloons which it is estimated operated in a six-blocks area included The House of All Nations (which still stands glum and vacant), the White House, Ivy, the Moulin Rouge, Turkish Cafe, Bear, the So Different, The Criterion, Dew Drop Inn, Squeeze-Inn, Cascade, Dutch Emma's, the Admiral, The Elko, and the California, said to be the first resort to allow Filipinos to dance with white girls.
>
> On the outer fringes of the Coast flourished three choice resorts of their kind: The Neptune Palace, The Jupiter and The Cave (on

Kearny Street). On Kearny Street around the corner of Pacific Street and above a large clothing store, Cissy Loftus, an opulent vaudeville blonde of the Della Fox period, is reputed to have run a "rooming house." It was at the Thalia and The Seattle Dance Hall (the first to open after the fire) that the percentage of girls worked the dummy key racket, selling customers keys for $2.00, keys that fitted no doors.[12]

The key racket had to be discontinued because dozens of drunken men were roaming the streets after midnight looking for the rooms the keys would fit and the girls who had promised to meet them.

During the era of the "Gay Nineties" San Francisco had the reputation of "The Wickedest City in the World." Writers of every era grappled with other places with which to compare the Barbary Coast. They usually passed quickly over any American city. The WPA project said, "As the Barbary Coast it was known around the world for half a century, more notorious than London's Limehouse, Marseille's waterfront, or Port Said's Arab Town."[13] The Barbary Coast was often favorably compared with Sodom and Gomorrah and not infrequently compared with Hell itself. Another name for the Coast was "The Devil's Acre."

Whatever the Barbary Coast offered in virtues and vices, it was a place that accepted the black man, danced and cavorted with black women, and listened to black music. The visitor to the Barbary Coast did not come to hear music by Mozart and Chopin. Instead, he appears inclined to a boot-stomping, heel-kicking, tub-thumping sound as wild and raucous as the place itself. If the music could be danced to and was in the spirit of the Barbary Coast, it was accepted.

All people, places, and times have their spring and summer, and likewise their autumn and winter. The time of winter came to the Barbary Coast in 1921. The *San Francisco Examiner* printed the following article on November 19, 1921, and it was preserved in Sid LeProtti's scrapbook:

> PACIFIC STREET DIVE OWNER IS FOUND GUILTY
> Proprietor of Thalia on Barbary Coast is convicted in Police Court; Resorts Are All To Go.
> Terry Mustain, proprietor of the Thalia, the most pretentious dance hall on Pacific Street, was found guilty yesterday of conducting a disorderly house by Police Judge Lile T. Jacks.

The revived Pacific Street, reopened as the International Settlement, c. 1934

This court ruling, the first genuine official ruling that has ever been aimed at the Barbary Coast region, is regarded as a staggering blow to resort owners on Pacific Street.

It is the culmination of a war which clubwomen, led by the Women's Vigilant Committee and Captain of Police Arthur Layne, in command of the central police station, have been waging against the Pacific Street dives.

Police Judge Jacks made his ruling without comment. The evidence in the case had been heard several days previous. He fixed next Tuesday as the date for passing sentence. The maximum penalty is a fine of $500 and a six month's term in the county jail.

300 ARRESTS

During the past two weeks more than 300 arrests have been made in Pacific Street resorts under Captain Layne, more than 200 of this number were women habitues, who were charged with either vagrancy or with being inmates of a disorderly house. Sixteen other proprietors of dives were charged with keeping such places. All of these other defendants have demanded jury trials. This was deemed advisable by them after the vigorous prosecution of John Orcutt, assistant district attorney, in the case of Mustain. Judge Jacks fixed December 1 as the date for the long list. Before that date the prosecution will select the particular defendant to try.

"Abatement proceedings will be started against owners," said Captain Layne yesterday, "unless the owners abate themselves. It is for them to determine. If the proprietors are willing to go out of

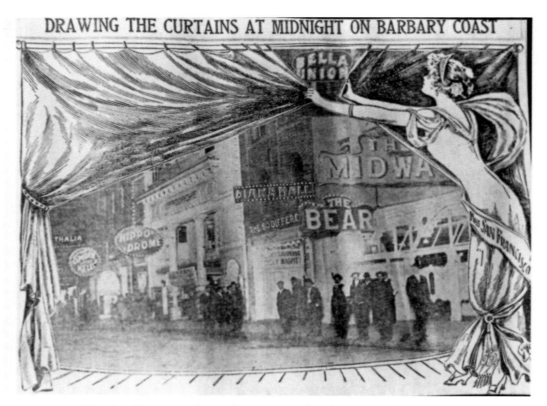

Miss San Francisco draws the curtains closed on the Barbary Coast. This image of Pacific Street appeared in the San Francisco Examiner.

business, so much the better. But if they act in defiance of the will of the people as it has been expressed then the abatement proceedings will be brought in the courts."

KNOWN THE WORLD OVER

For more than twenty years Pacific Street has been known the world over. It was the heart of San Francisco's notorious Barbary Coast region. It has been infested with dives that have harbored criminals and underworld women since its beginning.

"Barbary Coast" is a term that has been applied to this section of San Francisco since the early sixties, according to Captain Layne. The name was given to it at that time because the wholesale robbery of sailors reminded men of those pirate countries in the Mediterranean which brought this county into a naval clash at one time because American sailors were robbed so ruthlessly on their Barbary Coast.[14]

A few days later, a small article appeared headlined:

13 CAPTURED IN RAID ON "PURCELL'S CAFE"

Gillie Richardson, proprietor of Lew Purcell's Cafe and Dance Hall, 101 Columbus Avenue, and twelve visitors, were arrested early yesterday by Detectives Floyd and Mitchell for violating the 1 o'clock music ordinance.

The detectives say that when they entered the place at 2:35 o'clock music and dancing were in full swing.[15]

...And the Barbary Coast was dead.

Endnotes:
1. B.E. Lloyd, *Lights and Shades in San Francisco* (San Francisco: A.L. Bancroft and Company, 1876), 78–79.
2. Curt Gentry, *The Madams of San Francisco* (Garden City, New York: Doubleday, 1964), 26.
3. Lloyd.
4. *San Francisco News,* 1934.
5. *The Call,* San Francisco, 1869.
6. Gentry, 147.
7. Herbert Asbury, *The Barbary Coast* (New York: Alfred A. Kopf, 1933), 288.
8. Asbury, 292–3.
9. Writers' Program of the Works Progress Administration in Northern California, *San Francisco. The Bay and Its Cities* (New York: Hastings House, 1940), 134.
10. Writers' Program of the Works Progress Administration in Northern California, 245.
11. Asbury, 225.
12. *The San Francisco News,* 1934.
13. Writers' Program of the Works Progress Administration in Northern California, 214.
14. *The San Francisco Examiner,* 1921.
15. *The San Francisco Examiner,* 1921.

Jazzin' 'n Dancin'

It is a historical irony that the city that put "jazz" in jazz doesn't rate a mention in most jazz history books. The word "jazz" was first applied to music in San Francisco in 1913. Before World War I, San Francisco and the Barbary Coast gave America such popular jazz dances as the Texas Tommy, Turkey Trot, Grizzly Bear, and Bunny Hug. San Francisco is a city in which there was more musical diversity than in any other city in the world. It is the place where Lu Watters found fertile ground to start the Dixieland Jazz Revival and where Bunk Johnson was rehabilitated. In even more recent years, it has been a mecca for rock musicians.

The Depression Era WPA Project surveyed San Francisco's musical history and concluded that "few cities in America have such intensely variegated musical life as early San Francisco. Few have fostered and maintained its vital civic interest in the art. Nearly a century ago San Francisco became a mecca for musicians. In richness of background, New York and New Orleans can alone be compared with it."[1]

The gold rush abruptly ended California's "pastoral period" of Spanish haciendas, Franciscan Missions, and hide traders. After 1848, California was enveloped in a fury of new faces, industries, and entertainment. The occasional music of a family circle was replaced by a round-the-clock din from the gambling halls and saloons. This was soon followed by dozens of other musical presentations from opera and classical to minstrelsy and the celestial sound of the Chinese.

The 1849 advance man for the Cayuga Joint Stock Company noted San Francisco's business prospects and then the gambling halls: "The first thing that attracted my attention as I came into the place was the great number of gambling rooms in each of which was from one to a dozen tables loaded with gold and silver and surrounded by a crowd composed of men from every nation and clas (sic) under the heavens. Americans, English, French, Dutch, Mexicans, Indians, Chilanos, Sandwich Islanders (Hawaiians) and Chinese in all varieties of dress were mingled together bending over the tables and watching the turning of the cards with eager curiosity. The jingling of money, the clinking of glasses at the bar and the hum of voices were mingled with the music of the harp, guitar, flute and other instruments which are always in attendance at these places."[2] Another 1849 author noted the presence of "The Sons of Africa."[3]

The Englishman J.D. Borthwick gives us an inconsistent report of the music in San Francisco's gambling halls in 1851: "Auctioneers cried out their goods or rang bells to collect a crowd, and at the same time one's ears were dinned with the discord of a half-a-dozen brass bands, braying out different popular airs from many different gambling saloons." Later, he notes that in each of the gambling houses there "was a very good band of music, the performers being usually German or French." He also tells us: "In the mines Americans seemed to exhibit more tolerance of Negro blood than usual in the States. Negroes were permitted to lose their money in the gambling rooms,"[4] as "equal opportunity" suckers.

Recalling their gold rush years in San Francisco, Misters Barry and Patten tell us: "The Bella Union (temple of chance) in the days of '49 and '50 thronged with men playing against various games from about eleven o'clock in the morning until daylight the next morning. There used to be a quintet of Mexican musicians, who came here at night to perform. There were two harps, one large and the other very small, two guitars and one flute. The musicians were dressed in Mexican costume (which was nothing very noticeable as many of their auditors were in the same style of dress) and were quiet, modest men, with contented, amiable faces. They used to walk in among the throng of people, along to the upper end of the room, take their seats, and with scarcely any preamble or discussions, commence their instrumentation. They had played so much together, and were so similar, seemingly, in disposition—calm, confident and happy—that their ten hands moved as if guided by one mind; rising and falling in perfect unison—the harmony so sweet, and just strange enough in its tones, from the novelty in the selection of instruments, to give it a peculiar fascination for ears always accustomed to the orthodox and time honored vehicles of music used in quintet instrumentation. Their repertoire contained the popular waltzes and dances of the time and many weird, curious airs of old Spain; the listener knew the same sounds had centuries ago floated on a moonlit night in old Seville."[5]

The California Exchange was one of San Francisco's largest gambling halls and saloons. In 1850, it regularly employed a forty-piece orchestra for the customers' entertainment. Even more interesting was the, presumably, black bones player who was reviewed by the *Alta* newspaper: "There may be expression thrown into anything musical. We have heard even a drum, the next thing to a bagpipe for offenses against musical vibrations and responsive sympathies, leap out in the midst of abominable noise and make a desperate attempt for admission among the upper ten trombones. But that dry bones could become really musical and expressive we did not believe, until hearing the bones player of the band at the California Exchange. They were the very bones of Time himself—as delicately mournful in 'The Last Rose Of Summer' as full of fire and energy in 'Grey Eagle' or devil-may-careish in some wild rollicking Negro melody. With the mellow breathings of that exquisite flute, it is strange how the rattling of those dry bones can so harmonize."[6]

A black musical group was presented at the Aquila de Ora saloon and gambling hall in 1849. Their performances were described as "plaintive and moving."[7] This group, whoever they were, preceded abolition by fifteen years.

Not all strange and exotic instruments were appreciated. The Chinese had their own gambling halls in which celestial music was presented. *The Annals of San Francisco* sought to assess the music critically: "At the innermost end of some of the principal gambling places, there is an orchestra of five or six native musicians, who produce such extraordinary sounds from their curiously shaped instruments as severely torture the white man to listen to. Occasionally a songster adds his howl or shriek to the excruciating harmony. The wailings of a thousand lovelorn cats, the screams, gobblings, braying and barkings of as many peacocks, turkeys, donkeys and dogs—the earpiercing noises of hundreds of botching cork-cutters, knife-grinders, file makers and the like—would not make a more discordant and agonizing concert than these Chinese musical performers in their gambling houses."[8]

The exotic instruments of San Francisco were matched by several unusual performers. At the El Dorado gambling saloon, they offered a lady who alternated demonstrations of music and muscle. She hung from the ceiling on a trapeze on which she did gymnastics and played the violin. The El Dorado was one of the largest establishments and also hired a full orchestra that played the classic and popular airs of the day.

Across the street from the El Dorado, the smaller Verandah introduced a "one man orchestra."[9] This native of Sydney, Australia, played Pandean pipes hung on his chin; tied to his back, he had a drum which he beat with sticks attached to his elbows; with his hands, he played cymbal, triangle, and accordion; and, all the while, he performed an awkward tap dance with his huge hard-soled shoes.

"The lesser bars and shanties," of San Francisco, "issued a cacophony of singing, stomping and melodeon playing."[10] The name "melodeons" came to indicate a special kind of dive which took its name from the type of musical instrument installed in them. A melodeon was a small reed-organ worked by foot pedals that drew air in through reeds. These establishments did not have a dance floor and allowed women to enter only if they were hired by the dive. The customer was treated to melodeon music, simple female entertainment (sometimes quite lewd), and liquor. As time passed, the melodeon instrument was discontinued, but such establishments were still called melodeons. A number of melodeons catered to Mexicans and blacks.

Music in California was not confined to San Francisco, and at least one writer, Bayard Taylor said in 1850 that Sacramento surpassed San Francisco.

Frank Leslie's 1874 illustration of a San Francisco melodeon establishment

"The amount of gambling in Sacramento City was very great, and the enticement of music was employed even to a greater extent than in San Francisco. All kinds of instruments and tunes made night discordant, for which harrowing service the performers were paid an ounce* each...the wail of torture from innumerable musical instruments peals from all quarters through the fog and darkness. Full bands, each playing different tunes discordantly, are stationed in front of the principal establishments, and as these happen to be near together, the mingling of the sounds in one horrid, ear-splitting, brazen chaos, would drive frantic a man of delicate nerve. All one's old acquaintances in the amateur-music line, seem to have followed him. The gentleman who played the flute in the next room to yours, at home, has been hired at an ounce a night to perform in the drinking-tent across the way; the very French horn whose lamentations used to awake

---

*An ounce refers to an ounce of gold.

you dismally from the first sweet snooze, now greets you at some corner; and all the squeaking violins, grumbling violoncellos (sic) and rowdy trumpets which have severally plagued you in other times, are congregated here, in loving proximity. The very strength, loudness and confusion of the noises, which, heard at a little distance, have the effect of one great scattering performance, marvelously takes the fancy of the rough mountain men."[11]

The highlight of Taylor's musical observations comes when he describes Sacramento's Ethiopian melodists. "Some of the establishments have small companies of Ethiopian melodists, who nightly call upon 'Susanna!' and entreat to be carried back to Old Virginny. These songs are universally popular, and the crowd of listeners is often so great as to embarrass the player at the monte tables and injure the business of the gamblers. I confess to a strong liking for the Ethiopian airs, and used to spend half an hour every night in listening to them and watching the curious expressions of satisfaction and delight in the faces of the overland emigrants, who always attended in a body. The spirit of the music was always encouraging; even its most doleful passages had a grotesque touch of cheerfulness—a mingling of sincere pathos and whimsical consolation, which somehow took hold of all moods in which it might be heard, raising them to the same notch of careless good-humor. The Ethiopian melodies well deserve to be called, as they are in fact, the national airs of America. Their quaint, mock-sentimental cadences, so well suited to the broad absurdity of the words—their reckless gaiety and irreverent familiarity with serious subjects—and their spirit of antagonism and perseverance—are true expressions of the more popular sides of the national character. They follow the American race in all its emigrations, colonizations and conquests, as certainly as the Fourth of July and Thanksgiving Day. The penniless and half-despairing emigrant is stimulated to try again by the sound of 'It'll never do to give it up so!' and feels a pang of homesickness at the burthen of the 'Old Virginia Shore.'"[12]

These early black entertainers captivated their audience, and Taylor catches the flavor of both the audience and the performance. He notes several essential elements in black music: the cathartic effect of the blues; the satirizing of white morals, manners, and dress; and the "reckless gaiety." Finally, he concludes that this early black music is "the national airs of America" that "follow the American race in all its emigrations, colonizations and conquests." Few would deny that jazz and the blues have done just that.

At the diggings, there was music to be found. In the gold fields, an observer tells us, "Many good musicians are to found among the miners. Many had brought their instruments with them, and often at night could be heard echoing from the ravines and canyons the sound of fiddle, flute, accordion and clarinet."[13] One writer tells of a young Bostonian who brought his bugle and, at night, took it to a hilltop overlooking Hangtown (now Placerville) where he played "The Emigrant's Lament," "Oft In The Stilly Night," and "The Star-Spangled Banner,"[14] considerable accomplishments for a bugler. There were black entertainers in the gold fields, too. One early gold field diarist wrote on April 9, 1855, that he "went to a Negro concert with Miss H., poor performance. Went home in the rain and mud. Like to never got back myself."[15]

Minstrelsy and medicine shows are closely related and underexplored forerunners of jazz. Each of them is both a form of expression and a vehicle used for other forms of expressions. Reb Spikes's earlier description of medicine shows is one of the very few available. They were a popular entertainment that attracted crowds of suckers, who bought wormers, elixirs, and aphrodisiacs. The origins, flowering, and demise of medicine shows is largely unknown and is certainly a subject on which a serious jazz researcher could spend many useful years. Much the same is true of minstrelsy, except that, because it was paid for as pure entertainment, it was discussed in the popular press; several books and articles have appeared on the subject. None of these, to my knowledge, is devoted to the relationship between minstrelsy and jazz, although a book is now projected by a European researcher.

There are many overlapping elements in minstrelsy and medicine shows, including the very easy movement of musicians and entertainers from one form to the other. These two forms of entertainment are probably closely related in form and historical development. Because of these similarities, it is probable that the following short history of minstrelsy in California could be paralleled by a similar account of the development of medicine shows.

The first minstrel shows came to California with the gold rush, and they remained a popular form of entertainment until after the turn of the century. They differed widely in makeup, size, and quality. Some of the groups were only two or three people, using an abbreviated format for their shows; others went up to fifty or sixty persons, including musicians, comedians, and entertainers. Among the white minstrels were scattered individual black minstrels. Black minstrels blackened their faces along with the whites and would not have been easily distinguishable as genuine blacks to most observers in an audience. Probably some of the smaller companies which traveled the gold fields after 1849 were real blacks. The first record could be that of our gold field diarist who went to the "Negro concert with Miss H." in 1855. The first definite written record of black minstrelsy did not occur until 1862.

On February 5, 1852, Buckley's New Orleans Serenaders arrived on San Francisco's Long Wharf. The entire troupe was native New Orleanians, and they were definitely white. Four nights later, they opened at the Adelphi Theater. They were a hit and toured California for over a

The San Francisco Minstrels advertised their engagement at Sacramento's Forrest Theater, 1858

year before heading east. Through the years they returned to California for periodic tours. This group many have fashioned some of their music on the basis of the black New Orleans music of the times and brought it with them.

By early 1862, the San Francisco area had a large enough black population to support a black newspaper, *The Pacific Appeal—A Weekly Journal Devoted to the Interest of the People of Color.* The April 19, 1862, issue carried the headline, "Sam Pride's Original Colored Minstrels," and reported, "We have witnessed the performance of this troupe, and can speak favorable of their ability. They are equal, and in some ways superior, to any in their peculiar line. Their performances are amusing and highly ludicrous—exaggerated, of course; all such burlesques must necessarily be, whether Yankee, Irish, or Negro character, but with all calculated to excite the risible faculties. All who like to enjoy a good hearty laugh, should go and see them. There is nothing offensive or indelicate in their performances. Mr. Sam Pride is truly the Champion Banjoist of the world; he produces sounds from his banjo which we never thought an instrument so crude was capable of expressing; he imitates the entire Band, in fact, he almost makes the banjo play itself. His performances are inimitable."[16]

In the May 24, 1862, issue, a letter to the editor took minstrelsy apart at the seams, calling whites who performed it "foul dogs" and saving blacks who partook for an even lower niche in hell.

The next record of a large group of blacks entertaining a California audience is of the Tennessee Jubilee of Fisk University Singers. They opened on January 3, 1876, at the New Theater; the record of their performance is preserved because of a Civil Rights action brought by a black man, Mr. Charles Green. He was denied seating in the dress circle and sued the theater owner. The suit was lost on a technicality, but after that, San Francisco blacks were permitted to sit wherever they bought seats.

In May 1876, at performances of the Georgia (Colored) Minstrels, blacks were seated with whites. The Georgia Minstrels are the second group of black minstrels we know to have played California theaters. It is very likely they had been entertaining local audiences for years—since the show was owned by a Californian and wintered in San Francisco. This person also owned the New Orleans Minstrels, The California Minstrels, and several other shows. These other shows probably had individual blacks in them. The Georgia Minstrels are mentioned prominently by Sid LeProtti and Reb Spikes. We know that individual members of this troupe played in early black bands while they wintered in San Francisco. Some of them dropped out of the minstrel shows to live there, and replacements were undoubtedly recruited there. The show lasted for at least thirty-five years after 1876, and some of San Francisco's earliest black musicians came from the Georgia Minstrels.

Another black minstrel group was Charles Callender's Minstrels. Charles Callender started this group as a novelty for audiences tiring of the conventional white minstrels. They came to San Francisco in 1882 "direct from New York."[17] According to one inaccurate history, they were the first black minstrels and created great interest. The troupe had been recruited from the East and South: Billy Kirsander was a boot-black found in New York's Bowery; Sam Lucas was a coachman from New York; Billy Banks had been a longshoreman on the levee at Wheeling, West Virginia; James Grace was a waiter, also from Wheeling; Lew Brown had been a Philadelphia barber; and Bob Mackenloch was a roustabout from a Mississippi riverboat.

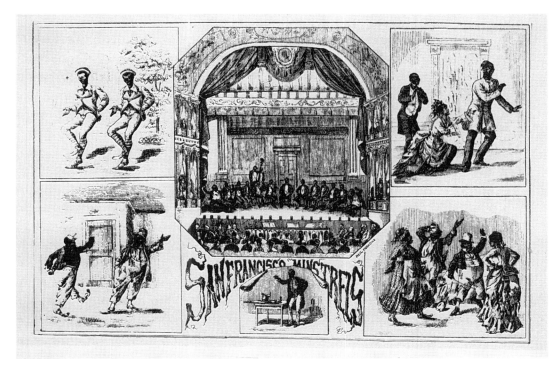

Advertisement from the late nineteenth century for the San Francisco Minstrels. The early development of ragtime and jazz had origins in the minstrel tradition.

It was reported that Callender, a white, schooled them in "Negro ways" and wrote the dialogue. Callender said that, "In jubilee songs and plantation dances they are superior to white men and have the advantage of a natural dialect, but they have scarcely any sense of humor."[18]

San Francisco's *Argonaut* newspaper covered their opening at the Standard Theater on May 1, 1882. Its critic wrote: "Are they real Negroes? There was the familiar burnt cork. They were, down to the last drummer. The minstrels came sauntering in the lazy way peculiar to the race and they were of all colors, from pale Mulatto to Guinea black. Of course they opened with the serious music which has come to be known as Negro melody. And it was only now and then that they drifted into the swinging rhythm which characterizes their own."[19]

This reference by the *Argonaut's* critic is most tantalizing for 1882 for any black music in any location. Since she knew the usual minstrel music was "spurious," though widely accepted as genuine by white audiences, she had obviously heard the real thing and had some appreciation of it. Furthermore, she had come to the performance to compare white minstrels with black minstrels, and she was waiting for the black minstrels to use the "swinging rhythm" of black music. She was obviously disappointed that they played the "spurious" music and was alert to those occasions when they "drifted into the swinging rhythm." Had this perceptive reporter ever visited the Barbary Coast?

In 1869, the Union Pacific and Southern Pacific railroads joined at Promontory, Utah, and the first transcontinental rail link was completed. A few years later, the Southern Pacific pushed its rails into New Orleans to join the West with the South. Blacks were employed in large numbers on the railroad, and there was considerable migration west. Many early black musicians of the San Francisco Bay Area tell how they or their parents came west to work on the Southern Pacific. Since New Orleans was the eastern terminus of the railroad, many of them came from Louisiana. We have already observed that some of the larger black productions came to the West after the railroad was completed.

The black minstrels and medicine show men were only some of the black artists who trod the California stage. The black newspaper, *The San Francisco Elevator,* in its issue of December 4, 1868, covered a black concert of operatic selections at Mozart Hall. The audience consisted of "many colored" and "some curious whites."[20] It was reviewed by some white newspapers, which the *Elevator* quoted. *The Call* is quoted as saying, "She was accompanied by Mr. Arthur C. Taylor, who, if he would drop the very unmusical habit of elaborating his accompaniments by adding little runs and arpeggios, would really entitle himself to high praise. Drop it Mr. Taylor." Taylor could have been an unappreciated early Fats Waller or Art Tatum, but he was definitely in the jazz mold. *The Call* continued: "The only other noticeable feature was the beautiful voice of Mrs. Smith—a voice of rare quality, rich, sonorous and of considerable register though lacking cultivation. Mrs. Smith's voice has natural grace and style, which renders her singing enjoyable."[21]

On May 5, 1873, Blind Tom, the famous and original black pianist, gave a concert in Virginia City, Nevada, that was reported in *The Gold Hill Evening News.*[22] It is unlikely he and his guardians came all the way west and did not come on to California to play, as he was to do in the 1890s. Presumably, he gave concerts in San Francisco and elsewhere in California, as Sid LeProtti has reported him doing in the 1890s.[23]

Sissieretta Jones, known as Black Patti, appeared with her Colored Troubadours in San Francisco in February, 1898. She carried a large company of black artists that included some blues singers. One blues singer who she used about 1910 was Tillie Sequin from Sequin, Texas.

The jazz dance has become the subject of more and more interest from jazz researchers studying the origins and development of jazz. Marshall and Jean Stearns wrote *Jazz Dance—The Story of American Vernacular Dance,* the nearest to a definitive work to date. They write, "Jazz dance evolved along lines parallel to jazz music, and its source is similarly a blend of European and African traditions in an American environment." While noting the oversimplification, they also write, "In general, European influences contributed the elegance, African influences the rhythmic propulsion." Jazz dance is *"American dancing that is performed to and with the rhythms of jazz*—that is, dancing that *swings.*"[24]

Tom Fletcher, in *100 Years of the Negro in Show Business,* says of the World War I period: "Dances that had been going on in the West and South for years invaded and rapidly became popular in the East. Dances that had hitherto been performed mainly in honky-tonks, dance-halls on the levee and in the Tenderloin districts, began to be seen regularly in New York."[25]

If the jazz dance is important in the development of jazz, and the West is important in the development of the jazz dance, the Barbary Coast undoubtedly played a large role in the development of both. The dance halls of the Barbary Coast were packed with enormous crowds of hoofers, of whom Herbert Asbury says, "They exercised a tremendous influence upon the dancing habits of the whole United States. In these dives originated dance steps which practically every dancing young man and woman in America strove to master. The turkey trot, the bunny hug, the chicken glide, the Texas Tommy, the pony prance, the grizzly bear and many other varieties of close and semi-acrobatic dancing, which swept the country during the half dozen years that preceded the World War, despite the scandalized roaring of the nation's pastors, were first performed in the dance halls of San Francisco's Barbary Coast for the delectation of the slummer. The birthplace of the best known terpsichorean masterpieces—the turkey trot and the Texas

Poster for Black Patti's Troubadours, 1897–98 season. Many musicians and dancers in her company lived and performed on the Barbary Coast.

Tommy—was the Thalia."[26] This latter claim is refuted by Sid LeProtti, Reb Spikes, and several other sources.

The WPA Writers' Project has this to say about jazz and the dance on the Barbary Coast: "To many, the Barbary Coast's unbroken hum of melodeon, piano, Mexican orchestra and singer was only San Francisco's brawling night voice. But one man caught in these sounds the musical implications of a future rhythm. This man was Ferdinand Rudolph Van Grofe—Ferde Grofe—incomparable arranger of jazz, composer of "Grand Canyon Suite" and other notable interpretations of the American scene. As an extra piano player on call at the Old Hippodrome and Thalia, Barbary Coast resorts, he recorded in his mind a medley of folk songs, Negro dance tunes, and sailors' chanties. 'The new music in the air along Pacific Street...did something to me!'

"When Grofe left the Barbary Coast to play the piano with Hickman's band at the St. Francis Hotel, the two arranged music that was different and sparkling. Other orchestra leaders who played in San Francisco—Paul Whiteman, Rudy Seiger, and Paul Ash—became conspicuous exponents of this new music.

"Along the Barbary Coast, the underworld whirled in fantastic steps to the rhythmic tunes of banging pianos, banjos, tom-toms, and blaring brass horns. It was the era of checkered suits, derby hats, and bright turtleneck sweaters. The police patrolled the district in pairs. Assisted by honky-tonk pianos grinding out 'Franky and Johnny,' gamblers fleeced their victims with inscrutable calm. From Barbary Coast dives to the Hotel St. Francis came the banjo, with Herman Heller as orchestra leader, soon to be followed by Art Hickman's introduction of the saxophone, which would bring jazz to the modern era.

"It was into this phantasmagoric atmosphere that Arnold Genthe brought Anna Pavlova (1885-1931) on a slumming tour. At the Olympia, a glittering dance hall, she watched the rhythmic sway of the dancers. Fascinated, soon she and her partner were on the floor. No one noticed them, no one knew who they were. Feeling the barbaric swing of the music, they soon were lost in the oblivion of the time-beats of the orchestra. One couple after another noticed them and stepped off the floor to watch. Soon they were the only dancers left on the floor, the other dancers forming a circle around the room, astonished, spellbound. The music stopped, Pavlova and her partner were finished, there was a moment of silence. Then came a

"I'm Thru With Love" sheet music cover featuring Paul Whiteman, 1931, Robbins Music Co.

thunderous burst of applause, a stamping of feet, a hurling of caps. The air was filled with yells of 'More!'"[27]

The Barbary Coast produced the Turkey Trot and the legend of how it captivated Anna Pavlova, the Russian prima ballerina. On November 29, 1910, The *San Francisco Examiner* reported: "San Francisco has produced, in the famous 'Turkey Trot' dance, a novelty in terpsichorean art, which is to be exported to the Imperial Palace of the Czar of the Russias for the entertainment of Nicholas II and his court. Anna Pavlova, who has dazzled at the Valencia Theater for the last week, was delighted with the novelty. 'I will take it to Russia,' she said, 'and I will introduce it throughout Europe.' Pavlova was on the 'coast' as a member of a big party [of]....society people....who admired the 'trot'. 'The Turkey Trot is a wonderful dance,' said Pavlova, after she had seen it, admired it, learned it and tried it in one of the Pacific Street dance halls. 'It is something quite different from anything I have ever known before. I like it. I will use it. I am going to dance it and introduce it in Russia and throughout all Europe. It is full of possibilities. The life and intensity of it appeals to me very strongly. I will have a great and beautiful ballet made of it, a ballet that will astonish the world. That is a wonderful dance. It is the only American dance I have seen that is original, in which there is no evidence of borrowing from something else. Such dances are rare, and I feel that I have made a discovery here.'"[28] The Turkey Trot was introduced to society and, from there, became a dance craze.

After the Turkey Trot had become popular, the Stearnses say "It varied from city to city and seemed to change weekly, but in general it consisted of a fast, marching one-step, arms pumping at the side, with occasional arm flappings emulating a crazed turkey. In 1910 the dance reached New York in a show from San Francisco called *Over The River,* accompanied by a tune entitled 'Everybody's Doing It.' The lyrics contain the repeated phrase, 'It's a Bear!' at which point the dancers are supposed to lurch like a grizzly bear—another dance from the West which became a hit a year later in the 'Follies of 1911.'"[29]

The Texas Tommy was another San Francisco-originated dance that swept the nation. In 1911, a tune titled "Texas Tommy Swing" was published, and, on the back, a "historical" summary was given under the headline, "The Dance That Made the Whole World Stare": "The Texas Tommy invades the North and East. The rhythm of the Grizzly Bear, the inspiration of the Loving Hug, the grace of the Walk-Back, and the abandon of the Turkey-Trot all blend in the harmony of the Texas Tommy Swing, which was really the parent of all the others. The dance originated more than forty years ago amongst the Negroes of the old Southern plantations. Southern darkies brought the dance and a suggestion of the melody to San Francisco several years ago, and there upon the Barbary Coast it was rounded into perfect harmony. It took the place by storm. Eastern people interested in dancing took it up. Stage favorites seized upon its absorbing rhapsodies. Society men and women adopted it. Pavlova, the Czar's favorite dancer, went into raptures over it and incorporated it into her repertoire. Leaders of the four hundred all over the country regard it as one of the sights of San Francisco and endorse it to their friends on their return."[30] Some of this is fact and other parts are obviously Tin Pan Alley imagination and puffery. It is far more likely the dance was created in Texas than "on the old Southern plantations," and the forty-year plus life span is pure fantasy dating.

Caroline and Charles Caffin, in *Dancing and Dancers of Today,* describe the movements of the 1912 Texas Tommy: "The dancers are perhaps more acrobatic than eccentric. The whirl which spins his partner toward the footlights with such momentum that without aid she must assuredly fly across them, must be nicely adjusted so that in neither force nor direction shall she escape the restraining grasp of his hand outstretched at just the right moment to arrest her. Poise and gentleness of handling must regulate the seemingly fierce toss of his partner, first in the air, then toward the ground."[31]

Ethel Williams, interviewed by the Stearnses, described the Texas Tommy as "a kick and a hop three times on each foot,"[32] followed by a slide. She was the substitute for Mary Dewson and was Johnny Peters's first new partner in New York City. According to several sources, the Texas Tommy was essentially the same as the Lindy Hop of the twenties and thirties, and the Jitterbug of the forties and fifties. According to black dancer Willie Covan, "it had a different first step than the Linday, or Jitterbug, that's all."[33]

The Stearnses, in *Jazz Dance,* have done an outstanding job of researching the Texas Tommy and interviewing various early black dancers. The Sternses say: "In 1910, when San Francisco was having a shipping boom, this dance, usually performed by teams of four to six dancers, became popular at Lew Purcell's."[34] Gene Harris, a white pianist who played the Thalia, told the Stearnses: "All the new dances came from Purcell's, which hired the best colored entertainers from coast to coast."[35] Susie Beavers told the Stearnses: "Johnny Peters brought the Texas Tommy to San Francisco in 1911 and then went East with the Al Jolson troupe of eight youngsters. His partner was Mary Dewson, and they were a sensation in Chicago and New York."[36] Nettie Compton told them: "When I danced at Purcell's in 1912, everybody was working out his own variations on the Texas Tommy. They told me that Johnny Peters brought it up from the South."[37] Will Mastin took a troupe of Texas Tommy dancers east. They were called *The California Poppies,* and featured, according to Mastin, Pet Bob Thurman, the fastest dancer of them all. Mastin told the Stearnses: "'Tommy' meant prostitute, and when we presented the dance at a San Francisco theater, the place was jammed— lots of cops, too, expecting a riot—but nothing happened because there wasn't anything bad about it, just a kind of acrobatics, with every step you could think of added to it."[38]

The Shimmy, or Shimmeshawobble, made an early appearance on the Barbary Coast. It possibly dates from as early as 1900; Sid LeProtti recalls Willard Jones playing the "Shimmeshawobble" in 1906. Another early reference to it is from Nettie (Lewis) Compton. She told the Stearnses: "We did the Shimmmy in San Francisco in 1910 and later called it the Shimme-Sha-Wobble."[39] According to both Sid LeProtti and Reb Spikes, Nettie Compton came to the Barbary Coast about 1910 and stayed several years.

Spencer Williams capitalized on the growing popularity of the Shimmeshawobble, and in 1917, wrote and published the tune "The Shimmeshawobble."

In the early years of this century, Bert Williams was the most famous black man alive. He was born in Nassau, Bahama Islands, in 1876, and was brought to Riverside, California, as an infant. Williams was raised in Riverside and came to San Francisco in the early 1890s to study civil engineering. As a teenager in San Francisco, he met and teamed up with George "Bon-Bon" Walker. Walker was a San Franciscan (born in Kansas) and, until he retired in 1907, was half of the famous Williams and Walker comedy and dance team. After Walker's retirement, Bert Williams continued on to even greater successes until his sudden death in 1922.

Sheet music cover from the San Francisco Examiner, *1898, for a song made popular by Williams & Walker*

By 1898, Williams and Walker had reached New York's Broadway, engaged in a forty-week run at the top variety theater. They were billed "The Two Real Coons," a very ordinary name for blacks in those days. Williams and Walker were concerned with the real representation of blacks and were pioneers in exposing the white puppeteering of minstrelsy. They were returning to the black "swing" our lady critic had recognized. They were depicting their race in a real and natural way, and were an immense success. Walker said of Williams that "My partner is the first man that I know of our race to delineate a 'darky' in a perfectly natural way."[40]

Basically, Walker did a Cakewalk (a subject to which we will return), and Williams did a slow, loose-jointed mooche dance or grind. The mooche or grind was like a flowing, swinging version of the modern twist and its variations; it may even be its ancestor. The way Williams did it reflected great grace and subtlety.

In an interview with the Stearnses, Walter Crumbly said of Walker's strutting: "George 'Bon-Bon' Walker was the greatest of the strutters, and the way he promenaded and pranced was something to see." Thomas "Chappy" Chappell told the Stearnses: "Walker was the man who turned the Strut into the Cakewalk and made it famous."[41] From here the Cakewalk became an international movement with French marquises, German barons, and English dukes doing awkward versions of it. It was probably the first dance craze based on black dancing. It was also the dance that put blacks in a vehicle in which they excelled and brought them before the entertainment public again. The Cakewalk is credited with bringing back authentic American art forms to the American stage. It began the displacement of stilted imitations of stylized European art forms like ballet and opera. The Cakewalk did little for George Walker, since he retired in 1907 and died in 1911.

Charles Johnson proclaims that he introduced the Cakewalk on Broadway in 1895, three years before Williams and Walker made their first hit at Koster and Bial's. The Cakewalk, like other dances we have discussed, probably originated in the San Francisco area, George Walker's home. The earliest written reference to the Cakewalk appeared in *The Stockton Evening Mail* on Monday, May 9, 1892. The headline read: "The Cakewalk—Stockton's Colored Four Hundred Will Be On Exhibition Tomorrow." This article followed: "A two-story cake topped by a dome is on exhibition in one of the show-windows of Holdon's Drug Store. It is the prize to be given to the successful cullid pussons (sic) at the Cakewalk at Masonic Music Hall tomorrow and Wednesday evenings. The couple that shows the best style in the contest will win the prize. A colored man from San Francisco is here for the purpose of arousing interest in the local colored four hundred and inducing them to turn out *en masse* and take part in the promenade. The general price of admission will be 50 cents. Reserved seats cost 25 cents extra."[42]

Stockton is about seventy miles due east of San Francisco. In a follow-up article done in a racially humorous vein on May 11, 1892, *The Stockton Evening Mail* noted that none of Stockton's black populace entered the contest. The entries consisted of "three colored ladies and twelve gentlemen from Oakland and San Francisco." Perhaps George "Bon-Bon" Walker was among them. Music was provided by the Stockton City Band; a pie-eating contest was noted with hilarity; and a bones player of considerable talent performed. "The bones playing by one of the members of the troupe was ahead of anything of the kind ever heard before in Stockton. The performer could almost make the bones talk, and he received rounds of applause."[43] The turnout to the affair was so poor that the Wednesday performance was canceled.

The first use, in print, of the word "jazz" in connection with music occurred in San Francisco on March 6, 1913. The term "jazz music" was possibly used earlier in the black dives of the Barbary Coast. The type of music called "jazz" originated in New Orleans, according to most experts, but most Crescent City citizens and musicians called the music "ragtime" until 1917. After that date, they slowly converted to the term "jazz." Some early New Orleans jazzmen never made the transition and, like Sidney Bechet, called their music "ragtime" until their march to the graveyard.

Pete Tamony, the scholar of Americanisms, tells us that the earliest recorded use of "jazz" in connection with any type of musical activity is in connection with the dance. This happened in 1910 on a Cal Stewart record (Victor 16145) titled "Uncle Josh In Society." He says, "One lady asked me if I danced the jazz and I told her, no, I dance with my feet. Heh, he, hah."[44] Marshall and Jean Stearns, in their book *Jazz Dance,* note several instances of "jazz" being applied to dances prior to 1913. These applications of the term to a dance or various dances are not surprising since the origin of the word "jazz" seems to be the French word "chasse." Chasse is a dance step and the word is also credited as the source of "sashay," which can be a dance step or a way of walking.

It is Tamony who tells us that the first written application of the word "jazz" to music occurred on March 6, 1913, in the San Francisco *Bulletin* newspaper. Art Hickman, who we've already seen associated with early jazz, took his band to Boyes Springs, about fifty miles north of San Francisco, to play evening dances for the San Francisco Seals baseball team, who were there for spring training. E.T. "Scoop" Gleason covered spring training for the *Bulletin,* and after returning to San Francisco, wrote a story about the encampment. Some quotations from the story are: "Come on there, Professor, string up the big harp and give us a tune....Everybody has come back to the old town full of the old 'jazz' and they promise to knock the fans off their feet while they're playing [baseball]....What is the 'jazz'? Why, it's a little of that 'old life', the 'gin-i-ker', the 'pep', otherwise known as eating your way through Twin Peaks....[The San Francisco Seals'] members have trained on ragtime and 'jazz' [provided by Art Hickman]....The players are just brimming over with that old 'Texas Tommy' stuff and there is a bit of the 'jazz' in everything they do."[45]

In a later interview, Gleason recalled that "As a feature, Hickman included a banjo player in his orchestra—someone said he got the notion from watching the Negro orchestras at Purcell's on the Barbary Coast." At the dances at Boyes Springs, "when Hickman's orchestra swung into action for the evening dances, it was natural to find it included as 'the jazziest tune tooters in all the Valley of the Moon.'"[46]

In 1903, a chamber of commerce-type booklet titled *San Francisco and Thereabouts* reported on the Barbary Coast when it said that "On the window of a saloony-looking restaurant was printed 'Sanquinetti's,' and three Bohemians doing the Barbary Coast entered. The Master of Ceremonies stood behind his counter, red-faced, bullet-headed, bull-necked, with one eye gone and the other betwixt a leer and a twinkle. He was in his shirt sleeves with a sort of apron tucked about his ample form. Two darkies strummed a banjo and a guitar, singing the while hilarious coon songs."[47] It was from this type of scene that Hickman probably picked up some of this ideas.

Bert Kelly, the early banjoist and leader, claims he led the first jazz band soon after he left San Francisco. He may have been the first to include the word "jazz" in a band's name, but it was after the Hickman reference quoted above. In 1916, the *Literary Digest* does state, "On account of the expense of hiring Bert Kelly's Jazz Band." Kelly himself says, "In San Francisco in 1914, I played the Tea Dances at the St. Francis (Hotel) for the Douglas Cranes in a dance group consisting of George Gould, piano, Artie Hickman, drums, and myself on ragtime banjo; tried out with Leon Carol, piano, Artie and myself for the Cliff House in 1914, then went on to Chicago and originated the Jazz Band."[48] The word "jazz" was first heard by New Orleans musicians in Chicago; Tom Brown, the trombonist, was probably the first to hear it. In 1915 he named his band Brown's Dixieland Jass Band. Brown's group was closely related to the later group known as the Original Dixieland Jazz Band (ODJB), which made the first jazz record in 1917 and popularized the term "jass" or "jazz."

The *Victor Record Review* of March 7, 1917, publicizing the first Original Dixieland Jass Band recording and the first time the word "jass" had appeared on a record, said, "Dixieland Jass One-Step/Livery Stable Blues. Spell it Jass, Jas, Jaz or Jazz—nothing can spoil a Jass Band. Some say the Jass Band originated in Chicago. Chicago says it comes from San Francisco—San Francisco being away across the continent. Anyway, a jass band is the newest thing...."[49] This piece, like the record, was produced in New York City. As with many researchers before and after, research ceased once the barrier of the North American continent was in place. In an April 1917 Honolulu, Hawaii, newspaper advertisement, Sid LeProtti's band was advertised as the "So Different Jazz Band" playing at the Alexander Young Cafe. "Jazz" is spelled as it is today, and it is noteworthy that this spelling survived. Reb Spikes clearly recalls Sid's band being a "jazz" band in 1914. Sid LeProtti's use evidently predates the ODJB's popularizing of the use in March 1917. It is possible that "jazz" was used in connection with black music on the Barbary Coast and may have been used by any number of black bands to describe their music before it first appeared in print in 1913.

As Sid LeProtti and Reb Spikes have told us, their band was inducted into the army in 1917, and they were later transferred to Nogales, Arizona. On September 4, 1918, they played at a concert in Nogales as The Young Hotel Jazz Band of Honolulu, Hawaii. The concert was presented by the Twenty-fifth Infantry; the local newspaper covered the concert and reported its critical assessment. Several things are apparent from reading the article: the first is that the type of music the band played was unknown to the local population, and they were bowled over by it; secondly, the black infantrymen were thoroughly familiar with the music and were a most receptive audience; finally, that the local writer is unfamiliar with the term "jazz," as he used quotation marks each time it is mentioned.

From what has been said, several things are clear. One is that a black band from San Francisco's Barbary Coast called itself a "jazz band" before any other black band. Another is that this band also played a brand of music different from the usual music heard by whites in Nogales, Arizona. We may suspect that this was also the case in Honolulu, Hawaii. Third, we know that Art Hickman, whose name was the first to be associated with the term "jazz music," visited Purcell's on the Barbary Coast and picked up some musical ideas there. Fourth, on the first occasion that the word "jazz"

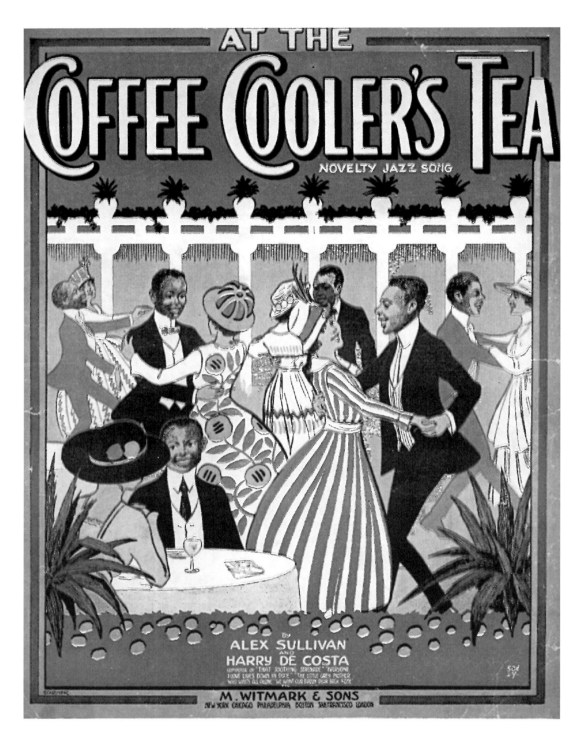

"At the Coffee Cooler's Tea" sheet music cover, 1918, shows an early use of the word jazz. The term would soon replace both rag and novelty to describe a wide array of popular syncopated music.

appears in print in connection with music, we also find a reference to the "Texas Tommy," a black dance popularized and nominally originated at Purcell's, a black saloon with black musicians and entertainers. From this evidence, it is not difficult to imagine the term "jazz" originating among black musicians and entertainers on San Francisco's Barbary Coast. It was then borrowed by white musicians, along with some musical ideas, and thus found its way into print. One of the San Francisco musicians went to Chicago and used the term in his band's name: Bert Kelly's Jazz Band. It was such a good word for the music that it was borrowed by Tom Brown to describe his band: Brown's Dixieland Jass Band. Then the Original Dixieland Jass Band adopted "jazz" and spread the name to the world.

There were other black bands playing in the San Francisco area prior to 1920. One that came from out of the area and has received a lot of attention was Will Johnson's Creole Band. It is difficult to pin down exact dates from the comments of Reb Spikes, Sid LeProtti, and others, but we are fortunately able to be definite about at least one date that they played. On December 21, 1907, *The Oakland Sunshine,* a black newspaper, carried an advertisement for a dance at the West Oakland Skating Rink with music by the "Creole Orchestra."[50] The date and names fit perfectly with Reb Spikes's description of the band's visit. They undoubtedly played Los Angeles about that time, and several histories note that Will Johnson became a permanent resident of Los Angeles before 1910.

The black newspapers of the period from 1900 to 1920 have advertisements for a number of black musical-social events. On December 27, 1913, *The Oakland Sunshine* carried an advertisement for a dance at the Bilikin Club, Page and Fillmore streets, San Francisco, with music furnished by the Orphean Orchestra, whose personnel is listed as E.E. Almond, Earl L. Near, Ed Harland, and Harry Pierson.[51] The paper's March 27, 1915, issue has nearly all the front page devoted to a photograph and advertisement announcing a "Grand All Night Exposition—Ball and Banquet." The band is identified as the Crescent Orchestra. The affair was "in honor of our Greatest Comedian Mr. Burt (sic) Williams," and was sponsored by the Colored Assembly Club of San Francisco.[52] This function was probably a different one from that recalled by Sid LeProtti as taking place in 1911. At least three members of Sid's band are in the photo, and Sid himself is probably in the back row.

The Oakland Western Outlook, in their March 15, 1915, issue, advertised an "All Night Southern Ball (Strictly Colored) May 3, 1915." Music was by "The Big Five—Roy Tabourne, Euphonium; G.D. Wells; Sid LeProtti; Pete Stanley, traps; Adam Mitchell, clarinet."[53] In December 1915, the same paper advertised the Orphean Orchestra playing at the Marion Social Hall with J. Bost, J. Thomas, H. Thomas, and H.L. Clarke. This personnel is altogether different from the personnel given for the Orphean Orchestra at December 27, 1913. The same issue of *The Oakland Western Outlook* advertises a dance played by the Philharmonic Orchestra led by Charles Strather.

Lester Mapp was the impresario for many of these early affairs, such as the Elks Day Dance on July 10, 1915. This bash included two bands, led by Harry Pierson and Jack Miller, and such entertainers as Nettie Compton, Maud Turner, Esmeralda Statham, Mary Dewson, Will Mitchell, John R. Davis, Evelyn Joyner, and Jerome FitzPrice. The advertisement noted "The Committee Guarantees Good Order."[54]

Other bands are mentioned in the period before 1920, but without any reference to their personnels. They include the Golden West Orchestra, Famous Ivy Orchestra, Athens Orchestra, Athens City Orchestra, Professor Black's Orchestra, and Summer Orchestra. Most of the groups listed appear again and again for various dances and social functions.

From the first available issue—that of November 7, 1914—for a number of years, *The Oakland Western Outlook* carried advertisements for Lester Mapp. They were for "The Ivy Cafe and Dance Hall, 468 Pacific Street, San Francisco, Lester Mapp, Proprietor—Charles Uter, Manager." This was Sam King's old place and the Famous Ivy Orchestra mentioned above may have had its headquarters there. Also advertised was "The Elite Cafe (formerly Purcell's), 520 Pacific Street, San Francisco, High Class Entertainment. A Specialty Orchestra of Six Pieces. L. Mapp, Proprietor—A.F. Shavers, Manager."[55]

Endnotes:
1. Writers' Program of the Works Progress Administration, *Theatre Research Series, Vol. XIII–Minstrelsy,* Notes.
2. Cauyuga Joint Stock Company, *A One Volume Journal of Voyage from Auburn, New York to California, Diary of a Member,* Isaac Shepard papers, Entry for October 13, 1849.

3. B.E. Lloyd, *Lights and Shades in San Francisco* (San Francisco: A.L. Bancroft, 1876), 79.

4. J.D. Borthwick, *The Gold Hunters* (New York: Outing, 1917), 54, 161.

5. T.A. Barry and B.W. Patten, *Men and Memories of San Francisco in the Spring of '50* (San Francisco: A.L. Bancroft, 1873), 118.

6. *Alta* newspaper, San Francisco, 1850.

7. Writers' Program, *Theatre Research,* 28.

8. F. Soulé, J.H. Gibson, and J. Nisbet, *The Annals of San Francisco* (Lewis Osborne, 1855), 213.

9. Writers' Program, *Theatre Research,* 28.

10. Writers' Program of the Works Progress Administration in Northern California, *San Francisco, The Bay and Its Cities* (New York: Hastings House, 1940), 140.

11. Bayard Taylor, *El Dorado or Adventures in the Path of Empire* (G.P. Putnam's, 1850), Vol. I, 223; Vol. II, 28, 29.

12. Ibid., 29.

13. C.W. Haskins, *The Argonauts of California* (New York: Published by the Author—Fords, Howard and Hulbert, 1890), 61.

14. Ibid., 61.

15. *California Historical Society Quarterly,* 1955. California's Bantam Cock, Vol. 8. The Journals of Charles E. Delong.

16. *The Pacific Appeal,* San Francisco, 1862.

17. Writers' Program, *Theatre Research,* 146.

18. Writers' Program, *Theatre Research,* 147.

19. *The Argonaut,* San Francisco, California, 1862.

20. *The San Francisco Elevator,* San Francisco, 1868.

21. *The Call,* San Francisco, 1868.

22. *The Gold Hill Evening News,* Virginia City, Nevada, 1873.

23. Tom Stoddard wrote a biographical sketch of Blind Tom: *Blind Tom, Slave Genius—Storyville 28* (London, England, 1970).

24. Marshall and Jean Stearns, *Jazz Dance—The Story of American Vernacular Dance* (New York: The Macmillan Company, 1968), XIV.

25. Tom Fletcher, *100 Years of the Negro in Show Business* (New York: Burdge & Co., 1954), 193.

26. Herbert Asbury, *The Barbary Coast* (New York: Alfred A. Knopf, 1933), 293.

27. Writers' Program, *San Francisco. The Bay and Its Cities,* 140.

28. *The San Francisco Examiner,* San Francisco, California, 1910.

29. Stearns, 96.

30. Val Harris and Sid Brown, *Texas Tommy Swing* (Jerome H. Remick, 1911).

31. Caroline and Charles Coffin, *Dancing and Dancers of Today* (Dodd, Mead & Company, 1912), 269, 271.

32. Stearns, 129.

33. Ibid., 128.

34. Ibid., 128.

35. Ibid., 128.

36. Ibid., 128.

37. Ibid., 128.
38. Ibid., 128.
39. Ibid., 105.
40. *The Real Coon on the American Stage,* The Theater, 1906.
41. Stearns, 122.
42. *The Stockton Evening Mail,* Stockton, 1892.
43. Ibid.
44. Peter Tamony, *Jazz: The Word and Its Extensions to Music* (San Francisco: 1868), 5.
45. *The Bulletin,* San Francisco, 1913.
46. *The Call Bulletin,* San Francisco, 1938.
47. Charles Keeler, *San Francisco and Thereabouts* (San Francisco: The California Promotion Committee, 1903).
48. *Variety,* New York, 1957.
49. *Victor Record Review,* New York, 1917.
50. *The Oakland Sunshine,* Oakland, 1917.
51. *The Oakland Sunshine,* Oakland, 1913.
52. *The Oakland Sunshine,* Oakland, 1915.
53. *The Oakland Western Outlook,* Oakland, 1915.
54. Ibid.
55. *The Oakland Western Outlook,* Oakland, 1914–1920.

COMMENTS OUT OF MY MIND

I have always thought that the best commentary on jazz is the music itself; next come the remarks of the jazzmen who create the music; last come the remarks of observers of jazz. This book has been primarily concerned with the remarks of jazzmen, and I have waited until the end to make a few remarks myself. These remarks are based on the text, general observations of jazz, tying some additional facts to the text, and a few personal opinions.

When interviewing black people, I have always been struck by their knowing what happens to friends and relatives over a period of years. The text of this book provides several instances of following the whereabouts of a person for a lifetime, seemingly by chance. A number of factors help to explain this phenomenon. First, blacks have a strong oral tradition and spend a lot of time when they get together discussing who has been where, doing what, and generally "catching up." Second, they are suspicious of whites and generally keep real communication among themselves. And, third, in most states outside the South, blacks are confined to very small areas. In California, for example, 99 percent of blacks live in less than 1 percent of the land area. This naturally makes running into each other a much more likely occurrence.

The photograph of the Silver City Cornet Band is unusual because it shows a black musician in an otherwise white band. The unknown black man is holding an alto horn beside six other alto horn players. The remainder of the group consists of three cornetists, two clarinetists, a snare drummer, a bass drummer, a valve trombonist, and a child piccolo player. The sixteen-man band would be a sizable group at any time and place; they were evidently a marching band, judging from the bass drummer's marching strap and the portability of the instruments. The back of the photograph states: "1863. Silver City, N.T. +8892." (N.T.=Nevada Territory.) Silver City was a silver-boom town of the era and is located between Carson City and Reno, Nevada. It now has a population of fewer than 200, but in the 1860s, the population might have been between 2,000 and 20,000. The photograph is forty years older than any other in this book and possibly predates any other photograph of a black American musician. The black man seems to stand by himself more than the others.

The photograph was discovered in a Reno, Nevada, antique dealer's store by Pete Clute, pianist of the Turk Murphy Jazz Band.

For those of us who spent our youths in darkened theaters watching oat-burner movies, the bond between ragtime piano and the Wild West is closer than between sin and good times. Between shoot-outs on Main Street, the gunning down of bank robbers as they back out of the money emporium, and the posse thundering off after bad guys, a garter-shirted, derby-hatted piano thumper knocked out some pretty wicked ragtime. Is this a myth perpetuated by 3,847 oat-burner movies locked in the grip of a successful formula, or is there some historical basis for the myth? The past has shown that many myths, when researched, turn out to be true. We have seen Reb Spikes's comments on Arizona and New Mexico, I have commented on the photograph of the Silver City Cornet Band, Ragtime Charlie spent time in Montana, Russ Morgan was a cowboy from there, Tom Turpin spent time in

The Silver City Cornet Band in Silver City, Nevada Territory, 1863

Nevada and California, and it is possible Scott Joplin did too. And, of course, this entire book is devoted to black jazz in the West. There may be a substantial connection.

I have purposely included in the text a number of references to jazz in the Far East. This is a subject that requires a great deal of investigation and might be worthy of a book. I recall that Sid LeProtti's band received an offer of an engagement in Shanghai or Hong Kong, China, after they finished their Hawaiian engagement; they could not take it because they were drafted into the army. The earliest reference I have of a black jazzman going to the Far East relates to Bill and Gene Powers, and Buck Campbell; they probably left between 1918 and 1922. The photograph of their band in Yokohama, Japan, was taken about 1925. Other bands that went were the Jack Carter Band with Teddy Weatherford, Bob Hill's and Frank Shievers's group, Earl Whaley's orchestra, and Sonny Clay's band. There were individuals who went, such as Bill Hegamin, the pianist, who died in China, and Freddie McWilliams, the dancer, who returned in 1935.

When black members of these groups left their bands, they were often replaced by Filipino jazzmen, who are reported to have a real flair and appreciation for jazz. At least one musician has told me that the Philippine Islands were a great place to play jazz in those days.

There were other areas where early jazz may have flourished in the West, and where useful research might be accomplished. One such area would be the Southwest—Arizona, New Mexico, West Texas, and Oklahoma. Another would be the Southern California area, with an emphasis on San Diego before 1920 and Los Angeles after 1920. A third would be the Northwest, including Seattle and Tacoma, Washington, and also Victoria, British Columbia (Canada), and Portland, Oregon.

They All Played Ragtime by Rudi Blesh and Harriet Janis reports that "in 1885, Tom [Turpin] and his older brother Charlie were off in Nevada, trying their luck at mining. It would not be until 1894 that they would both be back home [in St. Louis, Missouri] permanently."[1]

Most of the mining in this period was on the western edge of Nevada, around the Reno area and close to Northern California. California was also a prime mining location, and it seems natural that the Turpins would drift in and out of California during a ten-year stay. San Francisco was the mecca for miners, and like every other miner of this period, they probably came to San Francisco and the Coast to unwind. Harry Mereness reports that both Tom Turpin and Scott Joplin played the Coast but can't give dates or sources.

Reb Spikes says he saw Tom Turpin plying on the Barbary Coast in 1907. In *The Oakland Sunshine* of December 21, 1907, an F.L. Turpin advertised his saloon, The Royal House at Fourth and Howard streets in San Francisco. The Turpins were saloon keepers, the advertisement was in a black newspaper, and the area where the saloon is located is a partly black area. It is possible that this Turpin was a relative who the composer had come to visit in 1907. The 1906 earthquake and fire was the cataclysmic event of its era and drew rubberneckers from around the world. Thus, Turpin might have come to see the skeleton of the city he had known during the period of his mining adventure. For the visit circa 1907, we have a possible relative to visit, the remains of the greatest earthquake and fire in American history to see, and an eyewitness report from Reb Spikes. Spikes's account is highly credible because of his phenomenal memory, and because he knew the Turpin family and saw Tom Turpin on a number of other occasions.

In a letter to the author, Rudi Blesh states that Tom Turpin was in San Francisco, giving the date as circa 1914–1915, to visit the Panama-Pacific International Exposition. Turpin wrote the "Pan-Am Rag" in 1914 in honor of the event.

I conclude that Tom Turpin visited San Francisco and the Barbary Coast many times between 1885 and 1915. It is likely that the early visits were numerous and spread over a ten-year period. The ensuing trips were probably vacation excursions and probably didn't last more than a month or two each.

Harry Mereness also reports that Scott Joplin visited the Coast. The likeliest source of his information about both Joplin and Turpin is Wesley Fields, but he is now unable to confirm this. Joplin did travel west of his native Arkansas as a teenager (1881–1887) and could have gone as far west as California and the Coast. My letter from Rudi Blesh suggests that the most likely time would be 1906 and 1907, during Joplin's year of wandering after his break-up with his first wife, and before he moved to New York. This period also coincides with the rubbernecking period after the earthquake and fire, and Joplin could have succumbed to this lure. (So, incidentally, could Will Johnson's Creole Orchestra.) Joplin's visit remains conjectural.

Reb Spikes does not remember the story about Jelly Roll Morton conking his lady friend with the Colt .45. Either Sid LeProtti erroneously credited Spikes as the source of this story, or Spikes forgot the incident after telling Sid about it.

According to the comments of Sid LeProtti and Will Mastin, the Texas Tommy dance originated in Texas, and "Tommy" meant whore. The dance might have been a way of enticing customers, or "showin' your stuff," for Texas whores.

About 1933, there was a revival of the Barbary Coast on Pacific Street from Kearny Street to Montgomery Street. It was called the International Settlement but was widely known as the Barbary Coast. It was a collection of bars, B-girls, strip joints, and the like. During World War II, the area did a fairly efficient job of fleecing soldiers and sailors, but on the whole, it was

The Hippodrome, c. 1930, was one of the many Barbary Coast clubs that closed down around Prohibition, causing the music scene to shift south to Los Angeles.

tame compared with the original Barbary Coast. A number of black bands played in these revived night spots. This revival petered out in the late fifties, and the Barbary Coast is now an area of furniture stores and boutiques. I was misled a number of times by this revived Barbary Coast while researching this book.

Frank Withers appears briefly in the pages of history because he played on a few records. In 1921, he was with Noble Sissle in New York City where they recorded seven tunes for Emerson and associated labels. In 1922 and 1923, Withers was with Mitchell's Jazz Kings in Paris, France, where they recorded extensively. What happened to Withers after he played with these two groups is unknown to me.

The Pan Pacific Exhibition was a World's Fair that resulted in the filling of Francisco Bay mud flats and the creation of the Marina District of San Francisco on this site. The Exhibition was to celebrate the rebuilding of San Francisco after the fire of 1906 and the opening of the Panama Canal. The Exhibition opened on February 20, 1915, and closed on December 14, 1915. Reb Spikes's return to San Francisco can be closely dated from these dates and his own information. Sid LeProtti's band probably left the Coast in mid-1915 to play at the Exhibition. After that, they played the Coast again, interspersed with gigs in Los Angeles, Honolulu, the army, Porta La Louvre, Nogales, and so on.

In the twenties, the West Coast jazz scene shifted to Los Angeles. The Barbary Coast had closed and the center of Bay Area jazz disappeared. There were, of course, other spots in San Francisco, Oakland, and the outlying areas. These were mostly weekend gigs, and the full-time professional musician had to scratch pretty hard to stay in music. It was far easier to make it in Los Angeles, and many musicians went south, some staying for the rest of their lives. During the twenties, Los Angeles enjoyed a growth in the movie industry and a concomitant establishment of a recording industry. Both were added inducements for musicians to play there—a chance to record jazz for posterity. The recordings made there by Reb Spikes, Paul Howard, Harvey Brooks, Sonny Clay, Les Hite, and Curtis Mosby are the only recorded examples of the type of jazz played in the West. It is well known that the first black New Orleans jazz was recorded there by Kid Ory's Sunshin(n)e Orchestra.

The actual decline of the Barbary Coast began in 1913, led by the *San Francisco Examiner's* crusade to destroy "the open market for commercialized vice" and replace it with "wholesome fun"—similar to Sid LeProtti's ludicrous proposal to replace booze and women with baked ham and Southern fried chicken. To the voice of this powerful Hearst newspaper, whose owner had cavorted across the pages of history enjoying more than wholesome fun, was added the voice of a Methodist street preacher named the Reverend

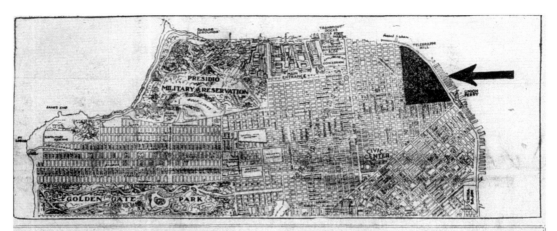

HERE IS THE ORDER CLOSING "BARBARY COAST"
❖❖❖ ❖❖❖ ❖❖❖ ❖❖❖ ❖❖❖ ❖❖❖ ❖❖❖ ❖❖❖ ❖❖❖
FIRST FRUIT OF CRUSADE BEGUN BY "EXAMINER"

*F*OLLOWING *is the text of the resolution wiping out the infamous Barbary Coast, adopted by the Board of Police Commissioners last evening:*
RESOLVED, That after September 30, 1913, no dancing shall be permitted in any cafe, restaurant or saloon where liquor is sold, within the district bounded on the north and east by the bay, on the south by Clay street and on the west by Stockton street;.
FURTHER RESOLVED, That no women patrons or women employees shall be permitted in any saloon in the said district;

In September 1913, the San Francisco Examiner *triumphantly reported on the passage of new city laws, which effectively shut down the Barbary Coast.*

Paul Smith, World War I, Prohibition, and a changed social milieu. Individual Coast dives were closed from time to time, and in 1917, a general closing stuck the area. Like a punchy fighter, the Coast kept coming back, in a weaker and weaker condition, and kept getting knocked down again and again until the final blow in 1921. Jelly Roll Morton's joint, The Jupiter, was probably buffeted by one or more of these blows. Morton blamed his troubles on vague enemies and competitors, but he was caught up in the final taming of the West by the law-abiding crowd.

The photograph that Harry Mereness reports seeing in Wesley Fields's room featured the usual New Orleans band line-up, plus violin. The traditional New Orleans line-up did in fact include a violin, as noted in many histories and confirmed by early photographs. The line-up was trumpet, trombone (first valve and later slide), clarinet, guitar, violin, string bass, and drums. We have to assume that the other four pieces were represented in Fields's photograph, as well as the drum, violin, and trombone noted by Mereness. Since Fields played the piano, it is difficult to fit him into the line-up, but presumably he was in the picture. Only one New Orleans band (Robichaux's) used the piano to any extent prior to 1920.

During the last years of his life, Sid LeProtti swept the city hall in the suburb where he lived, playing gigs as often as he could, and living comfortably with a lovely and loving wife. Mamie LeProtti is a careful and intelligent woman who saved Sid's early earnings and wisely invested them. It is my impression that they did not have the financial worries that attend most aging jazzmen. In the course of their life, they purchased an acre of land and built a lovely home where Sid spent the last thirty years of his life. While concluding my interview with Mamie LeProtti, I asked if she ever got lonely and wanted to remarry. She said she had had a perfect marriage and wouldn't take a chance on having anything less.

The reader will wonder, as I did, whether the noted copy of Sid LeProtti's "Sid's Rag" or "Canadian Capers" was copyrighted. I have had a search made at the Copyright Office of the Library of Congress. They searched under Sidney Louis LeProtti and LaProtti, and under George Bryant and Bryan in the period 1898 to 1954. They found nothing. I did have one report that a black woman nicknamed "Princess Bell," who played the piano and lived in San Francisco's Mission District, had a copy. She has been impossible to locate.

In the LeProtti's storage shed, there were a large number of papers which were passed along for my use in preparing this book. They included an unpublished tune titled "The Big Three Rag." The Vocalion record of "Maybe Some Day," cut by Henry Starr for Reb Spikes, has also proved impossible to locate.

Sid LeProtti mentions the banjo player Giles County. There are two counties so named along a common border of Tennessee and Virginia. One is in

Tennessee and the other in Virginia. Giles County may well have hailed from one of them.

Sid LeProtti says he played at a little town named Purisima on the San Mateo coast. This town has disappeared from current maps; it was a few miles south of Half Moon Bay.

Sid LeProtti recalls his band playing for Prince George of England, "who was to be King of England." Prince George of England did visit the United States and Canada in September 1928, aboard H.M.S. Durbin. This Prince George, whose father was King George V, did not ascend the throne, but his elder brother became King Edward VIII; on Edward's abdication, another brother became King George VI. Prince George became the Duke of Kent when his bother ascended the throne. Sid may have been confused by the two brothers having the same name and similar features. All of the brothers became avid jazz fans, and the Duke of Windsor (the former King Edward VIII) was a noted rare record collector.

According to Sid LeProtti, Reb Spikes, and Wesley Fields, there were black musicians playing the Barbary Coast before they arrived. We know that Lew Purcell and Sam King were on the Coast as early as 1901. According to San Francisco and Thereabouts, some of the white dives hired black entertainers. Black music existed on the Barbary Coast and in the Bay Area for years prior to the general period of this history (1900 to 1920). It has not been possible to obtain eyewitness accounts of the type of music played before 1900 or to develop some cross-verification for it. We do know that musicians like Jack Ross, Fred Vaughn, Willard Jones, Leroy Watkins, and Wesley Fields were around then. In my opinion, black musicians arrived during the Sydney Town era and stayed to close up the Coast some sixty years later.

The multi-cultural character of New Orleans is repeatedly cited as one of the essential preconditions of the creation of jazz there. The most casual visitor to San Francisco is immediately struck by the color spectrum of its citizens and the jabber of a dozen tongues. In San Francisco's short lifetime, there have been more distinct ethnic, racial, and national settlements than in any other city in the Americas. A brief list, for yesterday and today,

"Out'a the twenty years I played the Barbary Coast, fourteen years of it was all night."
—Sid LeProtti, 1953, as photographed by Harry Bowden

would include French, Hawaiian, black, Russian, Irish, German, West Indian (black), Chinese, Japanese, Mexican, South and Central American, East Indian, Italian, Greek, American Indian, Scandinavian, English, and American. San Francisco's Chinatown and Little Tokyo (Japantown) are the largest Chinese and Japanese populations outside the Orient. There have been San Francisco banking houses catering almost exclusively to French, German, Irish, Chinese, Japanese, and Italian populations. There were several West Indian cricket clubs at the turn of the century.

Many groups congregated in certain areas: the Hawaiians, Samoans, and American Indians in the central Mission; the Italians and Greeks in North Beach; the Russians, French, and Germans in the Richmond; the blacks and West Indians in the Fillmore or Western Addition; the Mexicans and South and Central Americans in the Mission. All these groups, plus the Irish, Scandinavians, English, East Indians, Americans, and individual members of the other groups, act as a paste holding the city and its elements together. If a diverse multi-cultural background is needed to create jazz, San Francisco can keep stride with the best of company.

New Orleans is the city most often mentioned in connection with jazz and is the almost sacrosanct birthplace of this unique music. There are a number of components of jazz, though, and surprisingly few of them are connected with the Crescent City. Ragtime is connected with Sedalia and St. Louis, Missouri. Rural blues are linked with backwoods Mississippi and Alabama. City blues are frequently associated with Memphis, Chicago, and New York. Improvisational music has been connected with almost every folk music from Hillbilly to Flamenco, and some of our early references indicate a free-wheeling improvisational style of playing in the West. Polyrhythmic music can be more easily found in Cuba and the West Indies than in any American city. San Francisco can easily claim a closer link with jazz dance than almost any other place. The point here is that perhaps early researchers were too myopic in their investigations of jazz origins.

I have long held the notion that black people in America and black music, such as jazz, were so widely scattered that it makes little sense to try to pinpoint the music's geographical origin, much less (as some researchers have done) to try to identify a particular person like Buddy Bolden or Jelly

Roll Morton as the source of the music. Rather, it is more likely the music was as widespread as blacks were, and that the development of jazz took place over many years, in different places, and involved many people. When black musicians traveled from one place to another, they were easily accepted by other blacks as playing their music of the times, whether blues, ragtime, or jazz.

Certainly there were differences in geographical styles, and there were a number of recognized great performers. Among these early greats were Joe Oliver and Freddie Keppard, and a legend has been made out of the recognition they received when they went to Chicago. Early researchers often cited this recognition as proof that Chicagoans had never heard jazz before. Two factors refute this interpretation. One, Keppard and Oliver were recognized as stars in New Orleans, and it is natural they would be accorded the same sort of recognition in Chicago. Two, their appearance in Chicago began one of the first instances of adulation by white youngsters, who spread their fame far beyond the black community. The same sort of recognition was accorded to two other New Orleans jazz giants, Louis Armstrong and Jelly Roll Morton, who exerted an even greater impact on early jazz. In my opinion, New Orleans had more active black musicians than any other city and therefore engendered more of the great exponents of jazz than any other place.

It is not my purpose in these short remarks to attempt to change jazz history or to claim that jazz originated somewhere other than New Orleans. It is rather to point out that early research focused very narrowly on New Orleans to the great loss of places like San Francisco, Detroit, Cleveland, Denver, Chicago, Kansas City, Oklahoma City, Seattle, Houston, New York, Washington, D.C., and San Antonio, to name a few of the more promising areas. When researchers did begin investigating in an area like California, they rounded up all the old New Orleans expatriates, recorded their playing, and interviewed them. Let me hastily add that I have done the same, because of my love for New Orleans jazz. At this point, however, much of jazz history outside New Orleans has been lost, and most of it will never be recovered. It is important to preserve what we can.

The text of this book relating to Sid LeProtti, Wesley Fields, and Reb Spikes, and the research references quoted, prove conclusively, in my eyes, that there was black jazz being played in the Bay Area by indigenous musicians prior to 1907. The creation of New Orleans jazz is usually dated to the late nineties or the turn of the century. When Will Johnson's Creole Orchestra came to the Bay Area, there were several things Sid LeProtti noticed about them. The first, and by far the most important, was the four-beat rhythm. This unique feature caused LeProtti to change the rhythm of his band and eventually caused the firing of his drummer. This feature is also cited by most jazz commentators as a unique feature of New Orleans jazz. The second was the excellent tunes, which LeProtti can't remember. This leads me to conclude that they weren't that exciting as tunes, and that his reaction was probably more related to their rhythmic propulsion. Third, was their use of the pizzicato bass. Reb Spikes did not find anything very remarkable about New Orleans jazzmen. It is evident that LeProtti and Spikes were both admirers of a number of New Orleans jazzmen, notably Jelly Roll Morton. Spikes clearly considers him the greatest piano player who ever lived.

The improvisational component of jazz follows two major trends: collective and solo. Collective improvisation, in which the rhythm section lays down the beat and everyone else improvises at the same time, is closely identified with New Orleans. There was probably no other type of improvisation in New Orleans until after 1920. The collective style of improvisation is credited with having a greater cumulative impact and with being closer to the African roots of jazz.

In solo improvisation, one member of the band improvises over a rhythmic foundation and/or over a diminished counter-melody by another member of the band. This style of improvisation has not been linked with any geographical school of jazz. Peter Tamony has stated that this style was first introduced in the music of Art Hickman and Paul Whiteman. Whiteman started his career as a member of the San Francisco Symphony Orchestra, which he soon left to join Hickman. Hickman was the first popular jazz leader to employ only reading musicians; we have already noted his early connection with jazz. With reading musicians it is easier to create the foundation or background music for a solo improvisation. Hickman's early bands are reported to have used, and probably originated, the solo style of jazz improvisation.

Whiteman went on to use this style with great success and became world-famous as the self-proclaimed "King of Jazz." The musicians who played and soloed with Whiteman are a "Who's Who" of early white jazzmen. They

Paul Whiteman and the original members of his band, 1919

include Bix Beiderbecke, Red Nichols, Jimmy Dorsey, Tommy Dorsey, Hoagy Carmichael, Frankie Trumbauer, Joe Venuti, Eddie Lang, Jack Teagarden, and, as an arranger, Ferde Grofe.

The solo style of improvisation has been the dominant style in jazz for the past forty years. It is possible that, like the other innovative musical ideas of Art Hickman, the solo style of improvising originated with black musicians of the Barbary Coast. Reb Spikes clearly identifies Slocum Mitchell as soloing over the counter-melodies of Reb's sax and Clarence Williams's bass. Presumably, Sid LeProtti and Gerald Wells also took solos. Buddy Mitchell, the cornet player, could have been another early soloist.

Endnote:
1. Rudi Blesh and Harriet Janis, *They All Played Ragtime* (New York: Oak Publications, 1966), 41.

BIBLIOGRAPHY

Books:

Aptheker, Herbert, ed. *A Documentary History of the Negro People in the United States.* New York: Citadel, 1963.

Asbury, Herbert. *The Barbary Coast: An Informal History of the San Francisco Underworld.* New York: Alfred A. Knopf, 1933.

Barry, T.A., and B.A. Patton. *Men and Memories of San Francisco in the Spring of '50.* San Francisco: A.L. Bancroft, 1873.

Beasley, Delilah L. *The Negro Trail Blazers of California.* Los Angeles: Times Mirror, 1919.

Blesh, Rudi, and Harriet Janis. *They All Played Ragtime.* New York: Oak Publications, 1966.

Borthwick, J.D. *The Gold Hunters: A First-hand Picture of Life in California Mining Camps in the Early Fifties.* New York: Outing, 1917.

Caffin, Caroline, and Charles Caffin. *Dancing and Dancers of Today.* Dodd, Mead & Co., 1912.

Cayuga Joint Stock Company Papers. *A One Volume Journal of Voyage from Auburn, New York to California. Diary Of A Member.* Isaac Shepard Papers, 1849.

Charters, Samuel B. *Jazz New Orleans 1885–1963: An Index to the Negro Musicians of New Orleans.* New York: Oak Publications, 1963.

Fletcher, Tom. *100 Years of the Negro in Show Business.* New York: Burdge & Co., 1954.

Gentry, Curt. *The Madams of San Francisco: An Irreverent History of the City of the Golden Gate.* Garden City, New York: Doubleday, 1964.

Harris, Val, and Sid Brown. *Texas Tommy Swing.* Jerome H. Remick, 1911.

Haskins, C.W. *The Argonauts of California.* Published by the Author. New York: Fords, Howard and Hulbert, 1890.

Katz, William Loren. *The Black West.* Garden City, New York: Doubleday, 1971.

Keeler, Charles. *San Francisco and Thereabouts.* San Francisco: The California Promotion Committee, 1903.

Leonard, H.T., Jr. *Scrapbook, Vol. I.* California Historical Society Library.

Lloyd, B.E. *Lights and Shades in San Francisco.* San Francisco: A.L. Bancroft, 1876.

Lomax, Alan. *Mister Jelly Roll: The Fortunes of Jelly Roll Morton, New Orleans Creole and "Inventor of Jazz".* New York: Duell, Sloan and Pearce, 1950.

MacMinn, George R. *The Theater of the Golden Era in California.* Caldwell, Id: The Caxton Printers, 1941.

Rust, Brian. *Jazz Records 1897–1942*. Chigwell, Essex: Storyville Publications, 1970.

Soulé, F., J.H. Gibon, and J. Nisbet. *The Annals of San Francisco*. New York: Appleton, 1855.

Stearns, Marshall, and Jean Stearns. *Jazz Dance—The Story of American Vernacular Dance*. New York: The Macmillan Company, 1968.

Tamony, Peter. *Jazz: The Word and its Extension to Music*. San Francisco, 1968.

Taylor, Bayard. *El Dorado, or, Adventures in the Path of Empire*. Two Volumes, G.P. Putnam's Sons, 1850.

Works, Monroe N. *The Negro Year Book*. Tuskegee Institute, Department of Records and Research, 1912–52.

Writers' Program of the Works Progress Administration in Northern California. *San Francisco, The Bay And Its Cities*. New York: Hastings House, 1940.

Writers' Program of the Works Progress Administration. U.S. WPA, San Francisco. *Theatre Research Series, Volume XIII–Minstrelsy,* 1939.

Periodicals:

California Historical Society Quarterly and *California Historical Quarterly,* California Historical Society, San Francisco, California, 1924–1971.

Population, Population Research Section, Budget Division Department of Finance, State of California, 1971.

The Real Coon on the American Stage, The Theater, 1906.

San Francisco Directory, H.S. Crocker Company, 1901–1905.

Variety, New York.

Victor Record Review, New York, 1917.

Newspapers:

The Alta, San Francisco

Argonaut Newspaper, San Francisco

The Call, San Francisco

The Call Bulletin, San Francisco

The Gold Hill Evening News, Virginia City, Nevada

The Oakland Sunshine

The Oakland Western Outlook

The Pacific Appeal, San Francisco

The San Francisco Bulletin

The San Francisco Call

The San Francisco Chronicle

The San Francisco Elevator

The San Francisco Examiner

The San Francisco News

The Stockton Evening Mail

Permissions

The photographs on the following pages are reprinted courtesy of Tom Stoddard's private collection: 45, 48, 65, 67, 73, 88, 89, 96, 108, 109, 115, 116, 120, 126, 128, 129, 131, 132, 134, 136, 139, 141, 143, 144, 146, 148, and 203.

The photographs on the following pages are reprinted courtesy of the San Francisco Public Library: 10, 11, 14, 24, 34, 38, 56, 59, 76, 94, 164, 167, 171, 172, and 206.

The photographs on the following pages are reprinted courtesy of the San Francisco Performing Arts Library and Museum: 16, 18, 19, 25, 33, 43, 101, 111, 178, 181, 183, 186, 188, 191, 196, and 215.

The photographs on the following pages are reprinted courtesy of the San Francisco Examiner: 62, 63, 168, and 208.

The photographs on the following pages are reprinted courtesy of the San Francisco Traditional Jazz Foundation—Charles Campbell Collection: 8 and 211.

INDEX

This "proper name" index is concerned principally with the musical aspects of the book; references to people and places which occur incidentally are not given. Page numbers in bold indicate material in photographs and/or captions. Where instruments played are noted in the text, these are given using standard abbreviations: as=alto sax; bar euph=baritone euphonium; bb=brass bass; bj=banjo; cl=clarinet; c=cornet; d=drums; f=flute; g=guitar; p=piano; pic=piccolo; reeds=reeds; sax=sax; sb=string bass; t=trumpet; tb=trombone; ts=tenor sax; v=vocals; vn=violin; vtb=valve trombone.

ABOUT THE AUTHOR

Tom Stoddard began interviewing jazz pioneers and collecting jazz photos in the 1950s and has written numerous articles on the history of jazz. His book, *Pops Foster—The Autobiography of a New Orleans Jazzman,* was published by the University of California Press in 1971 and won the 1972 ASCAP award. A former government official and vice president of Wells Fargo Bank, he is also the author of many articles on still and mechanical coin banks. His 1997 book, *Ceramic Coin Banks*, published by Collectors Books, is available from bookstores or for $22.00 postpaid. His 1993 book of miscellaneous writings, *Computer Cleanout* (a compendium of essays, aphorisms, short stories, and diatribes), is available for $5.00 plus $2.00 shipping within the United States. Send orders for *Ceramic Coin Banks* and *Computer Cleanout* to: Tom Stoddard, P.O. Box 71, Petaluma, CA 94953.